WESTERN TRAILS AND FRONTIER GRAFFITI

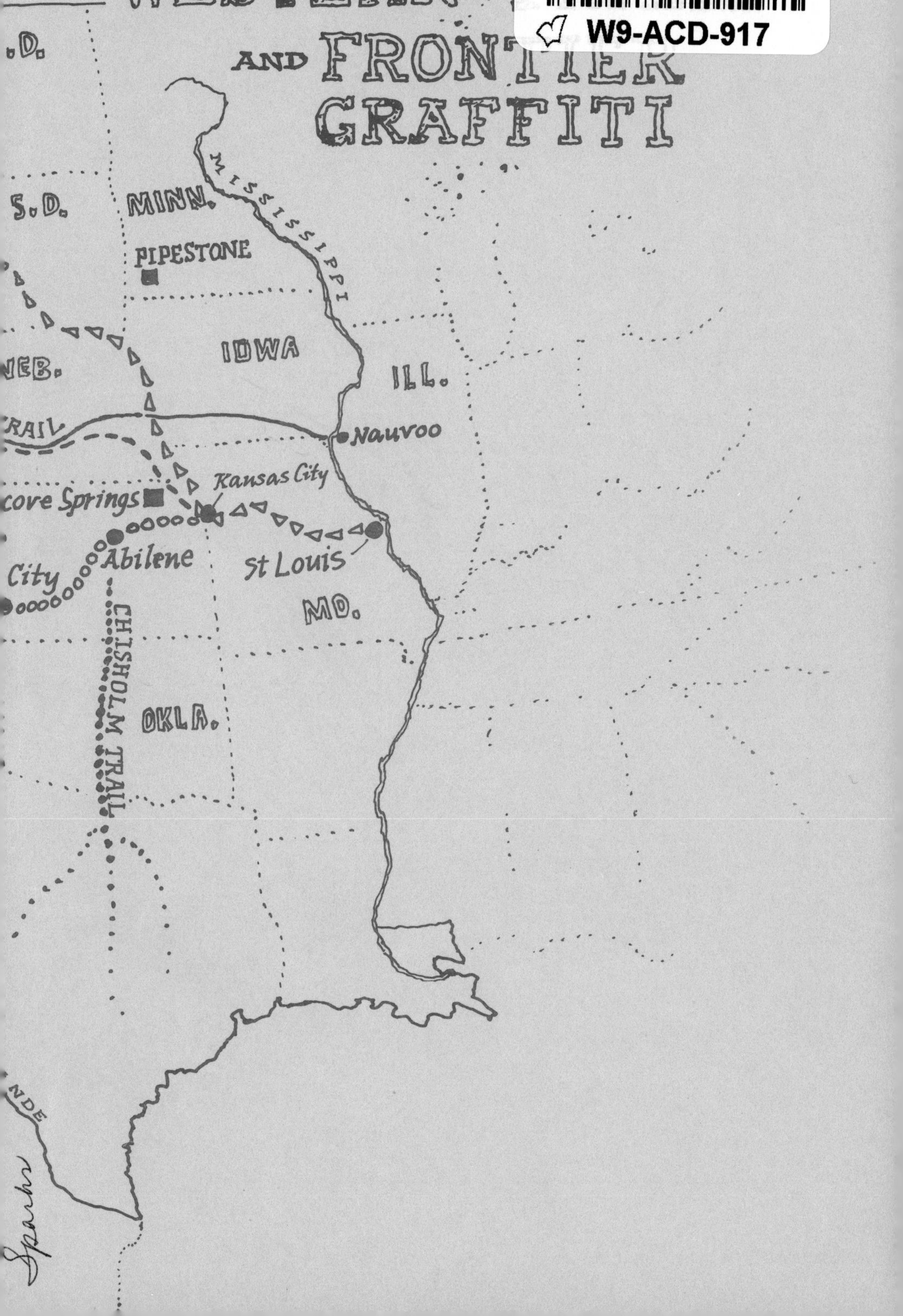

TOURING THE OLD WEST

TOURING the OLD WEST

KENT RUTH

**Maps and drawings
by Robert MacLean**

**The Stephen Greene Press
Brattleboro, Vermont**

In the Beginning

. . . a warm word of thanks to the many, many individuals whose kindnesses over the years have contributed in countless ways to the travel experiences from which this book has evolved . . .

. . . and a sincere dedication of the finished product to HELEN, who shares a love for the Old West and whose actual "touring" of it (in a variety of automobiles over an even greater variety of roads and near-roads) has made our exploration junkets possible—and doubly enjoyable.

This book has been produced in the United States of America: designed by R. L. Dothard Associates, set in type by The Book Press and printed and bound by Halliday Lithograph.

It is published by The Stephen Greene Press, Brattleboro, Vermont 05301.

MAR 10 '72

Library of Congress Catalog Card Number: 71-148620
International Standard Book Number: 0-8289-0129-5

CONTENTS

Who "We" Are

For the record, the *we* used hereafter is not the depersonalized editorial "we." It refers rather to myself and Helen, my sister, who has driven the car over virtually every mile of Western road discussed in the following chapters. And while we're on the subject, this is perhaps as good a time and place as any to establish the fact that we have, unless noted to the contrary, driven these roads, witnessed these sights, and experienced these events.

If the "we" is personal rather than editorial, so is the hodgepodge of facts, figures, and experiences a personal, rather than a library-shelf, distillation. Credit or blame, we must accept it.   K.R.

ONE FOR

THE ROAD

We weren't being morbid about it: it was time to eat, that's all.

And in southeastern Utah (as well as in other lonely corners of the West), when it's time to eat and you see a roadside café, it rarely pays to be fussy. The next establishment—not likely to be significantly different in size, service, or general decor anyway—may well be another hour or two down the road.

On this particular day, however, and at this particular truck stop, we confess that our physical hunger pangs were reinforced by a certain emotional titillation. Crescent Junction's café, as well as the T configuration of highways that spawned it, were familiar to us from previous trips. And for this reason we had followed recent news reports with more than usual interest.

A woman motorist and her daughter apparently had stopped to pick up a hitchhiker. And he, presumably, had murdered them, tossing their bodies onto the desert and fleeing in their car. A day or two later (maybe three, the details escape me now), police had spotted the car and given chase. At Crescent Junction, where U.S. 160 joins U.S. 50, the story ended as quickly as it had begun. The stolen car had skidded to a halt and, as police converged on it, the driver had shot himself to death.

"Yes," the waitress said softly, in answer to our inevitable question. "Over there. I heard the noise, looked up in time to see it." We talked a bit longer about the tragedy, the senselessness of it, then fell silent.

"I guess the worst thing is what it's doing to all of us," she said finally, her voice sad, almost plaintive. "Out here, you know, we've always prided ourselves on never passing a person in need. And now we're afraid not to. Even the truck drivers. It just isn't right."

Her words, and her tone—as if noting the passing of a family friend—tell much about her. They tell even more about the West she referred to as "out here."

1

It's a West of rugged terrain, of vast and underpopulated distances, and of harsh, often unpredictable, elements. And these combine to humble man, to remind him of his physical dependence on others, to sharpen his awareness of responsibility to his neighbors. These were the values she saw threatened, if not actually destroyed, by this brutal, meaningless crime. If in the future she was to respond to a stranger's wave from the roadside by pressing down on her car's accelerator, she seemed to be saying, what would happen to her the next time *she* needed help?

We knew the feeling. Some years before, on a quiet Sunday morning, we had jettisoned our battery on a lonely stretch of Wyoming highway. (A support brace had broken, actually, dropping the battery to the pavement where, still attached to the cable, it bounced along under the car, managing to create almost as much commotion as the string of tin cans and old shoes in an old-fashioned "shivaree.") We pulled off the road at once to reconnoiter. The first car to come by stopped, almost automatically, to see what could be done. As did the second, a semitrailer truck, and the third.

Soon we had shade-tree mechanics kibitzing shade-tree mechanics, all determined to diagnose our difficulty and come up with a practical solution. One truck driver, meanwhile, unable to get near enough to the raised hood to make his own diagnosis, assumed responsibility for directing highway traffic. And when emergency repairs were made (fittingly enough, with barbed wire, the all-purpose commodity generally credited with taming the West), the master mechanic insisted on following us to the next town, a mere thirty miles or so away, to make sure we didn't have any more trouble. We didn't; and a piece of pie and a cup of coffee was all we could pay him for his efforts.

But our waitress was right, of course. The West *is* changing— in many ways, and often with dismaying suddenness. That little tableau of latter-day Good Samaritanism in Wyoming, for example, isn't likely to unfold again any time soon on that particular road. (One can get killed on an Interstate these days by merely slowing down a bit, the better to appreciate a grazing antelope or a snowy peak against the horizon.) Yet it could take place on other roads in Wyoming—and, indeed, in many other parts of the West.

And this happens, happily, to be the whole point of all that follows here.

For change in the West is, we feel (and we feel it strongly), often more apparent than real. Cities have grown, become more tourist-conscious. Roads and accommodations, all visitor facilities and services actually, have been improved. And a certain amount of commercialization, varying widely from place to place, has inevitably followed. Yet these changes merely challenge one, making it harder for one to find the sights, activities, adventures—emotional experiences, if you will—that have not changed. But they are still to be found. It's just that limited access highways, posh hostelries, and the other now-to-be-expected niceties of travel in the last third of the 20th century often tend to obscure them.

THE MAGNETISM

Over the centuries the West has acted as a magnet, drawing people from over the world. And there's no simple explanation for it, no simple reason why. For the attraction has always been, and continues to be, a many-sided thing.

Non-Indians, we suppose, first pushed into the West because, like the mountain-climber's Everest, it was there. But when the excitement of the unknown was gone, or at least dulled, there were other equally potent lures. Visions of gold, whole cities of it, spurred on the Spanish as early as 1540. And the dream of striking it rich from a lucky hole in the ground—be it filled with gold, silver, even uranium—has drawn men to the West ever since.

From the end of the 18th century to well into the 19th, furs were the principal attraction, drawing the French and the English, the Russians, and, after the Louisiana Purchase in 1803, the Americans. Still other powerful lures were "heathen" Indians to convert, cities and railroads to build, virgin timber to cut, breathtaking expanses of waving grass to graze with sheep and cattle and eventually to sow to wheat.

Yet the dream of riches, or even the modest desire for a chance to earn one's livelihood, are common to any frontier. And the attraction of the American West has always been more than that of just another frontier to explore and exploit. Lewis and Clark recognized this unique appeal when they made their epochal trek from St. Louis to the Pacific Ocean and back in 1804–1806, as even a casual reading of their journals reveals. John Wesley Powell felt the West's magical

spell when he rode his boat through the awesome Grand Canyon
of the Colorado in 1869. And, most certainly, members of the 1870
Washburn-Langford-Doane Expedition to what is now Yellowstone
Park sensed this distinctive differentness, grappling with it in a way
that leaves all of us in their debt to this day.

Around a campfire the night of September 19 a century ago, near
the end of their journey of exploration, they discussed dividing the
area among themselves, knowing that in years to come people would
gladly pay money to see the natural marvels they had just verified
for themselves. It was a Montana judge, Cornelius Hedges, who
finally proposed that a treasure of this magnitude should be preserved intact for the enjoyment of all people. "Furthermore," he insisted, "each and every one of us should make every effort to have
this purpose accomplished." His plea won the enthusiastic support of
his friends. A year and a half later, on March 1, 1872, President U. S.
Grant's signature created Yellowstone National Park. It was the nation's first, and the world's.

The American West, then, was more than a frontier in the 19th
century, as the trans-Appalachian wilderness had been in the 18th
century, and the Atlantic seaboard itself in the 17th. It was a different

land, with a mystique all its own—no more likely to blend into the older coastal areas than Kipling's East and West. Never mind that most of the West's explorers, settlers, exploiters, builders, and hell-raisers came from the East. Often as not it was their *differentness* that sent them West in the first place (whether driven by a society to which they would not or could not adjust, or by an inner response to the challenge of excitement and danger). In any case, the West soon shaped them to its own mold.

THE DIFFERENCES

This East-West differentness is, of course, partly physical. There are such obvious phenomena as perpetually snowy mountain ranges, awesome river gorges, fancifully eroded buttes and mesas, bleakly forbidding deserts, trees of unimaginable girth and height, and eye-stretching sweeps of almost treeless plains.

These geographic features have, in turn, helped to create—or at least to emphasize—certain distinctive climatological differences. Influencing day-to-day life in many ways are such Western "surprises" as the ceaseless winds on the plains, midsummer frosts in the high mountain parks, the searing, dehydrating heat on the deserts, and that striking contrast between summertime sunshine and shade on the High Plains. "In Montana," a rancher friend insists, "you're never quite comfortable, you know: a little too hot in the sun, a little too cool in the shade." Visitors rarely fail to wonder that people in the West spend so much time talking about the weather. But why shouldn't they, in a land where the elements play such a dominating role in the day-to-day living of so many people? "Think it's going to rain?" isn't so commonplace when translated to "Suppose these hundred steers will put on enough weight to pay off the note at the bank?"

Ethnological factors also contribute to the West's distinctiveness. Centuries-old Spanish and Indian ways of life were encountered here by the first "Eastern" Americans in the Southwest. (Perhaps no single book details so dramatically the results evolving from this blend of differing cultures as the late Erna Fergusson's *New Mexico: A Pageant of Three Peoples.*) And there are so-called socioeconomic factors, too, none readily identifiable with developments east of the Mississippi. These would include the gold and silver booms which created "instant cities," the building of the transcontinental railroads, the "runs" into Oklahoma and other land rushes, the establishment of the unique cattle industry, and the white man's tragic final confrontation with a disillusioned and desperate red man.

The American West, in short, has always been different, offering unusual sights and experiences, unusual adventures and opportunities. And the non-Westerner has long recognized this differentness and sought to experience it, either firsthand as explorer, prospector, settler, or saloonkeeper, or secondhand, through the adventures and accounts of the more fortunate. Artists, from Charles Bodmer and George Catlin in the 1830's, through Frederic Remington and Charlie Russell, to today's growing band of serious moderns, have stoked this desire to see and know the West. And the "western" in all its various forms—Owen Wister's *The Virginian,* the pulp-paper *Wild West Weekly,* television's "Bonanza"—has fanned the same travel flame, proving itself a durable, not to say profitable, art form. Zane Grey was our own personal artistic evangel and we nod in his direction, with respect and gratitude, to this day.

EXPLORING TODAY

All right, then, what does it all boil down to?—what is it we're trying to say? Just this: (1) that the American West, distinctively different in terrain, climate, natural resources, and historic development, has attracted the traveler now for more than four centuries; (2) that this differentness is the West's essential attraction; and (3) that despite threatening clouds of change on the horizon, this attraction is as powerful today as it ever was. To experience it we need only to adapt our visiting pattern to changing circumstances. For if the West has changed, so has today's "typical" traveler in many and different ways. The automobile and the jet have seen to that.

For one thing, we are not likely to be seeing the West for the first time. The oftener we go back, the more critical, more sophisticated, more demanding we become, the more intolerant we're inclined to be of our fellow travelers who are responding to the same magnetic attraction. It's an all too human reaction. We understand it because we've been guilty of it all too often ourselves.

Colorado's Royal Gorge is one of the West's most magnificent sights—a 1,053-foot-deep, sheer-walled canyon, at the bottom of which the Arkansas River and the Denver & Rio Grande Western Railroad compete desperately for *Lebensraum*. (The contest is actually a draw. They both make it, although at one point the railroad must resort to the sheer engineering magic of a hanging bridge.) We were introduced to it under the best circumstances imaginable.

It was just before dusk on a quiet summer evening that we finally got the attention of the tollkeeper, paid our fifty cents (or was it just a quarter?) and pulled slowly onto the wooden-floored suspension bridge spanning the gorge. From pictures we knew what to expect, so far as the bridge itself was concerned; and from years of crisscrossing the West gathering material for our newspaper column and travel articles, we thought we knew what to expect from the top-down view into the gorge.

We didn't. Alone on the bridge, we stared down into the black chasm, awed by its grandeur, humbled by the thought of the millennia required by the river to scrape such a crevice from solid rock. Finally above the murmur of the wind in the nearby pines we became aware of the low, throaty growl of diesel engines. We watched as a long freight snaked its way up the canyon, so far below us it seemed little more than a realistic toy model. And a new dimension was added to our appreciation of the scene—a surge of shared pride that man could so successfully meet nature's challenge in such an awesome setting.

A number of years later we returned to the gorge, eager to recapture the pleasure and excitement of that first visit.

Amid the blare of music from parking-lot amplifiers we paid our toll (a dollar?) and inched through a garish entrance onto a bridge now choked with cars and people. The gorge was unchanged, of course, and so was the bridge itself; but the mood was shattered by the raucous music, the milling crowds, and the general carnival atmosphere. (Happily, we can report, most recently, a subsequent change for the better. The crowds are still there, true enough. But imaginative development the past few years has eliminated much of the carnival air. The spectacle must be shared with others—but it's worth the sharing!)

Each of you, we suspect, could counter our Royal Gorge experience with one of your own. The trouble, basically, is one of simple overcrowding: the spell of Yosemite Falls broken by the screech of transistor radios; the soul-restoring scent of redwoods tainted by exhaust fumes; the magic of Grand Canyon at sunset violated by the inanity of a viewer who might more profitably have remained home with color television. The trick, however, is not to berate others for doing, actually, just what one is himself doing. The trick is to out-maneuver them. To be there when they aren't. (Though we hate early rising, we transcend our prejudice on trips, get up with the sun and try to work in an hour or more of sightseeing before breakfast.) Or, perhaps even more desirable, to be somewhere else that's better—perhaps in part because "they" have not yet discovered it's there!

All of which brings us to the single, all-there-is-to-it point of this book: that we forthwith attempt to discover the whole by examining in greater detail the individual parts. That we, in effect, specialize.

This means that we learn of the Western explorers by retracing their trails. And get an insight into their just-like-us human frailty by examining their cliffside graffiti. That we learn of the fur trade by seeing historic trading posts. And discover the role of the military in winning the West by similarly visiting frontier forts, some of which simply evolved from the previously established trading posts. That we consider frontier pride and pretension by looking up the remains of famed old hostelries, nearly all of them touted at one time or an-other as "the finest west of the Missouri River." That we try to un-derstand and appreciate the magnitude of gold and silver fever by accumulating ghost towns (and those few rare towns that have re-fused to become ghosts). That we look at the challenge facing those who won the West by examining the mountain passes they used, the canyons they threaded, the railroads they built, and the cemeteries where they buried their dead.

But let's keep our perspective. There were Indians here in the West to greet the first Europeans. And they are still here. We'll try to appreciate their role in the history of the West by examining relics of the not unsubstantial culture they had developed, particularly in the Southwest, while Europe was enduring the Dark Ages—and by look-ing at what they are doing for themselves today.

And, finally, we'll attempt to round out our picture by taking some Western byways we've happened to miss in making our various other excursions. All, of course, can be made more real, more meaningful —and more poignant—by our personal involvement in the search.

Let's start with the trails.

A CLUTCH OF

WESTERN TRAILS

For many years, this over a century ago, a crude signpost is said to have stood at a fork in the rutted road near present-day Gardner, Kansas (west of Kansas City), offering slogging wagon trains a choice of arrows. One, labeled *Santa Fe,* pointed left. The other, pointing right, read *Oregon.* It may quite possibly have been the first highway marker west of the Mississippi River. Certainly it was one of the most important. Past it, first on this side, then on that, Bishop Berkeley's (and Bernard DeVoto's) "course of empire" flowed westward for several momentous decades.

All important as they were, though, in shaping the destiny of the American West, the Santa Fe and Oregon trails were neither the first nor the last of the destiny-making Western roads. Some, like the so-called Lewis and Clark Trail, were mere routes, owing their fame primarily to the stature of the men who first traveled them. Others, like the Chisholm Trail, embraced many separate and alternate routes rather than a single well-defined series of wagon ruts.

All had one thing in common, however. They helped to weld, for better or for worse, the trans-Mississippi West—its mountains and plains, deserts and fertile river valleys, its vast timber reserves and mineral resources, its Indians and Spanish-speaking peoples—to the then still predominantly Anglo-Saxon enclave that was the eastern United States. These trails carried the explorers westward and, later, the missionaries, miners, soldiers, saloonkeepers, trappers, gamblers, cattlemen, and farmers who followed them. They carried Bibles and whiskey westward, too, along with silks, square grand pianos, McGuffey readers, and fine Haviland china.

But traffic on the trails was not exclusively one way. They carried back furs to the East; and salted buffalo tongues and precious metals; and Indian children to educate in Eastern schools and an occasional disillusioned emigrant.

More importantly, perhaps, these trails carried intangibles east-

9

ward. They transmitted the historic "Macedonian call" for help from the Nez Percé and Flathead Indians in 1833, which released a flood of heathen-seeking missionaries and teachers. They broadcast the frenzied call of *Gold!* from the millrace of Sutter's Fort in California that opened the gates on yet another torrent of humanity. And they returned tall tales of unbelievable sights—trees as big as houses, mile-deep canyons, valleys that bubbled and boiled and erupted, buffalo herds that flowed across the prairie like a river for days at a time—tales that lured wondering travelers from Virginia log cabin and Bavarian castle alike.

As trails, they are gone now. But only in fact, not in fancy—and to appreciate just *how* fanciful they can remain, one has only to spend an evening before the television set. Today's traveler, given a real interest in history and a modicum of imagination, finds it relatively easy to retrace these storied routes in the family automobile, to re-create in his mind's eye much of the ever changing panorama they unfolded, to re-experience at least part of the excitement, dread, awe, anticipation, and wonderment they once inspired.

If their crude, man-made signs have disappeared (and there were precious few of them to begin with), not so their God-created landmarks, so eagerly or fearfully watched-for by the 19th century's traveler. Even today their names stir the imagination: Chimney Rock, in Nebraska, a giant finger pointing to heaven—in blessing? in warning?; the Rabbit Ears, first promise of the Rockies in New Mexico along the table-top smooth, and dangerously dry, Cimarron Cutoff; Council Grove in Kansas—wood and water, and the last trace of "civilization" before Santa Fe, and Pawnee Rock, farther on, with the possibility of Indians lying in wait; Raton Pass, linking Colorado and New Mexico, the bone-wearying mountain defile that, for all its ample supply of water, always made one wish he'd gambled on the "dry" route to Santa Fe; Devils Gate in Wyoming, with its sobering mounds of dirt and crude grave markers.

There are other trail relics, too: Signatures and initials carved on trailside rocks and ledges (these frontier graffiti are considered in the following chapter); deeply eroded ruts pounded into the rocky earth by untold thousands of iron-rimmed wagon wheels; tumbledown buildings that have somehow withstood the ravages of time; and a magnificent array of monuments, markers, and memorials erected by appreciative after-followers to record facts, recall feats, and pay respects to those who have gone before.

Retracing these old trails, then, can be a moving experience for the history buff. It takes but a contemplative moment or two beside Idaho's Lochsa River, its boiling white water compressed alternately between giant rocks and forested wilderness, to appreciate the enormity of the challenge Lewis and Clark faced in their way to the Pacific. Similarly, we never really felt the vast loneliness encountered by Oregon-bound wagon trains until we'd spent a day on the dirt and graveled ranch roads of southwestern Wyoming, beyond South Pass, where antelope outnumber cattle two to one and any permanent sign of habitation is as rare as a spring of cool water. And it wasn't until we had actually stood on Donner Pass in the High Sierras of California, and on the forested site below the summit where the Donner Party spent the tragic winter of 1846–1847, that we began to understand the awesomeness of seventeen-foot snowbanks in the middle of a vast mountain wilderness.

There are many such reminders, natural and man-made, along all these routes; and the individual traveler will of course react differently to each. But taken together they flesh out one's history-book skeleton of people and events, bring them to life, make them more understandable and meaningful. And because the crisscrossing trails themselves do create a kind of useful skeleton for the purposes of this book, we'll use them to begin our Western tour.

First, however, I would urge all travelers with Oklahoma on their itinerary to schedule a leisurely stop at the National Cowboy Hall of Fame and Western Heritage Center in Oklahoma City, if only for the museum's animated orientation map and lecture. So far as I know, it's the only one of its kind with such scope, and it offers the traveler a remarkably relaxing way to review his Western history.

As small colored lights flash across the contoured surface of the giant 45-by-37-foot relief map, and the docent (a ten-dollar word for "guide" we learned only when the new Center opened in 1965) makes her presentation, the viewer follows the course of the various trails that created the West and comes to recognize their interrelated, yet individual, roles in the development of the region. Afterwards, then, when he is able to explore for himself (to go on to the Chisholm Trail, for example, a branch of which ran within sight of the museum's Persimmon Hill location; or the Santa Fe or Mormon trails; or El Camino Real), he has a helpful field of reference.

And to enrich his preview of the West even further, he can partake of the visual smorgasbord offered by the magnificent Gilcrease Museum in Tulsa. There, in a somewhat similar way, he is given a graphic overlook at the West in all its variety and as seen by some of the world's great artists.

LEWIS AND CLARK TRAIL

President Jefferson told them "to explore the Missouri River, and such principal stream of it, as by its course and communication with the waters of the Pacific Ocean, may offer the most direct and practicable water communication across this continent, for the purposes of commerce." And Captain William Clark and Captain Meriwether Lewis did just that on their epochal 1804–1806 expedition to the Pacific and back.

They were not, admittedly, the first non-Indians in the area. Individual fur trappers and traders had come down out of Canada to explore various sections of the route they followed. But theirs was the journey that captured the imagination of a nation, and did much to influence the course of its development. It was a magnificent accomplishment; it takes nothing away from their undeniable abilities to note they were also incredibly lucky. For more than two years they led a party of forty-some people over a wildly variegated, virtually unexplored wilderness, populated with Indians of largely undetermined background and generally undeterminable disposition. Through it all they lost but a single party member, this not to Indians, but to what was probably appendicitis.

Too, Captains Lewis and Clark did their own cause no harm by keeping one of history's most minutely detailed and completely fascinating travel journals. These helped to prompt additional writings about the trip, further cementing its position in American history. Kansas City historian Fred L. Lee would seem justified in calling it the "writingest" expedition and at the same time the most "written about."

The 2,000-mile route they followed, however, is still pretty much that today: a route. No ordinary vacationing motorist is likely to attempt a complete rerun—even along the riverbanks (for most of the original route was made in a boat). Giant dams and their elongated reservoirs have flooded much of the historic Missouri River valley in North and South Dakota. As for the headwaters of the mighty Missouri ("in surch of which," Captain Lewis noted, "we have spent so many toilsome days and wristless nights"), they lie against the Continental Divide in southwestern Montana and are strictly off-limits for the automobile.

But the ten states whose present-day confines the expedition touched are now promoting the Lewis and Clark Trail: up the Missouri to the Bitterroot Mountains, then down the Lochsa, Snake, and Columbia rivers to Astoria, Oregon. And it's a rich route indeed in both history and scenery.

THE START, THE FINISH

Almost any trip into the Northwest lets one "cut" Lewis and Clark's trail, and several points along the way have been developed to give the traveler a keener understanding of the expedition. In St. Louis, where most of the Western trails actually started, Eero Saarinen's magnificent Gateway Arch now dramatizes the important role this Mississippi River town played—and to a certain extent continues to play—in this nation's westward expansion. The riverfront arch itself is part of the Jefferson National Expansion Memorial.

Another site preserved by the National Park Service is Fort Clatsop National Memorial near Astoria, the western end of the trail. A crude reconstruction here shows how the expedition spent the miserable winter of 1805–1806. As for the previous winter, it was spent among the friendly Mandan Indians near present-day Bismarck, North Dakota; and nearby Fort Abraham Lincoln State Park lets one clamber down inside a Mandan earth lodge, sunk into the ground for extra protection from the biting cold of the Northern Plains.

AND IN BETWEEN

Two other sections of the trail we've found particularly impressive are at the Floyd Memorial, on a ledge above the Missouri River just north of Council Bluffs, Iowa, and along the Lochsa River in the Idaho Panhandle. Floyd was the only member of the expedition to lose his life. His simple memorial here offers a magnificent panorama of the Missouri River valley. As for the Idaho road, it would thrill the traveler who had never even heard of Lewis and Clark (were such an unlikely creature to be found!). Long a wilderness, this area got its first road, U.S. 12 along the rock-strewn north shore of the turbulent Lochsa, only a few years ago. So rugged is the terrain through this area, so dense the forests descending to the water's edge, that the expedition was forced up onto the ridge to the north, as were centuries of Indian travelers before them, there to follow the Lolo Trail.

The latter-day traveler, however, has a choice of routes, if Lewis and Clark did not, and he should try to find the time somehow at least to sample them both. The new water-level route beside the Lochsa can be driven with extreme ease. The Lolo Trail ridge route is something else again: a high and narrow forest trail that doesn't shed all its snow until well into the spring. But the awesome panoramas of magnificent Idaho Panhandle wilderness it opens up are well worth the extra driving effort. Taken together, the two routes provide a dramatic yardstick with which to measure Lewis and Clark's remarkable accomplishment. (Write the U.S. Forest Service, Northern Region, Missoula, Montana, for excellent maps and descriptive information on this four-Forest stretch of the Lewis and Clark Trail. The individual states can also provide helpful material.)

OREGON TRAIL

This was the big one. If the Santa Fe Trail won for us the Spanish Southwest, the Oregon Trail assured us the Northwest, which might otherwise have remained in British hands. (Along the way, needless to say, the Indian lost out too—as he always did. He called this trail the "White Man's Big Medicine Road," not figuring out, until too late, how such an endless stream of covered wagons could snake westward year after year with virtually no traffic in the opposite direction.) Kentucky-born Jesse Applegate, heading for Oregon with his famed "Cow Column" (adding 1,800 cattle to the great migratory flood of 1843), called it the Path of Destiny. Historian Howard R. Driggs called it, simply and accurately, the trail of American Home-Builders. Stretching some 1,800 miles from the Missouri to the Columbia, it drew as many as 300,000 Americans westward in the three decades from 1840 to 1870.

How does one go about recapturing the spirit of such a long, history-rich trail? Well, to begin with, you can, if so inclined, drive the entire route, virtually every mile of it. Geographically that would be up the Platte and the Sweetwater across Nebraska and Wyoming, down the Snake and (after a fashion) the Columbia across Idaho and Oregon. By highway, it's roughly U.S. 30 across Nebraska, and several state routes in Wyoming, and then U.S. 30 again. You can accomplish this motorized survey in as little as three days—without, admittedly, seeing very much. Or you can profitably spend a full three weeks on the project; in which case you may be obliged to change your "buff" status to one of "fanatic," at least in the eyes of your friends.

Three sections of the trail, however, strike us as particularly rewarding: the Chimney Rock/Scotts Bluff area in western Nebraska; Independence Rock in central Wyoming; and historic South Pass on the Continental Divide, about 100 miles farther west. We're admittedly traditional in this, for these were among the stretches most familiar to the weary trail-travelers themselves, the ones they most often, and most dramatically, noted in their diaries and journals.

If you would leave your car and get a feel for the trail by actually walking a section of it, Wyoming is your happy hunting ground. Topography and climate have combined here to slow the ravages of time and preserve vestiges of the trail along almost its entire course. Near Guernsey, for example, you can stand in one trail rut, cut man-deep into the gray sandstone by wagon wheels and then worn deeper and deeper by a century of rain and wind. The defile, its sheer walls just beyond one's outstretched fingertips, is an impressive monument to perseverance on the part of man and nature alike.

CHIMNEY ROCK
(NEBRASKA)

The weirdly eroded shaft of reddish sandstone called Chimney Rock stands beside State 92 in western Nebraska. Rearing up out of the relatively flat prairie like a giant, storm-shattered tree trunk, it's an exciting hint of the Rockies on to the west. And rare indeed was the literate traveler over the years who passed this way and failed to note and try to describe it.

Boston merchant Nathaniel J. Wyeth thought it "a work of art," and even Richard F. Burton, that globe-trotting eccentric, found it "picturesque." The ubiquitous Father De Smet, more analytical, called it an "inverted funnel," gave it "a few more years" before erosion would reduce it to "a little heap on the plain." (The good Father knew people, fortunately, better than he did his geology.) And one matter-of-fact emigrant saw the truncated monument merely as "a haystack with a pole through its top."

SCOTTS BLUFF
(NEBRASKA)

Scotts Bluff National Monument, just west of Gering and also on Nebraska 92, protects Scotts Bluff, Chimney Rock, and other important trail sites in this area. To get the most from your visit, begin it with a leisurely tour of the visitor center's three exhibit chambers. In the Landmark Room you learn that the fur-seeking Mountain Men were Johnny-come-latelys along this particular stretch of the Platte: artifacts found here indicate Indians traveled the valley for at least ten thousand years before the white man appeared. The Oregon Trail Room dramatizes the long trek westward and its meaning to the nation. As for the William Henry Jackson Gallery, it salutes both the trail and one of the West's outstanding artists. An accomplished painter and, in later years, an imaginative photographer, Jackson crossed the plains in 1866 as an ox driver, making landscape sketches along the way. From these sketches he created—authentically re-created, actually—the West he had experienced. Two score of his original watercolors are on display at the museum.

With the visitor center behind you, you're ready for the drive to the top of Scotts Bluff itself, 750 feet above the river plain, and an unexcelled panorama of the Platte valley. In yet another section of the monument is Robidoux Pass, a low sandy ridge above one of the trail's finest springs. The French fur trader Basil Roubidou (the spelling varies) built a trading post and blacksmith shop here in 1848 to become the earliest settler in western Nebraska. Ruts of the rumbling Conestogas are still visible in the pass, this despite the fact that after 1852 most of the covered-wagon traffic used Mitchell Pass, through which Nebraska 92 continues westward from Scotts Bluff.

Independence Rock, in central Wyoming, was Father De Smet's famed Register of the Desert, a turtlelike mass of smooth rock beside the trail that tempted the graffito-minded traveler to try his hand. And few indeed of the passers-by seem to have resisted. But we'll go into that in the following chapter.

SOUTH PASS
(WYOMING)

On Wyoming 28 in the southwestern quarter of the state lies one of the most celebrated of all pioneer passes, largely because it was also one of the easiest to negotiate. The altitude of South Pass is only 7,550 feet, remarkably low for the Continental Divide in this area. Historians like to speculate that had it been more "typical" of the Northern Rockies—that is, with snowy heights and tortuous near-inaccessibility—the whole course of American expansion to the Pacific could have been altered. Home-seekers would have been shunted southward and thus the development of the nation drastically altered. But South Pass drew travelers to its grassy slopes and at least a few of them seemed unconsciously to grasp its significance. Joel Palmer, captaining a wagon train in 1845 (and author of an 1847 Journal that served for many years as a helpful emigrant guidebook), halted on the pass to note solemnly, "Here Hail Oregon." Standing astride the Continental Divide, he was justified in savoring the moment: Independence (Missouri) lay 947 miles behind him, Fort Vancouver (Washington) on the Columbia about that far ahead.

A few years later, "color" was found in California, and Oregon home-seekers were joined by a surge of frenzied gold-seekers. A marker here on the pass commemorates the Parting of the Ways. It's yet another historic junction, with Oregon lying off north, Utah and California to the south and west. In 1852, the Oregon Trail's peak year, an estimated 40,000 emigrants came to this die-casting fork in the road. Pause, if you would, to soak in the drama. It takes only a little imagination to visualize the good Dr. Marcus Whitman, equally devout and patriotic, kneeling here with Bible in one hand, American flag in the other, to offer up a grateful prayer. Of such simple, straightforward stuff the West was built.

Curiously, South Pass is no well-defined gorge. Instead, it's a broad, treeless, almost level flat some twenty miles wide. And if you're confused (as we were) as to the actual Divide, we're all in good company. In the early 1840's it bothered even such doughty pathfinders as John G. Frémont and Kit Carson, who served as his guide. The ascent was so gradual, Frémont wrote afterwards, that "we were obliged to watch very closely to find the place at which we had reached the culminating point."

OVERLAND TRAIL

Or call this one the *California Trail,* if you like. Basically it followed the older, well-established Oregon road as far as South Pass. Beyond, it struck southwest across the bleak deserts of Utah and Nevada, then vaulted the awesome Sierra Nevadas to reach the northern California gold fields. An excellent point from which to get the feel of this trail is California's now idyllic Donner Memorial State Park. Here just below the summit of what is now called Donner Pass (beside Interstate 80, some 35 miles southwest of Reno, Nevada), the tragically ill-prepared Donner-Reed Party was caught by snow in the early winter of 1846.

The memorial is movingly effective, even when viewed in shirt-sleeves on a warm sunny day. Extensive snowsheds protect long stretches of Southern Pacific tracks along the canyon wall just beyond the park, chilling reminders of the fierce winter storms that frequently paralyze this section of the High Country. Inexperience and poor judgment were primarily responsible for the Donner Party's misfortunes, of course. Delayed by a combination of circumstances, and caught by an unusually early storm, they were forced to spend the winter on the snow-buried mountainside. Some forty of the party died, despite eventual resort to cannibalism (it was the great arctic explorer Vilhjalmur Stefansson who discovered that cannibalism can actually hasten the death of the starving cannibal). And while the Donner experience was certainly not representative of travel on the Overland route, the tragedy remains one of the West's epic dramas.

MORMON TRAIL

Across Nebraska and Wyoming the emigration route of the Latter-Day Saints bound for Zion—Utah—roughly paralleled the Oregon Trail, though for the most part it stuck to the north rather than south side of the Platte. But the Mormons, driven from Nauvoo, Illinois, and striking westward some 1,300 miles for a new homeland in a desert no one else presumably wanted, blazed a trail of their own across southern Iowa to the Council Bluffs/Omaha area on the Missouri River, and again across southwestern Wyoming.

The Mormons, with their great respect for history, are long on noting, marking, and commemorating. Many monuments and memorials thus honor this heroic trek, and at least two stand out. The first is a sorrowful mother brooding over her dead in the Mormon Cemetery in North Omaha. Here in so-called Winter Quarters—a crudely constructed, yet painstakingly organized settlement—thousands of Saints waited out the cold, snowy months of 1846–1847 and 1847–1848. Some six hundred of them died and were buried in this vicinity. Their graves and the Arvard T. Fairbanks bronze of the grieving mother are moving reminders of the hardships they endured in the cause of religious freedom.

A far happier memorial stands near the end of the trail. It's the heroic "This Is the Place" Monument, beside Utah 65 on the flank of the Wasatch Mountains only a few miles east of Salt Lake City. From the mouth of what is now called Emigration Canyon the monument overlooks much of the desert-flat Salt Lake valley. It was from here, on July 24, 1847, that Mormon leader Brigham Young first saw the promised land. And when he uttered those historic words, "the place" is said to have boasted only a single cedar tree: Zion was a barren desert flat stretching westward from his feet to the gaunt Oquirrh Mountains beyond Great Salt Lake. The lush, trim greenness of modern-day Salt Lake City underscores his vision, and the zeal and perseverance of his hard-working followers.

SANTA FE TRAIL

Are you unhappy from time to time with the tolls charged by the new turnpikes? Then console yourself by considering for a moment the lot of the Santa Fe Trail traveler of 1865 pulling up before the gate of Uncle Dick Wootton's toll road over what is now Raton Pass on the Colorado-New Mexico border.

If we don't like the $1.45 or $2.15 tariff, chances are we can drive on to our destination by a variety of free (if not quite as fast) roads. But our roaming compadre of a century ago had no such simple freedom of choice. He had mountains all around him. And a brawny two-hundred-pound Mountain Man standing in front of him, rifle slung casually in the crook of his arm.

Richens Lacy Wootton was the man who lived in a house by the side of the road. And collected his toll, or else. He'd used his own money to build the twenty-seven miles of what even then was charitably called a road. He had no bondholders or rating boards to consult before setting his tolls: he collected what the traffic would bear. When you consider the fact that there wasn't another road within a hundred miles (and this alternate was a waterless trail across the Oklahoma Panhandle, the so-called Cimarron Cutoff), and the fact that Uncle Dick had a rifle he knew how to use, it isn't too surprising that what the traffic would bear came to $1.50 a wagon. (In the 1860's and 1870's there was considerable traffic bound for Santa Fe: Uncle Dick kept his money in a whiskey keg and, so they say, more than paid for his road the first year.)

And then in 1878 came the Santa Fe Railroad to replace treacherous ruts with smooth, parallel ribbons of steel (this gave rise, apparently, to that familiar expression, *sic transit gloria Wootton,* or "there went Wootton's glorious transit"). Today, driving Interstate 25 over the new Raton Pass and holding to an even 70 mph all the way, one finds it hard to realize that two miles a day was not bad in a prairie schooner, and anything less than a week for the Trinidad-to-Raton leg of the journey was considered a wanton flaunting of the laws of God and man.

"From civilization to sundown" is the way one early observer described the nearly 1,000 miles of ruts on the prairie that made up the Santa Fe Trail. Without a single bridge, it stretched (originally) from

Franklin, Missouri, to Santa Fe, New Mexico. Almost by itself it pried the rich Southwest from the grip of Mexico.

Over the plains it wound, at times over 400 feet wide, packed so hard—by as many as 3,000 wagon trains and 50,000 yoke of oxen a year—that traces of it still remain. (They're especially easy to spot northwest of Boise City in the Oklahoma Panhandle and near Fort Union in New Mexico.) U.S. 56 parallels much of it across Missouri, Kansas, Oklahoma, and New Mexico—this of course on the Cimarron Cutoff; the main route followed the Arkansas River into Colorado before swinging southwest along the Purgatoire River to Trinidad and Raton Pass.

Along the way remain enough natural and man-made monuments to give one the atmosphere of the trail. There are missions (Shawnee, Kaw), old forts (Larned, Dodge, Nichols, Union), and familiar landmarks (Council Grove, Pawnee Rock, Rabbit Ears Peak, Wagon Mound). Running down even a few of these brings Southwest history alive as no textbook possibly can.

If you're a purist, you'll want to begin your rerun at Franklin, Missouri, on the river of the same name, some 25 miles west of Columbia. Finding Franklin will be your first chore; it's almost gone now. But it was a thriving frontier settlement in 1821 when William Bicknell led a string of loaded pack-mules westward to try his hand at trading with the Spanish settlements. The first wagons rolled westward in 1822. And as riverboat traffic, railroad construction, and other factors changed, the point of debarkation moved progressively westward. In its latter years of usefulness the trail began on the Missouri waterfront in what is now downtown Kansas City.

JESSE CHISHOLM, AMONG OTHERS

This only scratches the surface. There are many more once important trails that played a role in developing the West. One could spend days, even weeks, in the steps of the good Fathers along California's famed *Mission Trail* from San Diego north to San Francisco. And there is *El Camino Real,* "the royal road" that carried soldiers, missionaries, and traders from Vera Cruz in Mexico up through Chihuahua to what is now El Paso, Texas, then along the east bank of the Rio Grande to, eventually, Santa Fe.

Then there are the various cattle trails, most storied of which is, ironically, the Chisholm Trail. From 1867 to 1887 it fed perhaps as many as 3,000,000 Texas cattle northward across Indian Territory to a succession of raw railhead towns in Kansas. The hardy longhorns, pretty much forgotten during the troubled Civil War years, had multiplied greatly. Getting them to eager markets in the East rescued impoverished Texas, made the railroads prosperous, and created the Western cattle industry. In the process Indian Territory was prepared for eventual white settlement.

But why "ironically" the Chisholm Trail? Because Jesse Chisholm, who gave it his name, was primarily an Indian trader: he never drove a single cow up the trail. Indeed, he died (March 4, 1868, only a few miles from where we write this) before the route he blazed for his freight wagons had actually begun to play its role in history. If you would begin to comprehend what these cattle trails meant to the West, try to visit the National Cowboy Hall of Fame and Western Heritage Center in Oklahoma City, mentioned earlier.

So much for trails. Log these and you will have discovered many more for future trips. That's the beauty of exploring for yourself. The more you work at it, the more you learn, the more places you find out about and decide you have to visit.

The next chapter is a case in point. Follow the old trails and you soon discover that yesterday's traveler, like today's, was wont to scratch his name and date of passage for the edification of those who followed. Kilroyism, it seems, is ageless. Only our name for it changes.

FRONTIER GRAFFITI

"Paso por aquí . . ."

Scratched into the soft, creamy sandstone of a striking New Mexico headland west of Albuquerque, the inscription could well be just another evidence of mindless vandalism, something of a Kilroy-was-here defacement with a Spanish accent, so to speak. Were it not, that is, for the rather exalted stature of the defacer. And the date of his scratching.

"There passed by here," the inscription reads, in translation, "the Adelantado Don Juan de Oñate, from the discovery of the Sea of the South [the Gulf of California] the 16th of April of 1605."

The passage of three and a half centuries has transformed this particular trailside graffito into priceless Americana. Here, preserved for all to see and marvel at is a bit of history recorded by *perhaps* the first European to—shall we say it?—leave his mark on the West: and this, fifteen years before the doughty Pilgrims stepped foot on Plymouth Rock.

We say *perhaps* the first European visitor. The Spanish in present-day Florida antedated the Pilgrims by some forty years. As for who may or may not have beaten Columbus to the New World—the Norse? the Etruscans?—we leave that to the scholars. (Along with determination of the authenticity of Minnesota's controversial 1362 Runestone. And, for that matter, similar rune-inscribed stones recently uncovered in southeastern Oklahoma.) For our purposes here, Oñate's inscription on El Morro is the oldest completely-agreed-upon literary relic of a European yet found in the West.

Oñate, however, was no pace-setter in this respect. For Kilroyism —unlike alcohol, smallpox, and syphilis—is not one of Europe's unique contributions to the culture of the American West. Indeed, the leaving behind of a record of one's passing probably began (if archeologists would only get busy and dig up the proof) with Adam and Eve's expulsion from the Garden. Certainly the Indians indulged in this innocent exhibitionism long before Columbus. Or Leif Ericson. (The Indians, needless to say, were our first "discoverers," and that by many centuries. How many, anthropologists are not yet ready to say with absolute certainty. It was almost surely two thousand years before Christ that they first probed the Aleutian land bridge from Asia to North America; it could easily have been six or eight thousand years before that.)

FOUR EARLY INDIAN ROCKS

In any case, examples of this pre-European artwork can be found throughout the West, whether incised in stone as petroglyphs or painted on rocks as pictographs. If you would examine an excellent one, and readily accessible, make it the so-called *Newspaper Rock* in Arizona's Petrified Forest National Park.

Another one, more spectacularly set, is in the rugged *Capitol Gorge* section of Capitol Reef National Monument in Utah. Back some years ago when one could still drive through the gorge by removing a few boulders here and there we stopped to examine it. And found it still impressive, despite the fact it had only recently been defaced— ironically, on the previous Easter Sunday. This underlines, of course, the problem of protecting these invaluable bits of Americana. So long as travelers, like Oñate, either walked or rode a horse, preservation was pretty much self-enforcing. Today, with almost total mobility, the problem is much more acute.

Only recently has North Dakota's *Indian Writing Rock* (north of Williston), its inscriptions still not definitely interpreted, been protected with a stone shelter and grate-type enclosure.

But delinquents with spray paint or pocket knife are not the only threat to valuable early-day graffiti, Indian or European. There are also the dam builders. Fortunately, historical and archeological "salvage" is now a recognized part of almost every major dam project. A recent success here is preservation of central Oregon's eighteen-ton *"Water Monster."* One massive petroglyph, it was saved from a watery grave behind Round Butte Dam on the Deschutes River by being hauled up out of the river canyon to a new state park near by. We can only hope that the original artists, looking down on the laborious, not to say costly, project from their Happy Hunting Ground vantage point, get at least a measure of gratification from the trouble they put Portland General Electric Company to.

But enough right now for Indian art. In this chapter we'll limit ourselves chronologically to the handiwork of more recent European and American inscribers, and geographically to some of the then more popular—and hence today more valuable—inscription sites. Isolated carvings, like elusive pockets of gold, are where you find them, and running them down can be both exciting and instructive.

Three sites, however, are outstanding:

El Morro—Don Juan de Oñate's two-hundred-foot-high bulletin board—stands beside New Mexico 53, some 45 miles south of Interstate 40.

Independence Rock—which we mentioned in the previous chapter while retracing the Oregon Trail—is beside Wyoming 220 about 50 miles southwest of Casper.

Pompeys Pillar—the third—is a dramatic reminder of the epochal Lewis and Clark expedition. A Yellowstone River landmark, it is visible from Interstate 94 in Montana, 30 miles downstream (east) from Billings.

EL MORRO

New Mexico's "great stone autograph album" is a three-century record of comings and goings in the Southwest. Juan de Oñate was merely the first, so far as one can tell at this late date, to leave his mark. (Coronado, who may well have been the first Conquistador to see El Morro—in 1540, while capturing the nearby Zuñi pueblo of Hawikúh [Cíbola]—apparently failed to sign the register.)

Autographing the rock did not stop until President Theodore Roosevelt established El Morro National Monument in 1906. In the intervening years the bluff's sheer east face proved irresistible to explorers, priests, emigrants, traders, Indian agents, soldiers, artists, surveyors, and pioneer settlers. More than five hundred of these signatures are still legible today.

At El Morro, too, one can examine Indian petroglyphs. Two large mesa-top pueblos were occupied here as early as 1175, so the Indians' rock writing probably predated Oñate's by nearly a half-millennium. Such is the material of history. And grist for the stone autograph collector's mill.

In 1629 Governor Francisco Manuel de Silva Nieto took pains to record on the rock his role in carrying the Faith to the Zuñis. Three

Oñate's historic "Kilroyism" on New Mexico's El Morro in 1605—the earliest known non-Indian inscription in the West.

years later El Morro absorbed this cryptic inscription: "They passed on March 23, 1632, to the avenging of the death of Father Letrado. Lujan." Thus was noted for historians the rejection of Christianity by the selfsame Zuñis (a rejection which was in many ways final). Other Spanish signatures one can "collect" at El Morro include such notable ones as De Vargas (1692), Governor Martinez (1716), and the Bishop of Durango (1737). The last decipherable Spanish inscription is dated 1774.

Among the first "modern" North Americans to sign in at El Morro —following the conquest of New Mexico in 1846 by General Stephen Watts Kearny—were Lieutenant James H. Simpson and the artist Richard H. Kern, in 1849. Among the more unusual visitors were the ungainly, humpbacked stars of Edward F. Beale's camel caravan on their way in 1857 from North Africa, via the Texas Gulf Coast, to California's Fort Tejón. The U.S. Army Camel Corps, a curious experiment in military transportation, was ordered by the Secretary of War, Jefferson Davis.

He thought, not illogically, that the desert animals would be perfect for supplying isolated army posts in the arid Southwest and, at the same time, for providing greater mobility to soldiers on patrol duty against hostile Indians. Beale shepherded the twenty-eight-camel caravan across the Southwestern deserts in five months, thought so highly of their performance that he recommended wider use for them. However, he and Jeff Davis both failed to take into consideration the army trooper's apparently inborn repugnance for the Near East's favorite beast of burden (among other things he considered the camel smelly and untrustworthy). The outbreak of the Civil War ended the experiment for good.

INDEPENDENCE ROCK

Though not nearly so venerable a ledger, a turtle-shaped mound of virtually vegetationless rock beside Wyoming 220 approximately 50 miles southwest of Casper, is the American West's most celebrated autograph album. Beside the busy Overland and Mormon trails, Independence Rock was called "the great registry of the desert" by the indefatigable Father Pierre Jean De Smet in 1840. (The "Black Robe" had come up the Missouri River in 1838 to establish a mission near what is today Council Bluffs, Iowa. For the next thirty years he crisscrossed the Upper Missouri River country, establishing additional missions, assisting other priests in their work, acting as a friendly intermediary between the War Department and hostile Indian bands.) Though the good Father's first visit came years before the great Oregon- and California-bound migrations of the 1840's and 1850's, he confesses that "my name figures amongst so many others."

Artist Alfred Jacob Miller, whose 1837 paintings were the first of Independence Rock, thought it resembled "a huge tortoise sprawling on the prairie." He noted in his journal that it contained "the names of Sublette, Wyeth, Campbell, Bonneville, Pilcher &c., many carved deep into the stone." (William Sublette—he spelled his surname *Sublett* on the Rock—and Robert Campbell built famed Fort Laramie in 1834; Joshua Pilcher was a veteran fur trapper and Indian agent; Nathaniel J. Wyeth was the Boston trader who came west in 1834; Captain B. L. E. Bonneville of the U.S. Army took the first wagon over the Oregon Trail's South Pass on July 24, 1832.) And then Miller adds: ". . . the temptation was too strong not to add our own;—to make amends for this assumption, and show our zeal for others, we found a man by the cognomer of Nelson had carved his name, and to insure *him* immortality we added to it, 'Of the Nile!' . . . what a pity it is he will never know his benefactors."

Unfortunately all evidence of this curious bit of frontier horseplay has been lost—either to the erosion of the elements, or to a boisterous Fourth of July celebration in 1847 when a thousand or so westbound emigrants set off a tremendous charge of gunpowder on Independence Rock as a fitting salute to the Founding Fathers.

Another fascinating bit of history, now lost, was "a symbol of the Christian faith . . . a large cross." So reads the 1842 journal entry of John C. Frémont, who "engraved" it on the rock. Curiously, his well-intentioned piety may possibly have cost him the Presidency: talk of the cross helped inflame feeling against him in 1856 when he ran unsuccessfully for President on the Republican ticket.

Far happier was the experience of the Mormons. Shrewdly capitalizing on the vanity of Gentile emigrants—most of whom lacked both the knack and the patience to memorialize their passing—Brigham Young's Zion-bound Saints assigned a few experienced stonecutters to the rock. The one dollar to five dollars they collected for each name chiseled on De Smet's register were duly deposited in the Mormons' depleted treasury.

These names are among the thousands still decipherable on Independence Rock. Also of interest to the visitor today: memorial plaques embedded in the stone to honor Narcissa Whitman and Eliza Spalding (the first white women to cross Wyoming), Father De Smet, the Mormons, and pioneer Ezra Meeker.

POMPEYS PILLAR

The striking bluff beside the Yellowstone River about 30 miles northeast of Billings, Montana, is yet another fascinating autograph album in stone. It is perhaps most important historically because it preserves one of the oldest non-Spanish inscriptions thus far discovered. And, for added significance, it is the only known physical evidence yet found of the magnificent Lewis and Clark trek from

St. Louis to the Pacific Ocean and back in 1804–1806. Here is the way Captain William Clark records the event in his Journal:

> . . . at 4 P.M. arived at a remarkable rock situated in an extensive bottom of the Star. [board] Side of the river & 250 paces from it. This rock I ascended and from it's top had a most extensive view in every direction. This rock which I shall call Pompy's Tower is 200 feet high and 400 paces in secumpherance and only axcessable on one Side. . . . The nativs have ingraved on the face of this rock the figures of animals & near which I marked my name and the day of the month & year . . . and opposit to a large Brook I call baptiest's Creek.

Almost surely Clark wanted to honor Sacajawea's son ("Jene Baptiest," in the Captain's spelling), born the previous winter. He had nicknamed the boy Pomp—Shoshone for "chief" or "first-born." *Wm. Clark July 25, 1806* is now preserved under glass, an irreplaceable treasure of American history.

Pompeys Pillar received many more inscriptions over the years. The Yellowstone was an important artery of travel (and remains one today: first the railroads, then the auto roads have followed this water-level route into the mountains). One of the Pillar's best-known visitors arrived in 1873—General George A. Custer with several hundred men. While swimming and playing in the river they were ambushed by Indians. No one was wounded. Three years later, however, and only a few miles away, the outcome of another ambush was far different.

SIX SCATTERED REGISTERS

These are but three of the West's better-known collections of trailside autographs. There are many other crowded registers, plus countless isolated rocks and ledges containing only a name or two.

Register Cliff, for example, is an impressive bluff guarding the south bank of the North Platte River near Guernsey, Wyoming. (Inquire locally. The road picks its way across a rickety one-lane wooden bridge—or did when we were there—then swings left along the foot of chalky cliffs to the rock itself.) The Overland Trail passed beneath it and by looking closely we found a few of its ruts, visible as depressions in the rank grass. Near by is a simple concrete monument, studded with horseshoes, spurs, and rings. It marks the site of an early-day stage station. The cliff itself has been badly vandalized. But there is a fence against one section, enclosing the weed-grown grave of an unknown pioneer. The site is nonetheless pretty and seems essentially unchanged from what it must have been a century ago. One can soak in the atmosphere, accept the experts' word for it that almost seven hundred inscriptions, dating back to 1842, are still legible. (An 1880 one was the best we could do, but we didn't try too hard; in situations like this our exploring is often more emotional than academic.)

Also in Wyoming, on *Names Hill* south of La Barge (beside U.S. 189), is the weathered carving, "James Bridger 1844 Trapper." It is believed to have been cut by the famed Mountain Man himself.

West of Pueblo, Colorado, in the Wet Mountains beside Colorado 96, there's the so-called *Kit Carson Rock.* On it the highly respected trapper and scout carved his name and the initials "J. J." for his wife, Josefa Jaramillo. The inscription, quite dim but still legible when we were there, is protected by an iron grating.

In rugged *Horsethief Canyon* near Brookville, Kansas, the hiker can (or could) find the rock on which William F. ("Buffalo Bill") Cody etched his initials in 1874.

Also in Kansas is a reminder of one of the West's most poignant dramas. It's at *Alcove Springs,* a modestly developed memorial park near Blue Rapids on the old Overland Trail. (The unnumbered access road is somewhat hard to find and it saves time to ask for directions in Blue Rapids.)

The faint inscription at the springs reads "J F R 26 May 1846."

J. F. Reed was with the ill-fated Donner Party. Here occurred the death of Sarah Handley Keyes, Reed's mother-in-law—memorialized on an impressive monument above the springs. It was the first of several delays that led to the party's being trapped by snow in the High Sierras. Even without the historical excitement, the site would merit a stop. An easy trail leads from the Keyes monument down into a wooded gorge from one wall of which the springs seep. The Reed inscription is in an overgrown "alcove" beside it.

For an even older inscription (1838), go to *Pipestone National Monument,* just off U.S. 75 in Minnesota's far southwestern corner. Here, still legible, are the initials "C. F.," for the same pathfinder John C. Frémont who, in 1842, engraved the "large cross" on Independence Rock. Four years before, as a young lieutenant, he'd been in this area with an exploratory party under Joseph Nicollet.

Today we hold no brief for those who deface public property with names and dates. Yet these defacements belong to yesterday, and the day before that. They are the signatures of men—there's no denying it—who did indeed leave their mark on the West, who played more than walk-on roles in its exploration and development.

Because of this—what these men made of their lives rather than what they did with their pocket knives—their idle "vandalisms" have now become cherished artifacts, and are, in a very real sense, living museums of Western Americana. Looking them up, re-creating the contemporary scene and reliving the historical dramas they recall, thus becomes both exciting and rewarding.

Much the same thing is true of what still remains of the fur trade. Larger, more numerous, and relatively easier to find, they unlock for the visitor yet another turbulent era in our history.

RELICS OF
THE FUR TRADE

PLACED BY THE CHEVALIER DE LA VÉRENDRYE
LO [LOUIS] JOST [JOSEPH VÉRENDRYE]
LOUIS LA LONDETTE
A MIOTTE
THE 30TH MARCH 1743

That's the message, scratched in French on one side of the small lead plate. On the other, prepared more professionally two years before, the neat Latin inscription reads: "In the 26th year of the reign of Louis XV the most illustrious Lord, the Lord Marquis of Beauharnois being a viceroy, 1741, Peter de La Vérendrye placed this." Together they mark something of a formal opening of the fur trade in the Upper Missouri country. And if one would explore the role furs played in the development of the American West by "tracking down" still extant fur-trade relics, the La Vérendrye brothers' lead plate is as good a starter as any.

To see the plate itself—6½ by 8½ by 3/16 inches, for those who cherish such footnote-ish details—you must go to the South Dakota historical museum in Pierre (not a bad idea when visiting any state, regardless of one's historical predilections). Uncovered by accident in 1913, it is now on permanent display as a small but priceless piece of Americana. Fully as exciting, however, is the discovery site, a low gumbo hill across the Missouri from the capital city. Developed as a modest memorial, with flags snapping gaily above a traditional granite slab of pertinent information, the grassy knoll offers the traveler-in-a-hurry an unusually fine view of the fabled "Big Muddy." But the more leisurely—and imaginative—visitor is offered much more: a picturesque observation point, suspended above time and space, from which to consider the fur trade *in toto*.

The Upper Missouri, now domesticated behind a chain of giant dams, lies placidly at one's feet. Aside from its hydroelectric generators, the river is primarily a single elongated recreation area serving a half-dozen states. But it was not ever thus. Until the coming of the railroads to this region in the last third of the 19th century, its importance extended into every area of man's endeavors. To the east and south, downstream, one can trace its bluff-lined course for many miles. On beyond, just over the horizon—out of sight, to be sure, but still in the mind's eye—are the physical reminders of that all-pervading importance.

Above Omaha lie the carefully preserved ruins of military Fort Atkinson, established on the upper river to protect and promote our Manifest Destiny. Downriver from Kansas City a few miles are the painstakingly reconstructed buildings of Fort Osage, the only official government trading factory west of the Mississippi. And at the mouth of the Missouri, beside the Mississippi, lies St. Louis itself, the acknowledged center of the American fur trade from the city's founding in 1763 down to the present. Up the Missouri from St. Louis came Lewis and Clark in 1804. Right behind them came the trappers and traders.

The posts they established once beaded the Missouri below and above our La Vérendrye Hill view. Fort Pierre, one of the American Fur Company's finest, lay a few miles to the north of where we stand. It has disappeared completely now; as has Fort Union, another important A.F.C. post near the mouth of the Yellowstone in northwestern North Dakota—not to be confused with *military* Fort Union, New Mexico, described in the following chapter. (The site, however, now belongs to the National Park Service, and plans are under way to reconstruct the once bustling establishment.) And with them have vanished scores of lesser trading posts owned by half a dozen different companies. But much remains, despite the ravages of man and the elements over the past hundred years and more.

In Montana, a tower of old Fort Benton still stands, and a building at Fort Owen. Physical remnants of trading establishments can also be found, in varying stages of disintegration, in Colorado, New Mexico, and California; in Utah, Nevada, and Washington. Nor are Osage and Union the only posts to be favored with restorations; there are others. And some excellent fur-trade museums have been set up to memorialize this vital aspect of our Western heritage.

If you are a fur-trade fancier, then, or would become one, you can map out a figurative course from atop La Vérendrye Hill, where it all can be said to have started. True, running down the specifics—the historic sites, preserved ruins, careful reconstructions, and excellent museums—may well fill your summer. But it will be a pleasant one. With your history you'll get scenery. Beaver country means water and woods implicitly. And that's still a pretty good vacation combination, regardless of one's travel tastes and prejudices.

HEART OF THE FUR COUNTRY

If La Vérendrye Hill and its long-buried lead plate provide an ideal starting place, symbolically, for one's fur-trade safari, Grand Teton National Park in Wyoming can claim the honor on purely practical grounds. Not only does the park offer the best static museum of the fur trade we know of, but it also presents it against a backdrop of some of the continent's most spectacular scenery—all in the setting of fabled Jackson Hole, which was loved by the Mountain Men themselves. For here on the upper Snake River they found the perfect "hole" or "park," the sheltered mountain valley offering water and grass for the horses, plenty of game for food, wood for the cookfires, and easy access.

The magnificent Tetons need no touting. One can describe them, if at all, only in clichés. Even to see them, we learned, isn't necessarily to believe them. Our first view was from Togwotee Pass, on the east. They were awesomely beautiful, yet somehow unreal . . . jagged cardboard cutouts in black against a dazzling blue sky . . . caricatures of mountain peaks as created by an earnest, but not too imaginative, fourth-grade art class for the next P.-T.A. open house. They were unreal to us then, almost incomprehensible. And they remain so to this day. We can only console ourselves with the thought that the Mountain Men themselves probably couldn't comprehend them either, if indeed they gave them a second glance. They'd come for beaver after all, and this was prime beaver country. Like the Mormon rancher who dismissed Utah's Bryce Canyon as "a helluva place to lose a cow," the typical trapper probably accepted the Tetons towering above him as a damned good windbreak and let it go at that.

This was indeed the heart of the fur country. And the source of three of the West's great river systems: the Colorado (via the Green, across a range of low hills to the south), the Columbia (via the Snake itself), and the Missouri (via the Yellowstone and the Wind to the north and the east). The Mountain Men were as familiar with the tributary streams and mountain passes of the region as housewives today are with the aisles and counters of their neighborhood supermarket. And in this general area in the 1830's were held most of the great rendezvous, the fur trader's annual social, cultural, and commercial whing-ding.

Alfred Jacob Miller's memorable "Rendezvous," painted in 1837, gives us our finest contemporary picture of these frontier soirées. He spent a month at that year's rendezvous on the Green (the site is near what today is Daniel, Wyoming, which re-creates the scene each summer with a colorful pageant) and left an equally graphic word picture of the event:

> At certain specified times during the year, the American Fur Company appoint a "Rendezvous" . . . for the purpose of trading with Indians and Trappers. . . . The first day is devoted to "High Jinks," a species of Saturnalia, in which feasting, drinking, and gambling form prominent parts. . . . The Fur Company's great tent is raised;—the Indians erect their picturesque white lodges;—The accumulated furs of the hunting season are brought forth, and the Company's tent is a besieged and busy place.

But you get all this and more, creatively conceived and effectively presented, in the Fur Trade Museum at the Grand Teton visitor center. There are helpful maps, a meticulously detailed diorama of the 1832 rendezvous at nearby Pierre's Hole, and a score of helpful panels on every phase of the fur trade—from the trails, rendezvous points, fur posts, weaponry, trade goods, Indian artifacts, and trapping techniques, to the experiences of Jim Colter, Captain Bonneville, Lewis and Clark, and the Astorians. All in all, this is one of the finest specialized museums you'll find anywhere. Give it a couple of hours and you'll be much better prepared to get the most from the balance of your fur-trade collecting. (Other excellent museums dealing primarily with the fur trade are at Fort Vancouver National Historic Site and at Fort Okanogan, both in Washington.)

A GEM IN MISSOURI: FORT OSAGE

Even more dramatic at times than the museum is the restoration or reconstruction. When authentically done, and on the original site, it adds another dimension to one's enjoyment. While still a museum of sorts, it serves to re-create a larger scene. And here Fort Osage, on the Missouri a few miles below Kansas City, is a prime example.

Osage was established in September 1808 on a promontory marked "Fort Point" on the Lewis and Clark map of 1804. "Found the river could be completely defended and the situation elegant," Clark wrote in his Journal on May 5, 1808. "This situation I had examined in the year 1804 and was delighted with it and am equally so now. Fixed a spot for the fort and other buildings and ordered the militia to build four blockhouses."

The fort was part of a noble experiment that failed. The plan was for the government to take over the Indian trading business to—in the words of Thomas Jefferson—"undersell private traders, foreign and domestic, driving them from competition and rid ourselves of a bad class of men." To do this, twenty-eight government trading "factories" were established. Osage was the only one west of the Mississippi (and is today the only one to be rebuilt). George C. Sibley was appointed factor and for a time he presided over a rather impressive establishment. It became a popular stopping place for travelers up and down the river.

Distinguished visitors in 1811 were the English naturalists John Bradbury and Thomas Nuttall. There were fur traders like Manuel Lisa and explorers like Major Stephen H. Long. The first steamboat arrived in 1819. Boon's Lick Trail, Missouri's first east-west highway, reached Fort Osage that same year. Regular stage service from the east came in 1821.

But private fur traders like John Jacob Astor persuaded Congress to scuttle the factory system in 1822. The post was abandoned and by July 6—a "Satterday"—Major Jacob Fowler described "the Shattered Setuation of Every thing We See." The garrison, he noted, "Was Commanded by one officer of the United States armey—Haveing two men under His Command Both of them Haveing disarted a few days ago and carryed off all His amonition."

The "setuation" remained bleak until quite recently, when the Native Sons of Kansas City spearheaded a quarter-million-dollar

Distillation of the romance of the fur trade: Fort Osage, near Kansas City, as it looks today.

reconstruction. Now a high white-oak stockade, guarded by block-houses, encloses the officers' quarters, an interpreter's house, and huts of the soldiers, all furnished with historic displays. In the yard is a staff flying a fifteen-star flag. The factory itself stands just outside the main gate. Painstakingly reconstructed according to specifications supplied from Washington, it is as authentically furnished as when in use, beautifully complete with hand-blown window glass, period furniture, and Indian trade goods. The visitor comes away with increased understanding of the life of the trader and his role not only in the fur trade but also in the development of the entire North American West.

SIX WORTH A VISIT

There are other somewhat more modest preservation, restoration, and reconstruction projects. One of the most fascinating—because it represents the "high-water mark" of Czarist Russia's attempt to colonize North America—is *Fort Ross,* on the Pacific some 90 miles northwest of San Francisco. The Russian-America Company established "Colony Ross" in 1812 and at one time the bustling stockaded post boasted fifty-nine buildings and a sizable population. Finally abandoned in 1841 (had the colonists proved better farmers, California might today be a Russian outpost), Fort Ross is now a state historical monument. Carefully restored are the stockade, two blockhouses, and the commandant's house, which serves as a museum. The original Russian Orthodox chapel, dating from 1824, was destroyed by fire in 1970.

Fort Benton, on the Upper Missouri (in the Montana town of the same name), was another American Fur Company post. Established in 1846 and operated until 1870, it witnessed the heyday of the steamboat era on the Big Muddy. A picturesque small-town ruin today, its single adobe blockhouse quietly guards the now quiet river. A handsome modern building nearby houses a small museum.

Bent's Fort, in Colorado on the Arkansas River between present-day Las Animas and La Junta, was elaborately built and honestly operated by some of the West's most reputable fur traders (a class of entrepreneur not widely acclaimed for outstanding moral integrity): William and Charles Bent, and Ceran St. Vrain. They built up the 100-by-150-foot, high-walled establishment between 1829 and 1832; until 1852 it was the Southwest's biggest, busiest, and most important trading post. Today it is Bent's Old Fort National Historic Site (18 miles east of La Junta) and one can, pending completion of a proposed restoration project, tour the ruins and view the bastion's exposed foundations.

North of Bent's Fort, in the South Platte River valley of Colorado some 40 miles north of Denver, is *Fort Vasquez,* one of four trading posts established in the area in the 1830's. It has now been reconstructed, a massive adobe affair in the median strip of U.S. 85 some 18 miles south of Greeley.

Fort Nisqually, in Washington, is yet another important early-day (1833) trading post that has been reconstructed in Tacoma's Point Defiance Park. It contains two restored original buildings (granary and the factor's house), moved here from the original site about 17 miles to the south. Curiously, Nisqually was a Hudson's Bay Company post property until 1867, though the area became a part of the

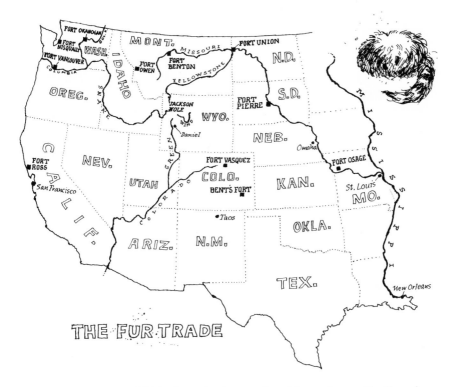

THE FUR·TRADE

United States in 1846 when the international boundary with Canada was pushed northward to the 49th parallel.

Fort Vancouver (a National Historic Site on the Washington side of the Columbia River opposite Portland, Oregon) is interesting to the fur-trade buff because it served as headquarters for all Hudson's Bay Company activities in the Pacific Northwest from 1824 to 1846, when "Oregon" passed into American hands. Nothing tangible remains of what was a prepossessing establishment—two dozen major buildings surrounded by a 325-by-732-foot log stockade, and guarded by a single bastion. Stockade and buildings, however, are marked with asphalt and concrete curbings and visitor center exhibits interpret the company's role (a generally benign one) in the Northwest fur trade. Factor at Fort Vancouver was the gracious and courtly John McLoughlin, who became the "Father of Oregon" after leaving H.B.C. (So ubiquitous were Hudson's Bay Company posts throughout the Northwest that its distinctive flag was readily recognized by travelers. The letters H.B.C. on the emblem, it was said, stood for "Here Before Christ.")

THE MEN OF TAOS

If Fort Vancouver was the center of activity in the Northwest, the rendezvous for the Southwest was definitely *Taos.* Few indeed are the old Mountain Men who did not at one time or another operate out of this friendly Spanish-Indian pueblo in the hills of north-central New Mexico. "Darn the white diggins," Lewis H. Garrard quotes John Hatcher as saying, "while thar's buffler in the mountains. Whoopee! Are you for Touse? This hos is thar in one sun, wagh!" The sentiment was widely shared, and the roster of Taos habitués included such doughties as Milton Sublette, brother of William, the Robidoux brothers, Uncle Dick Wootton (who later built and operated the toll road over Raton Pass), the highly respected Bents, Ceran St. Vrain, Jedediah Smith, Lucien Maxwell (of the famed Maxwell Land Grant), the colorful Jim Beckworth, and the one and only Kit Carson.

It was logical, therefore, that as the fur trade began to decline in the mid-1830's many of the Mountain Men chose to return to the congenial New Mexico village for good. Some married Spanish women and they naturally retired to the Taos area. Kit Carson himself had married Josefa Jaramillo, a New Mexican heiress; he stayed on to become a landowner, businessman, and U.S. Army colonel specializing in "troubleshooting" chores. (While post commander at Fort Garland, up in Colorado's San Luis valley, his understanding of the Ute language—and psychology—was a strong peace promoter. "In any dispute," one contemporary notes, "when violence seemed inevitable, all could be allayed by offering to send for 'Kitty,' as they termed him.") Charles Bent married an elder sister of Josefa's; he was appointed governor of New Mexico by General Stephen Watts Kearny.

Where do you best get the feel of the town? Well, try the Bent Home, a one-story Spanish Colonial building just north of the plaza, on Bent Street. Here in 1847 occurred one of the town's real tragedies. Indians from the Taos Pueblo, stirred up by Spanish residents still unreconciled to General Kearny's takeover the year before, revolted briefly, and attacked Governor Bent. He was scalped alive, then murdered here in his home. That he was one of the best friends the Indians had merely compounds the tragedy. There's a poignancy about the house, set on its quiet cottonwood-shaded side street; and a refreshing air of authenticity. Taos, happily, does not believe in hoking up its shrines.

Kit Carson's home is also preserved, just east of the plaza—a clutch of buildings, actually, grouped around the traditional patio. It was his home, office, and headquarters from 1858 to 1866. The parlor is particularly appealing. On one wall is a portrait of his brother-in-law, Governor Bent.

For yet another impression of Carson the man, walk the few blocks northeast to the town's old cemetery. Even your path through the towering cottonwoods is rich in history. The plaza you have left was laid out in the early 1600's, some three miles south of multistoried Taos Pueblo. The pueblo, or Indian village, was already well established when Hernando de Alvarado first saw it in 1540. Moccasins and soft leather boots have beaten down the path over the years, and the solemn Pueblo Indian you chance to meet, on his or her way to work, is a pleasant reminder.

In the cemetery you'll find a plot surrounded by an old-fashioned iron fence. In it are the graves of the Mountain Men, Josefa, and several other family members. And near by is the grave of retired U.S. Army Lieutenant Colonel John J. McGurdy. A Kansas lawyer, in 1958 he was buried there at his own request. On his stone is the simple inscription: "I am at Rest for Eternity by My Idol Kit Carson." Kit Carson was that kind of man. He earned and held the respect of all who knew him—if only by reputation.

It's a touching tribute to Carson the man. If all the Mountain Men could not have merited such a tribute, at least some of them could. They were a tough, individualistic lot. Had they not been, they would never have survived their first season in beaver country. They were also a colorful lot. Some day, we suspect, movie and television writers will "discover" them and, perhaps, give their stereotyped "cowboys and Indians" a well-earned rest.

A fitting place to end our fur-trade hunt, then, is Taos. The years have been good to the village. They have merely mellowed it, made it even more comfortable, more congenial. Actually, the most significant item missing from the Mountain Man scene would appear to be "Taos Lightning," by all odds the Southwest's most notable potable. Garrard called it "the 'mountain dew' of New Mexico— *aguardiente de Taos*," and noted that its fame was so widespread that "it is imbibed before attaining a very drinkable age, by both foreigners and residents, with great avidity." And if contemporary reports on its potency are to be credited, perhaps even that slight subtraction from the Taos scene is, today, all for the best.

WHERE THE
SOLDIERS LIVED

"You know the best place to dig for relics in an old frontier army post like this?"

The questioner was Nick Blesser, administrative assistant at Fort Union National Monument, the famed Santa Fe Trail military post in northeastern New Mexico (far from the former Fort Union *trading post* on the North Dakota-Montana border).

We saw the twinkle in his eye, and promptly gave up. And told him so.

"In filled-up privy holes!"

Then, to prove he wasn't putting us on, he began telling of experiences they'd had there at Fort Union. Not only was the latrine a handy trash bin, he explained. It also provided a convenient cache in an emergency. "Take the carbine we found recently in a pit on officers' row."

Records of the fort mention one that was stolen and never recovered. What happened to it? No one is ever likely to know for sure, he concedes. But he's willing to bet the man who took it suddenly got scared, simply dumped it into the nearest two-holer—other than his own, of course—he could find.

Post latrines have also yielded whiskey bottles (another example of disposing of the evidence, perhaps?), buttons, military insignia, and—discovered just before we were there—a Wedgwood pitcher with a small piece broken from its lip. One can almost see the hapless officer-husband knocking over the cherished possession in his wife's absence, then hurrying out to hide the proof of guilt so he could safely profess his innocence when accused.

But all the buried excitement and drama around a once important post like Fort Union is not confined to filled-in toilet pits. Established in 1851 to guard the busy Santa Fe Trail, it served as both military and social center until abandonment finally came in 1891. And one can apparently uncover reminders of its four-decade past anywhere he digs, even when not actually relic hunting.

Take the four skeletons uncovered a few years ago during construction of some Park Service residences. All non-Caucasian, they were buried in a single grave—each with a bullet hole in the head. There's still no official explanation; or wasn't when we talked with Blesser. But again he had an educated theory.

Barring evidence to the contrary, he imagines an officer telling his sergeant: "Take these so-and-so Indians out on work detail. If they try to escape, shoot." The sergeant did; they tried; and he shot. And that was that.

He could very well be right. The Southwestern frontier was not quite as pacified as it is now. Human life was on the cheap side, especially when it came to Indians, some of whom were still naive enough to think that because they'd once roamed this land, it was theirs and they should be allowed to keep it.

They are much more sophisticated today, thanks in no small measure to the tutelage of the white man's lawyers. They now recognize they'll never get their land back. (Indeed, in many cases they probably wouldn't accept it if it were offered, such is the nature of some of the white man's "improvements.") Instead, they have discovered (1) the Indian claims court; and (2) the fairly substantial monetary value that can be affixed to the white man's belatedly aroused conscience. As a result, in case after case involving most of the nation's Indian tribes, Uncle Sam has been recognizing the validity of the treaty granting the red man his land—usually in the quaint language of these flowery documents: "so long as the water runs and the grass grows"—and then agreeing, in lieu of return of the land, to make a per capita cash settlement.

But to get back to Fort Union. Obviously the quickest, surest—and most satisfying—way to come to know such an historic army post is under the personal guidance of a man like Nick Blesser. And happily there are many like him in the National Park Service. It is an amazingly dedicated group of men and women. Most of them not only love the particular area they're serving at the moment, but are eager to share that love with the interested visitor.

Even without a guide, however, these old posts can be completely fascinating. No matter if one hasn't visited too many of them before. Books, movies, and television shows have made us all pretty well aware of what they looked like, how they were run. To see a reconstructed blockhouse, a restored barracks, or even the crumbling

MONT.

FORT KEOGH •

• FORT BUFORD

N.D. • FORT ABRAHAM LINCOLN

WYO.

FORT LARAMIE •
• FORT BRIDGER

• FORT ROBINSON

NEB.

FORT ATKINSON

FORT LEAVENWORTH
FORT RILEY •

KAN. • FORT LARNED
FORT DODGE • FORT SCOTT •

NEV.

• FORT CHURCHILL

COLO.

FORT GARLAND •

FORT GIBSON
FORT RENO OKLA. •
FORT WASHITA • FORT SMITH
• FORT SILL ARK.

FORT WHIPPLE •

FORT UNION •

ARIZ. N.M.

FORT BELKNAP •

• FORT BLISS TEX.

• FORT DAVIS

WHERE
THE SOLDIERS
LIVED

ruins of a wall is often enough to help us re-create in our mind's eye the entire post as it existed in its heyday.

They all differed some, of course, in appearance, function, and importance. And because their role, taken together, was so vital in the overall development of the West, collecting them is both exciting and—as one learns more about them—enlightening, for it was in and around these early-day military installations that much of the history of the Western frontier unfolded. So visiting them today gives one not only a picture of 19th-century military life, but often an insight as well into some of the problems of civilian life in the 20th century.

By the late 1830's and early 1840's the fur trade was definitely on the decline. Many formerly important trading posts were beginning to disappear. Several others were being taken over by the government for use as army posts. In either case the influence of the trader—never, so far as the Indian was concerned, particularly ennobling (with an occasional exception)—was giving way to that of the U.S. Army. For better or worse, the last half of the 19th century in much of the American West came to be dominated by the military.

No one needs to be told that it isn't a pretty story, this seemingly endless account of Indian-white man conflict. The Indian can be forgiven for preferring the fur trappers and the traders. True, the trappers often took up with his prettiest women; and the traders frequently cheated him on his goods and supplies. They did, however, usually keep him supplied with whiskey so he could, if but briefly, forget his troubles.

If the situation wasn't nearly as good as it should have been, neither was it quite as bad as the movie and television writers would have us believe. And no one was actually to blame. The white man was simply doing what he was told to do: going West. And the Indian, for his part, was following the most basic of human impulses: protecting his homeland and his way of life. The clash was inevitable. And so, perhaps, was the cruelty, the killing and torturing, the treachery and broken promises, the heroism and occasional flashes of pure nobility. In the main, admittedly, it was a sorry tale. In some instances it was inexcusably sordid, as in the tragic "Trail of Tears" that uprooted the so-called Five Civilized Tribes from long-established homes in the Southeast and moved them onto new lands in the near wilderness that was then Oklahoma.

Nevertheless the military phase of the development of the West is past now: our regrets here, no matter how sincere, won't change the record. At best, they can only influence the course of the future by encouraging more enlightened attitudes and, perhaps, by awarding claim checks. To the historian, then, we leave the drawing-up of moral assessments for our past sins. We'll concentrate instead on the more physical legacies of our military past. We'll see how these now peaceful forts, each of which wrote its own brief paragraph in the history book, can make our Western travels today more enjoyable and more rewarding.

For the purposes of touring, let's consider them in three categories: (1) forts that are still active military posts; (2) forts that survive but in a nonmilitary capacity; and (3) forts that have been restored or are at least being preserved as "stabilized" ruins. Each category has its especially fine examples. Each has its particular satisfactions.

ACTIVE MILITARY POSTS

There are at least four important forts in this category and you can easily spend an enjoyable day at any one of them. (An inquiry to the Information Office at the individual post should bring all the descriptive material one needs.) They are Oklahoma's *Fort Sill,* one hundred years old in 1969; *Fort Bliss,* the El Paso (Texas) outpost that dates back to 1849; *Fort Leavenworth,* the first to be established (1827) in Kansas and now, because of its Command General Staff School, widely known as "the mother-in-law of the Army"; and, also in Kansas, *Fort Riley,* established in 1853.

Each has its own legitimate claim on one's time and attention. At Riley, now completely restored and operated as a museum by the Kansas State Historical Society, is the building that was Kansas's first capitol. The handsome stone structure was built in 1855. Bliss and Leavenworth both maintain excellent museums, too. And Leavenworth, with its tree-shaded Missouri River-bank setting and mellowed buildings, may very well strike the visitor as the "delightful cantonment" George Catlin found there in 1832.

As loyal Sooners, however, we are partial to Sill. It boasts not one, but three, fine museums, including one which, befitting its status as the nation's Artillery and Guided Missile Center, displays as complete a collection of American field artillery as can be found anywhere. Another is in the post's Old Stockade, a partly rebuilt stone affair that dates back to 1870 and is one of the reservation's oldest buildings. It houses an excellent selection of 19th-century vehicles, both military and civilian. The third, containing important Indian materials, is housed in the two-story stone Old Post Guardhouse, not the least fascinating feature of which is the bleak-walled dungeon that once contained Geronimo, the fierce Apache chieftain.

But Fort Sill's charm and interest extend well beyond museum buildings. For one thing, there are its fascinating old cemeteries. In them lie buried many of the Indians whose names are known and recognized across the land—old warriors like Geronimo, Satanta, Satank, Quanah Parker, and others. And this was, and is, Indian country: Fort Sill was established to keep peace among the various tribes. There are still thousands of Indians living around the reservation.

Also adding interest to the Fort Sill area is the Wichita Mountains Wildlife Refuge, which adjoins the reservation. Established in 1907 to protect the American buffalo, then nearing extinction, it was the nation's first, and has served as a model and proving ground for those that followed. Along with some 1,000 buffalo, it shelters 350 elk, 300 Texas longhorns, many deer, and other animals. The Wichita Mountains themselves offer lakes for fishing; picnic and camper areas; a rugged red-rock mountain one can drive to the top of; and Holy City, setting for one of the nation's first Easter pageants.

STILL ACTIVE, BUT NONMILITARY

In this category we would like to be similarly chauvinistic. *Fort Reno* is only a few minutes from our home. As kids we crossed the reservation, by train or by car, every time we went to "the city" (that is, Oklahoma City). It has always had a very special appeal as my first military post (which it was until 1949), and still a favorite among all those seen later. In many ways it deserves my affection, too, particularly on historical grounds.

Reno was established in 1874, near the North Canadian River west of present-day Oklahoma City in what was then the heart of the Indian country. After the Cheyennes and Arapahoes were finally pacified (albeit with extreme reluctance and not without a last heroic try for freedom—the epic 1877 flight of 937 Northern Cheyennes under Little Wolf and Dull Knife), the post became a cavalry remount station. Our childhood memories include the polo field, a fashionable clubhouse, and thousands of acres of horses. Later we came to appreciate some of the importance Fort Reno shared with Darlington, the Cheyenne and Arapaho Indian Agency across the river (and for whose protection the post was established). Together they represented a white outpost deep in Indian Territory. The *Cheyenne Transporter* became the first (1880) newspaper in western Oklahoma. From here the Territory's initial mail and stage lines fanned westward as far as Texas and its first telephone line provided a welcome link to the outside world.

Today we still enjoy roaming about the tree-shaded parade (the reservation is now an agricultural experiment station) and visiting the lonely, walled cemetery on a grassy knoll a half-mile to the west. It's an altogether satisfying exercise in nostalgia—and one the unhurried traveler can easily share simply by turning off Interstate 40 some 30 miles west of Oklahoma City. (Footnote to history: Fort Reno soldiers fired the shots on April 22, 1889, that started the fabled "run" of home-seekers into Oklahoma Territory, and in the process heralded the end of the Western frontier.)

Fort Robinson, however, of all the still active nonmilitary posts in the West, has perhaps the most to offer the casual visitor. This is especially so if one would absorb the maximum of Indian frontier atmosphere in a minimum of time. Not that we would encourage this hurry-up approach to sightseeing. Travel pleasure, generally, goes to the light-footed and carefree. But at Fort Robinson everything is spread out conveniently for one to enjoy; you waste no time hunting for the sights and moods you came to find.

In extreme northwestern Nebraska, it has a record of founding and development remarkably similar to that of Fort Reno. It too was established in 1874 to keep an eye on Indians (the Sioux in this case) not yet ready to give in to the white man. It too avoided abandonment, when the Indian threat had disappeared, by becoming a remount station. And when the army finally did give up on the post (in 1949, as with Fort Reno), it too was turned over to the U.S. Department of Agriculture for use as an experiment station.

The Nebraska State Historical Society set out in 1956 to preserve the post's historic values. (It was here that the Sioux's famed Crazy Horse, hero of the Little Big Horn, was killed in September 1877 while being taken to the guardhouse.) And today, while still a U.S.D.A. facility, it is operated as a state historical monument. The post headquarters building serves as a museum. A two-story galleried brick barracks serves as a lodge, with pleasantly decorated dining room and lobby gift shop. Several original officers' houses—sprawling, comfortable affairs under lofty cottonwoods—also provide visitor accommodations. Fort Robinson, in short, is a thoroughly fascinating living museum, an old army post where one can browse for an hour amid musty relics of the Indian-fighting frontier West, or spend an entire vacation.

Fort Keogh, beside the Yellowstone River just west of Miles City, Montana, is yet another U.S.D.A. facility. One of the West's classic examples of "too little, too late," it was established in 1877, the year after the watershed Battle of the Little Big Horn and named for one of Custer's captains killed in that celebrated encounter. Its role in the pacification of the Sioux was thus a relatively minor one and the post was de-activated in 1900 after the Spanish-American War. Today it is a quiet livestock experiment station, with a half-dozen or so of its original log buildings remaining, plus many of the old officers' homes fronting the unused parade ground. These structures, the historical markers erected to note long-vanished buildings, the ancient trees, and the ruins of the old power plant down by the Yellowstone all help to re-create for the visitor the post's brief heyday.

Two additional troves are *Fort Whipple,* on the northeast edge of Prescott, Arizona, established in 1864 to provide a measure of insurance against being scalped by the Apaches, and now a Veterans' Administration facility; and *Fort Dodge,* four miles southeast of present Dodge City, Kansas, one of the most important of the military posts built (in 1864) to protect the Santa Fe Trail. Although considerably modified, at least four of its very early buildings are still in use at what is now a state soldiers' home.

PRESERVED AND/OR RESTORED

Thanks primarily to the National Park Service and various state historical societies, the Western traveler finds his richest pickings in this category. At least three important Indian posts are now national historic sites, their ancient buildings scientifically preserved (in a few cases, painstakingly restored). Their role in Western history is dramatized with museum exhibits, slide presentations and, in the case of *Fort Davis,* such electronic extras as regulation bugle calls, martial music, and the roar of a 12-pound Napoleon!

This old fort lies nestled against the Davis Mountains of southwestern Texas. Founded in 1854, it was named for Jefferson Davis, then Secretary of War, who had ordered it built to protect California-bound gold-seekers from the Apaches. (In 1857 it was on the route westward of the famed Camel Corps, another brainchild of Mr.

Davis's.) Cattlemen moved in when the Indian threat disappeared. Its usefulness outlived, the post was finally abandoned in 1891. Yet so durable were its adobe and limestone buildings (and so dry the climate) that most of them were still recognizable—and altogether impressive—ruins when Congress recently declared the 447-acre reservation a National Historic Site. That's when the Park Service decided to amplify its traditional preservation techniques with electronic gadgetry.

The ruins were stabilized, and information signs erected. A barracks was carefully restored to serve as visitor center and museum. But the unique offering consists of two audio tapes—produced for N.P.S. at Fort Sill, interestingly enough. One is a daily program of regulation bugle calls, blown on an authentic "period" bugle and heard throughout the fort at the appropriate time (roughly every twenty minutes). The second program—more elaborate, but presented only on special occasions and at times of heavy visitation—is an eighteen-minute re-creation of a full 1875 formal retreat parade. To hear it while standing on the parade looking out over the old homes, barracks, commissary, and other buildings can be a moving experience.

Fort Union (visited at the start of this chapter) some 25 miles northeast of Las Vegas, New Mexico, and *Fort Laramie,* in southeastern Wyoming, are additional N.P.S. preserves that, as indicated above, can transform the often dry facts of history into exciting drama. From 1851 to 1891 Union was the largest military post on the Southwest frontier. An eighty-acre collection of rock and adobe buildings, unprotected by either stockade or blockhouse, it served as a base for a combined military/civilian population that at times reached 3,000 persons. Extensive tracks of the Santa Fe Trail still surround the post. We consider its visitor center's telling of the Fort Union story outstanding.

Fort Laramie has an even longer and more dramatic tale to tell. Several decades of existence as an important American Fur Company trading post preceded its years of service (1849–1890) as a military establishment to protect the Overland Trail. Twenty-one structures remain on the site, only a few of them restored. Most notable of these, without doubt, is "Old Bedlam," the one-time headquarters building. A real showpiece, its refurnished interior units represent various periods of its history. Equally impressive, we think, are some of the fort's less glamorous attractions: the restored sutler's store (authentically stocked with everything from black powder to bustles); the single-lane steel bridge thrown across the North Platte in 1875 (and believed to be, when finally retired in 1961, the oldest west of the Mississippi still in use); deeply eroded ruts of the Overland Trail; and the stark, sobering remains of five 3-by-5-foot windowless rock cells that once restrained the post's incorrigibles.

Yet another interesting N.P.S. exhibit is *Fort Smith,* in the Arkansas city of the same name that grew up around it. Its site was an elevation above the Arkansas River overlooking Oklahoma to the west —the wild Indian Territory it was established to supervise. And it did just that, from its founding in 1817 until well after its abandonment in 1871, four years before the arrival of the town's best-known figure: Judge Isaac C. Parker. The Park Service offers an ivy-clad old commissary, dating from 1838 and now filled with frontier relics and mementos, and, in a nearby building, Judge Parker's restored courtroom, from which sounded one hundred and fifty-one death sentences that led, eventually, to eighty-three hangings. His "multistage" gallows, as we would say in this missile age, has also been reconstructed near by, for those who go in for such grisly relics.

The various Western states have also done an admirable job of preserving still other historic military outposts. Oklahoma protects as state parks two of her oldest and most important: *Fort Gibson,* dating from 1824 and boasting, with the stone ruins of a later date, a stockaded reconstruction of the original building; and *Fort Washita,* established in 1842 and now being partially restored.

Colorado's *Fort Garland,* in the San Luis valley, though comparatively small is well cared for; it houses an interesting state historical society collection.

Nebraska also has, east of U.S. 73 a few miles north of Omaha, the archeological remains of *Fort Atkinson,* the first U.S. military outpost on the Upper Missouri River.

North Dakota's primary entry is *Fort Abraham Lincoln,* from which General Custer and the Seventh Cavalry marched away that gala May day in 1876 for the fateful rendezvous with the Sioux on the Little Big Horn. The state park, across the Missouri from Bismarck, is also noteworthy for Slant Village, five carefully reconstructed earth lodges of the Mandan Indians, the friendly tribe with whom Lewis and Clark spent that first winter of 1804–1805.

Other state parks worthy of inclusion in anyone's collection: Nevada's *Fort Churchill,* a picturesque and extensive ruin in the desert east of Carson City; Wyoming's *Fort Bridger,* of particular interest for its Pony Express associations. Local historical groups are responsible for preserving still other formerly important military posts, notably *Fort Scott* and *Fort Larned,* both in Kansas, and *Fort Belknap* in northern Texas.

These are but a handful of the old military posts that dot the West. If hunting them up proves exciting, you'll have no trouble building a list of additional ones to log. And by this time you're likely to have discovered the special pleasure that comes from the chance encounter with a native who shares your interests and who, as often as not, becomes a firm new friend. It happened to us when we were poking around the remains of North Dakota's *Fort Buford,* which the U.S. Army established at the confluence of the Missouri and Yellowstone rivers after the American Fur Company abandoned its trading post of Fort Union, near by.

A request for directions from old-timer John Mellon and his wife led to an animated discussion of history. A few more questions and answers and the chat moved from the corral to the Mellons' sitting room, where the table was soon filled with relics they had picked up over the years from the fort/trading post area. "Many's the time," he was soon reminiscing, "I've swum a horse across the Yellowstone in flood."

It's then that history, no longer confined to a book, suddenly leaps out at you. This is what memorable vacations are made of.

THOSE GOLD
AND SILVER CAMPS

We run into trouble right off on this one. Do we visit only those old mining camps that have now lapsed into complete ghosthood—or at least give every evidence of ghosthood in one of its more terminal stages? Or do we concentrate instead on those camps that are still going strong, even stronger in some cases than when they were in their heyday? And what about these in-between communities, the proud, once important little mining towns that have fallen on hard times yet refuse to give up, relying blindly on the hope that seemingly springs eternal in the hearts of all who search for gold?

But you get the idea. The problem here is not *what* to explore so much as it is what *not* to explore. Otherwise we're in the awkward position of the little boy who was curious about penguins. Remember how he went to the library, told the nice lady what he wanted, and was soon handed a tome so big he could barely lift it? How he thumbed through it awhile, dutifully, then confessed to the lady he hadn't really wanted to know *that* much about penguins?

Well, that's almost the way it is with ghost towns. Certainly the list of old gold and silver camps alone (not counting lumber-mill towns, railroad-construction camps, coal towns, and farming/ranching communities, many of which are also pretty well ghosted today) runs into the thousands. If you doubt it, ask that nice lady librarian to haul out for your inspection such ghost-town bibles as Muriel Sibell Wolle's *Stampede to Timberline* or *The Bonanza Trail,* Perry Eberhart's anecdotal *Guide to the Colorado Ghost Towns and Mining Camps,* or one of the recent photographic studies by Lambert Florin. If you're not already a ghost-town buff, you could be seduced by any of them into becoming one in short order. Each has its own mix of fact, legend, maps, and illustrative material. But the result is invariably the same: itchy feet. And that urge to run down "ghosts" is one of the nicest things that can happen to the Western traveler with a little extra time on his hands.

WHERE THE PAY DIRT WAS

"Gold is where you find it!" That was the cry. And it offered both consolation and reassurance. No matter that you arrived too late for a good claim in the latest rush. There would always be another one. A bigger one. Try that next creek—the other side of the mountain. Gold is where you find it. The biggest bonanza of them all is still waiting to be discovered.

So the miners—and would-be miners—crisscrossed the West. They stampeded up deep canyons, scrambled over forbidding mountain ranges, trudged across bleak and deadly deserts. And behind them they left brawling, boisterous discovery camps, newborn towns that boomed overnight into reasonable facsimiles of cities—complete with saloons, gaslights, dancehalls, hotels, churches, funeral parlors, and cemeteries—most of them to collapse, just as suddenly, into picturesque ghosts when their precious metals were exhausted. They were established haphazardly, wherever two or three lucky prospectors were able to locate paying claims. And so most of them are rediscovered today by the curious motorist, haphazardly, more often than not found tucked away in a breathtakingly beautiful canyon, occasionally at or near the dead end of a somewhat less than secondary road. (If you dislike leaving the pavement, you may well prefer to limit your jaunts to the "lively" ghosts discussed in the next chapter.)

This felicitous development—felicitous, that is, so far as the shunpike lover is concerned—is Mother Nature's contribution to our enjoyment. For by creating her precious minerals deep underground in a chemically sealed mass of lesser materials, then resorting to cataclysmic subterranean convulsions to expose them to the forces of erosion, she assured most mining camps a rugged, mountain-locked site. And this, in turn, promises the hunter dramatic scenery plus exciting history in seeking out his own Tombstones, Ophirs, Silver Cliffs, Tincups, and Cripple Creeks.

On top of this the camps themselves come in all shapes and sizes, which adds to the fun. A few fortunate ones, having apparently whipped the boom-and-bust cycle, still boast a certain importance, if not in the old mining-center tradition, then (as is more often the case) as a holiday resort. But these are our "lively ghosts" and we consider them separately later on. Here we concentrate on their more numerous brethren, the economically less fortunate, though often more interesting.

BEFORE THEY'RE GONE COMPLETELY

In both categories, however—the quick and the dead, so to speak— the dedicated buff will soon find himself driven by a stern, inevitable urgency. For the old mining districts, bustling or somnolent, are changing. Changing rapidly. The continuing travel boom, along with something we reluctantly concede to be "technological progress," combine to assure that. Here's what we mean.

Time was—and that but a few years back—when relative isolation protected these mining areas from all but their natural enemies of fire, flood, and decay. Not so today. To these time-honored adversaries have now been added a handful of modern ones.

First of all there's the automobile, to give us mobility. It permits us to come in ever increasing numbers to see and to enjoy; and, in the process, to sow the seeds of change. For our coming creates the need for better roads. And soon we must have the bulldozer to shape the "improvements" our being there demands. And thereby, ironically, we often obliterate much of that same aura we have come to see and enjoy.

Few areas of Colorado (or anywhere else, for that matter) could rival for number, variety, and picturesqueness the mining relics that once dotted Clear Creek Canyon near Idaho Springs, west of Denver. Yet much of its distinctive charm (or scarified ugliness, by today's Keep America Beautiful standards) has now been destroyed to make way for Interstate 70. Not all of the charm, to be sure; this stretch of road is still an open-faced textbook dramatizing a century of Colorado mining history. But if the unwary motorist isn't careful to get off onto service roads, he can easily find himself rocketing through this fascinating section at a speed that permits him to appreciate little more than the latest in automobile taillight design.

Then there's the tax collector. He's a destroyer too, though a largely unwitting one. Only a few years back you could poke up almost any canyon in Colorado with a 50–50 chance of discovering a rusty, stair-stepped mountainside mill, an abandoned cable or railway system, or perhaps a multistoried dormitory stuck precariously like an abandoned mud-dauber's nest to the side of a perpendicular cliff. Today many of these ghostly relics of the mining era have been razed because their owners seek to reduce their tax liabilities on property no longer productive.

But an end to tears. Enough remains to fill a lifetime of vacations for the history-minded, or camera-laden, friend of "ghosts." So what follows is no guide—no catalogue of possibilities—but rather a series of notes and suggestions on some of the areas we've found particularly rewarding over the years.

COLORADO

Colorado alone can keep one busy for years on end. Certainly it has us. And there's no easier place to start casting around than in the vicinity of the state's more lively ghosts, which we'll presumably visit later on anyway.

ASPEN-GUNNISON AREA

Let's go first to Aspen.

You approach this charming little center of sport and culture from the east, on the Independence Pass road, and suddenly you are directly above the true ghost camp that gave the pass its name.

Independence is a clutch of crude, tumbled-in log cabins on a denuded mountain slope: peacefully idyllic or cold and frightening, depending on your own mood at the moment. Either way, it's an altogether appropriate starter for one's tour.

Drive south of Aspen a few miles and you can log crumbling *Ashcroft,* with a soaring high-meadow view of the Taylor Pass country thrown in for good measure. (In season you might like to extend your explorations—by Toklat dogsled!)

And southwest of Aspen, up the Crystal River on an abandoned railroad grade, are two more "collector's items": the vaguely Grecian ghost of *Marble* (perhaps the country's only town ever able to boast an all-marble jail) and *Crystal City,* now a tiny, end-of-the-road summer colony.

Immediately across the Continental Divide to the south the various headwater streams of the famed Gunnison River make up another rich ghost-hunting ground. (But Schofield Pass, like Taylor Pass to the east, is impassable to passenger cars, so you'll have to go around.) Gunnison provides a convenient headquarters for exploring the entire area.

Schofield itself, almost on the Divide and virtually the end of the road, is reduced now to a few weed-filled cellar holes. (In 1880 General Grant rode in on a white mule—fittingly enough, if history is to be trusted—and joined the townsfolk around a barrel of whiskey to celebrate its brief silver prosperity.) But the town's top-of-the-world panorama is more than enough to repay the steely-nerved motorist for the somewhat hairy ascent.

Gothic lies just below the worst stretch of the road, and the cautious hunter may well choose to turn around here. A biological laboratory keeps Gothic's few remaining houses occupied. The number and variety of wildflowers here offer a colorful extra.

Crested Butte, however, is the real prize in this area. Started as a gold camp, it was long a prosperous coal town, and almost died when the mines closed in 1952. But it had, in better days, spawned one of the state's first ski clubs, and it is skiing today—with some lead and zinc mining—that threatens to put the picturesque old camp into the lively ghost category. A downtown block or two of false-fronted stores, hotels, and public buildings give it a real charm. A one-time mine company boardinghouse has been made into a pleasantly comfortable lodge.

Tincup, too, is a choice one, a near-ghost that gives its handful of summer residents high-altitude isolation, a unique name, and fond memories of the Gold Cup Mine (operated as late as the mid-1930's). Special feature: the curious four-section cemetery (for Jews, Catholics, Protestants, and Boot Hill-ers).

Latter-day summer popularity also keeps alive *Lake City, Ohio*

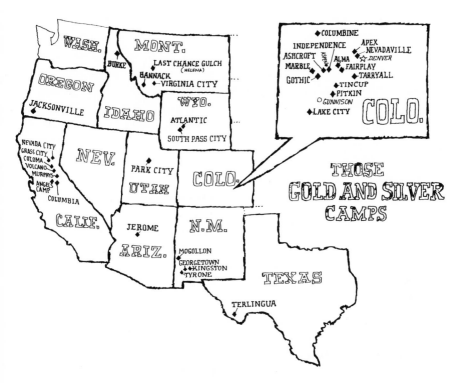

City, Pitkin, and several other camps once served by the area's many narrow-gauge railroads.

CENTRAL CITY AREA

Only a few minutes west of Denver lies Central City, perhaps the best known of the "lively" ghosts. And here, as at Aspen, a score of once prosperous satellite camps challenge the collector. *Nevadaville* and *Eureka* perch precariously above Central.

Beyond Eureka, past a pair of old cemeteries and along a dimly defined high-meadow trail that rewards one with a hundred-mile-long panorama of snowy Continental Divide, lies *Apex,* quite satisfyingly ghosted.

From this actual apex you drop precipitously into *Tolland.* One can easily loop back into Blackhawk/Central City from here or spend another day looking up a dozen or more old camps in this area. Or start the breathtaking climb over Corona Pass on the abandoned right-of-way of the Denver & Salt Lake Railway.

SOUTH PARK AREA

Incredibly flat South Park lies virtually in the center of Colorado. (In the West, a "park" is a mountain-rimmed valley varying in area from a few acres to many square miles.) The famed Bayou Salado of the Mountain Men (because of its salt marshes), it is carpeted with lush wild grasses that nourish some of the state's finest beef cattle. And hidden away in its crevices and canyons lie many old mining camps famous in their day.

Individual homes, stores, and other buildings from many of these once-thriving settlements have been brought into *Fairplay* to create South Park City. And you might well start your explorations here. It's a fine evocation of the early-day gold camp; not a real town, to be sure, but a collection of authentic structures in a realistic settlement. As such it should not be compared to the completely synthetic "Six Gun City" amusement parks now springing up over the country. (One even opened recently in Paris!) But Fairplay itself is fully as fascinating as its make-believe "city," with enough old buildings, mining atmosphere, and genuine frontier friendliness to put you in the proper mood for tarrying to explore the Park's less fortunate camps.

Alma, along the Hoosier Pass road to the north, is best known today for Silver Heels, the storied "Angel of Mercy of South Park." In the very best of mining-camp tradition, this now anonymous dance-hall girl—her beauty exceeded only by the deep-down goodness of her soul—stayed behind when a smallpox epidemic emptied the town of women, "respectable" and otherwise. She nursed the stricken, comforted the dying, and then, as the legend has it, came down herself with the disease, losing not her life, but her former beauty.

Near Alma are *Quartzville,* one of the state's oldest standing ghosts, and *Buckskin Joe* (not to be confused with the commercial attraction of that name near Pueblo). Here one can still find several Spanish *arrastras,* relics of one of the earliest methods man had for grinding ore to recover the gold it contains.

Leavick lies west of Fairplay, and not too many years ago it still boasted the ruined Last Chance Mill with an abandoned aerial tram from which rusty ore buckets groaned and squeaked in the wind.

On South Park's east side are the true ghosts of *Tarryall* (site of the area's first substantial gold strike) and *Hamilton.* Still visible at the former is the deep pit known as Whiskey Hole, a placer claim worked one winter by one hundred and fifty miners who spent most of their earnings for whiskey. During boom days, they say, men who lacked the wherewithal to assuage their thirst were permitted to pan gold on the premises just for drinks.

But ghost towns dot much of the western two thirds of Colorado. Wherever you roam, you're rarely more than a few minutes from one or more of them—hence the advantage of a Wolle volume on the seat beside you. Naturally the bigger and richer districts were soon served by a railroad; and some of them are now best reached by driving roads laid on abandoned railroad rights-of-way. Cripple Creek attracted no less than three rail lines (a richly rewarding field of its own, as we'll try to show in a later chapter); all three are now auto roads. But many other mining areas simply didn't produce long enough to rate rail service. Among these is the fascinating Elkhead country north of Steamboat Springs.

A forested semiwilderness served by meandering, graveled by-ways, it features the weathered—and, in some cases, virtually un-recognizable—remains of such pleasantly named camps as *Royal Flush, Columbine, Clark, Hahns Peak* (also known as *Poverty Bar*), and *Whisky Park*. For an extra, the unhurried motorist gets back-country vistas of a Colorado that 95 percent of the state's visitors never see.

WYOMING-UTAH-MONTANA-IDAHO-OREGON

Other states, needless to say, have prime ghost-hunting preserves, too. (Miss Wolle proves this handsomely with her *Montana Pay Dirt,* which does for the Treasure State what *Stampede* does for Colorado.) Wyoming offers no more historically interesting byway than State 28 southwest of Lander, highlighted by picturesque *At-lantic* and *South Pass City.* Both, as their names imply, lie near famed South Pass, that remarkably gentle crossing of the Continental Divide used by the Oregon and Overland trails.

South Pass City, however, deserves her footnote in history for yet another reason. Her gold, discovered in 1867, was exhausted within a few years. But not before she had played her role in the emancipation of women. On December 10, 1869, Wyoming's first territorial legislature granted equal rights to women, the nation's first state or territory to do so. The bill, introduced by South Pass City-man William H. Bright, was strongly supported by another resident, Esther Hobart Morris, who that same year became the country's first woman justice of the peace.

The Atlantic/South Pass City area represents Wyoming's first significant gold strike. And this suggests a kind of specialization-within-a-specialization: a collection, not just of any gold camp, but of the *first* important discovery camp in each state. (For Colorado that would be Central City, as we'll see in the next chapter.)

Park City is Utah's biggest, handsomest prospect for ghost-hood. Or was, until winter sports came along a few years ago to capitalize on its picturesque, mine-scarred Wasatch Mountains setting, abundance of snow, and overabundance of empty houses and buildings ripe for resort conversion into shops and living quarters. The district boomed in the 1870's, mostly on silver, has had its ups and downs ever since.

We saw it first from the downslope of Guardsman Pass, before the skiers arrived and when the *Utah Guide* was calling it "still the slightly uncouth mining camp of yore." Though impressively large, the canyon-bottom town was eerily empty, as if two thirds of its population had fled precipitously the day before. Some of that mood is gone now. But the town is still both charming and exciting. Access is easy from Interstate 80 at Kimball Junction.

In Montana the prime item would be *Bannack,* famous as one of the targets for the Plummer Gang until the Vigilantes caught up with and hanged their leader. It boomed into existence in 1862, thus antedating the better-known *Virginia City* and *Last Chance Gulch* (now Helena). As a state historical monument, its structures still standing are now guaranteed the protection they deserve. To appreciate the scene completely, drive to the old hillside cemetery above the camp.

For Idaho our first choice would have to be *Burke,* near the north end of the Panhandle. And this despite the fact that they've torn down the Tiger, the unique five-story hostelry so effectively plugging the narrow canyon that the railroad was forced to steam *through* it! All of which made it a bit trying for offduty miners trying to catch up on their sleep, but extremely convenient for hungry trainmen (and magnificent for ecstatic rail buffs).

Oregon's finest mining relic is *Jacksonville,* only a few miles west of Medford. Its ancient homes and business buildings, scattered along dusty, tree-shaded streets, create a handsomely authentic Western "set" even Hollywood would be hard pressed to improve on.

CALIFORNIA

And we've only scratched the surface. The Mother Lode was one of the great gold discoveries of all time, and the Forty-niners established scores of towns along the west slope of the Sierra Nevadas, many of them today virtual museums in themselves. *Columbia* is perhaps the prize here. It's a kind of Mother Lode Williamsburg and the state has now taken a hand in preserving and reconstructing it.

But *Coloma,* where it all began with the finding of gold flecks in Captain Sutter's millrace, has its share of lures and partisans.

And after taking another look just a few months ago, we're now ready to add *Murphys* and *Volcano* to our lengthy list of runners-up.

Follow California 49 from *Chinese Camp* north to *Grass Valley* and *Nevada City* and you can relive the entire Gold Rush era. But watch for road improvements that represent relocations. Where given a choice of Route 49 *Alternate* and the regular Route 49, opt for the former. It will be the old road—admittedly slower, but much more interesting, as it threads the main street of every town along the way. By hurrying one could perhaps drive the entire length of

Route 49 in a couple of days. By poking off onto the various side roads, and investigating the additional gold camps they serve, you could spend two weeks on the project. Or two months.

The Mother Lode's Golden Chain Council (P.O. Box 596, Jackson, California) sends excellent maps and other materials to would-be visitors who want to do a bit of homework before their trip. The region can be enjoyed without them, of course, but we're convinced you'll find your enjoyment doubled by knowing what to look for, and where, and having some background information on the many towns, old buildings, millsites, abandoned ferry slips, and other sights encountered along the way.

Once famed mining camps that are now bustling—though still pleasantly small—include *Placerville* and *Sonora*. As for *Angels Camp,* it relives its glory once a year with a flamboyant Jumping Frog Contest. (Mark Twain and Bret Harte, incidentally, are still very much alive in the Mother Lode. You stumble over references and monuments to their journalistic careers in the region everywhere you turn.) Many of the other camps, like their counterparts throughout the West, are sustained in great measure by summer residents, retirees, big-city refugees, and others who have decided simply to exchange the hectic pace of the "outside" for the relative peace and quiet of the Mother Lode's semighost-hood.

ARIZONA-NEW MEXICO-TEXAS

If and when your roaming takes you to Arizona, don't overlook *Jerome.* Not a gold or silver ghost, but a copper one, it dramatizes the fate of the substantial "company town" when the company moves out, which is just what Phelps-Dodge did in 1953. Population in the mountainside town, which had once been as high as 15,000, promptly dropped to a baker's dozen. We were lucky. We saw it, for the first time, just after this had happened. Not only was the town a virtual ghost, but there was an actual ghostliness, even to the atmosphere. Now you marvel at the size and complexity of the semideserted town, thrill to the beauty of its setting and the proud magnificence of its decaying buildings; then we could only stare, and shudder. It was a ghost in fact as well as in name.

Now the fates would appear to be smiling again. The availability of still usable buildings (fine Victorian homes as well as sturdy com-

mercial structures), a generally mild climate, undeniable picturesqueness (a precipitous pitch that allows much of the town to slip un-
evenly down the mountainside, inch by inch, year after year, and which
prompted insurance companies to cancel out policies long before
Phelps-Dodge left)—all these factors have combined with the efforts
of stubborn, history-proud Jerome natives to give the town a kind
of precarious near-ghost stability. Museums have been established.
The state has lent a hand in preservations. And that tortuous stretch
of U.S. 89–A which threads its way up Mingus Mountain through
the mass of stair-stepped homes, stores, and mining-era relics that
comprise modern Jerome is one of the state's most fascinating.

New Mexico's Jerome is *Tyrone*. Or was. For Tyrone, near Silver
City in the southwestern corner of the state, has been resurrected,
almost literally. And we rather preferred its first incarnation! Our
introduction to "old" Tyrone was much like that to Jerome. We
stared at its substantial Mediterranean-style stores, offices, and public
buildings, grouped graciously around a weed-grown plaza, and had
the eerie feeling of having stumbled onto a recently excavated Roman
ruin. The town was obviously dead, yet it appeared to have breathed
its last only a few days before.

The "new" Tyrone has the same fine mountain setting. And some
of its old homes. But a multimillion-dollar open-pit copper development has brought instant boom to replace instant ghost-hood. And its
magnificent business plaza—long a model of company-town munifi-
cence—has disappeared into the open pit itself!

Dust devils and desolation make Mogollon, in southwest New Mexico, one of the most evocative ghosts of the Rocky Mountain West.

This southwestern corner of New Mexico has other worthwhile items, less or more fortunate than Tyrone, depending upon your viewpoint.

Georgetown, above Santa Rita, is the complete ghost, with only remnants of stone walls and cellar holes to help you re-create the scene.

In the crumbling-relic stage are *Kingston* and *Hillsboro,* which you can log by continuing your Black Range explorations along New Mexico 90.

But the real gem, in our opinion, is *Mogollon.* Down to an old-timer or two when we last saw it, it was surrounded by an almost staggering array of sagging buildings, abandoned mine heads, rusted-out mills, and entire mountain ranges of waste and tailings dumps. Having read a bit of its turbulent history beforehand, we simply pulled off the road at our first vantage point, and tried consciously to recapture the scene at the time when a dozen or more stamp mills operated around the clock and thousands of people scurried about in the web of now virtually deserted canyons below us.

But only one's time and energy put a limit on the ghost-town hunting possibilities. Were we forced to choose but a single entry for each state, we'd have to select *Terlingua* for Texas, a "mercury ghost" in the spectacularly eroded Big Bend Country. It's had its ups and downs, determined primarily by the world demand for mercury.

But such, alas, are the hazards of collecting ghost towns: turn your back and someone tears down a landmark. Or opens a new mine and rearranges the landscape. But—to be philosophical about it, you then have a built-in excuse for going back. So hunting for ghosts actually becomes a never-ending quest. The more old gold and silver (copper? mercury?) camps one logs, the more he learns about what must wait for the next trip. At least that's the way we've always found it.

For a starter, mention your interest in old mining camps to the state tourist office when you write for information. Arizona, Colorado, Utah, California, Montana, and several other states have already prepared ghost-town lists for you. Get them and you're on your own. But go forewarned: it's addictive. Once you've stumbled on a treasure like Jerome or Park City, you could well be hooked for life.

A LOOK AT
LIVELY GHOSTS

"This may look like a thrift shop," the sign in the cluttered shop window blandly announced. "But it isn't."

And that pretty well sums up what has happened to Aspen in the two decades or so since industrialist Walter Paepcke "discovered" the sleepy little Colorado mining town beside the Roaring Fork and decided to wake it up. Awaken it he has. And though in many ways it still manages to resemble a gold and silver camp—despite the Rocky Mountain equivalent to urban sprawl—a thrift shop it most definitely is not.

Aspen has, for the moment at least, whipped the boom-and-bust cycle. It has added another upswing boom on the end—a prosperity based on culture, winter sports, spectacular scenery, a certain nostalgic romanticism that responds automatically to quaint Victorianism, and the obvious affluence that allows travelers to indulge their whims and fancies in all these fields of pleasure. The phenomenon is not unique to Aspen, by any means. With a varying mixture of attractions and appeals, a dozen or more other once dormant mining camps have similarly stirred to life after awakening to the happy fact that today's gold is to be found not in underground seams of rock or isolated gravel bars, but rather in the pockets of appreciative visitors. Aspen, however, was one of the first to make the discovery. And it has done more to capitalize on it to date than any of our other now lively ghosts.

ASPEN: BLUEPRINT FOR PROSPERITY

The first time we saw Aspen its multistoried old brick business buildings and tree-shaded streets were virtually deserted. Historic Wheeler Opera House was silent. The ornate Jerome Hotel was a picturesque relic of mining-boom opulence. And most of the town's many fine Victorian houses were unpainted and neglected. Aspen, in short, appeared much as it must have looked in 1893 when the collapse of the silver market undermined its justification for living. It had struggled on for another half-century, like scores of other once booming camps through the Rocky Mountain West, sustained mainly by the fervent hope that sometime, somehow, the "good old days" would return.

Today they have, though hardly in the way the grizzled old prospectors could possibly have imagined. For once again Aspen hums with activity, night and day, winter and summer—but as a resort, rather than as a mining town.

Walter Paepcke first saw Aspen in 1946, immediately after World War II when the long pent-up travel urge was only beginning to express itself. He fell in love with the town's ancient buildings and its mountain-locked setting. As a businessman, he recognized its long-term potential as a year-round recreational and cultural center. But to his everlasting credit he also recognized the importance of its mellow Victorian atmosphere.

And so, while ski lifts and other facilities were being built, he was giving free paint—in painstakingly determined authentic Victorian colors—to all homeowners who would agree to spruce up their properties. The town has been booming ever since, but in a controlled, intelligently planned way that has been amazingly successful in preserving what, for want of something more original, we'll call its quaint charm. A county ban on indiscriminate signs and billboards has received almost total co-operation, making the highway approaches to Aspen virtually clutter free and a genuine motoring thrill. Inside the town the ban on neon tubing has been almost as successful. Last time we were there a single oil company (national, not local) was attempting for some inexplicable reason to defy the ban. Should it be successful in keeping its neon banner, we're confident the good sense of the citizenry will be sufficient to handle the situation, if not through the courts, then through the cash register.

In 1949 Paepcke consolidated his sound beginning by incorporating the Aspen Institute for Humanistic Studies and staging a prestigious six-week Goethe Bicentennial Festival, attended by the late Dr. Albert Schweitzer and other notables. Since then artists and scholars from around the world have swarmed regularly to Aspen every summer to perform, to give lessons, and to conduct seminars. And this judicious blending of culture and sport, in a magnificent mountain setting that offers coolly invigorating air all summer and excellent snow all winter (not to mention such extra amenities as dependable trout fishing and some of the fascinating true ghost towns we mentioned last chapter), has made Aspen, if anything, almost *too* lively. At least its fantastic proliferation of lodges, inns, and condominiums, with the restaurants, shops, and other enterprises needed to serve them, continues unabated. And this despite the recent development of Snomass-at-Aspen, a new year-round play area competing only a few miles away.

MEDORA, NORTH DAKOTA

But our lively ghosts come in a variety of sizes and shapes. And they owe their current affluence, such as it is, to a variety of factors, or *bene*factors, as in the case of Aspen. At least two others in this category come readily to mind.

Medora, until a few years ago, was a relatively somnolent little cattle town on the edge of the North Dakota Badlands (far less publicized, but fully as fascinating as those of neighboring South Dakota). It had boomed briefly in the 1880's, with the development of the Western cattle industry, but it was best known perhaps for its brief and rather casual association with the colorful Theodore Roosevelt. The President-to-be came to hunt buffalo in 1883, fell in love with the area, and bought a ranch and brand, the Maltese Cross, within three weeks. He stayed long enough to lose a sizable amount of money (taking his lumps with the other ranchers in the awful winter of 1886–1887, the year of "the big die-up"), and gained a rugged, self-reliant maturity in return. "I never would have been President," he wrote later, "if it had not been for my experience in North Dakota."

Make an overnight stop of it and see *Teddy Roosevelt Rides Again,* an historical musical that plays nightly during the summer in a nearby amphitheater and retells much of the T.R. story. The original outdoor show was titled *Old Four Eyes,* recalling the story, perhaps apochryphal, of how the bespectacled greenhorn won his spurs in the West. An obvious Easterner from the moment he stepped from the train in his well-tailored clothes, and with the added handicap of unusually heavy glasses, he was promptly dubbed "that four-eyed dude from New York" or just plain "Four Eyes." And the name stuck, until the night he finally flattened one of his surprised tormentors with his naked fist. After that the nickname metamorphosed subtly and he was referred to, with respect and grudging admiration, as "Old Four Eyes."

Roosevelt left North Dakota for good in 1897 to fight the Spanish in Cuba. His ranches (he bought the Elkhorn in 1884), along the rolling breaks of the Little Missouri River northwest of Medora, are now included in Theodore Roosevelt National Memorial Park. The nation's only such memorial, the 70,000-acre preserve is not only a striking scenic attraction but a fitting monument to the man whose name has become synonymous with conservation of natural resources. His two-room, log Elkhorn Ranch home, now restored, stands at the park visitor center near Medora.

Despite the Roosevelt lore, the town itself dozed quietly until the state restored the twenty-six-room Château de Mores as an historical monument, and businessman Harold Schafer, a proud native son, spent considerable money refurbishing the Rough Riders Hotel (1885) and several other old establishments to help fuel a modest revival. The château, its plain exterior belying the lavishness of its furnishings, was built in 1883 by the Marquis de Mores for his young and beautiful wife, Medora. De Mores himself was an eccentric, colorful figure, a Frenchman with ideas that were sound but a bit ahead of his time. The Northern Pacific Railway had just linked the Northern Plains with the rest of the nation. He proposed to slaughter Western cattle in the West where they were raised, then ship them East in refrigerated railroad cars, instead of on the hoof as had previously been done. And had he managed to pull it off, Medora might well have been another Omaha, Kansas City, or Sioux Falls. But the scheme eventually failed, for personal as well as economic reasons.

He gave it up, leaving behind for today's visitors a chimney of his ambitious packing plant and the mansion with its French appointments. Go through it, then take a leisurely swing through the colorful Little Missouri Badlands formations that comprise the national monument. Top off all this with a performance in the Medora amphitheatre and you've spent a full and enjoyable day.

CALICO, CALIFORNIA

Another lively ghost that combines scenic and historic interest is Calico, California. Just off U.S. 66 on the desert east of Barstow, it owes its resurrection (and it is that, almost literally) to the fact that among its early-day residents was one Walter Knott, a failure as a miner but a spectacular success in the berry-pie and chicken-dinner business. Knott's Berry Farm and Ghost Town is a family-oriented amusement park, like its better-known neighbor, Disneyland. But Calico, the loving tribute of a man who remembered, and respected, his hardscrabble origins, is at least a reconstruction of a "legitimate" ghost town. It counted as many as 3,500 people in the late 1880's and early 1890's at the height of the mining boom, then declined rapidly with the collapse in the price of silver. It had nearly disappeared when Mr. Knott started to work.

Fully as interesting (indeed more so) are the spectacular desert canyon byways one can explore in the immediate Calico vicinity.

VIRGINIA CITY, NEVADA

You don't know whether to laugh or cry when you see Virginia City. The queen city of Nevada's famed Comstock Lode has fallen on good times or evil, depending upon your taste in ghosts. If you don't mind insistent commercialization, there are old mansions and opera houses to tour, abandoned mines to visit, cemeteries to poke around in, and gargantuan engineering feats to marvel at. There's even that Virginia City trademark, a clutch of fine old saloons (including the Bucket of Blood), to enjoy—as museums, if not as sources of inner warmth and contentment.

If you *do* mind—well, many of the natives don't particularly like

it either. But what are they to do when travelers come in increasing numbers to "see" Virginia City: ignore them? refuse to serve them? Proposals have been made to preserve and/or restore this lively ghost as a kind of mining camp Williamsburg. And certainly the Comstock would warrant such treatment historically; its vast wealth in silver virtually built San Francisco.

Be that as it may, Virginia is *still* something to see, feel, marvel at. As we do, every chance we get.

MONTANA'S ALDER GULCH

For a real gem, go to Montana and 10-mile-long Alder Gulch. Rich in both history and gold ($10 million of it in all), it too owes much of its new "lively" status to zealous restoration/reconstruction efforts. Montanan Charles Bovey helped push things along initially by restoring part of the main street of *Virginia City*. After that he moved into nearby *Nevada City*, by then almost completely ghosted, genuine old buildings from even less fortunate settlements in this southwestern corner of the state. In these are now reproduced (much as in Fairplay's South Park City, mentioned in the previous chapter) such authentic frontier institutions as a jail, schoolhouse, livery stable, firehouse, and saddle shop.

But Virginia City was—and is—no ghost. She's a working county seat, if an extremely small one. She has pride: one of the state's oldest settlements, she served as Territorial capital until 1876. And more than a score of her restored buildings are original structures dating back to Gold Rush days. In them are still other representative frontier enterprises—newspaper office, photographic studio, drugstore, express office, and saloon.

So don't get put off by the carnival atmosphere that pervades the gulch on a hot summer afternoon when the tourists are out in force. Be tolerant of the "period" touch that is just a bit too-too—like, say, the headboard in the cliffside "Boothill" that appears too freshly painted. (The nearsighted visitor on the horse-drawn sightseeing coach wants to see, too, you know.) The overall effect is surprisingly satisfying. For the town emerges as something of a museum piece—if not a completely real town, then a lively and not totally unconvincing representation of what the successful mining camp of a century ago *might* have looked like.

Before making a final judgment, drive around a bit, off the main street. Go up onto the rolling residential streets above the business section (which naturally sprang to life along the gulch where the action was). The town itself is real enough. If the boothill markers are suspect, not so were the Vigilantes whose extrajudicial handiwork made graveyards necessary. Following the discovery of gold here on May 26, 1863, the gulch soon seethed with an estimated ten thousand people living in a half-dozen or more ragtag settlements.

But if the district was long on miners and gold, it was short on law and order. Shipping out the gold safely soon became almost as big a problem as panning it from the creek in the first place. And so men and circumstances, meeting fortuitously at the right time and place, brought into being the storied Vigilantes. And brought into a state of *non*being—by virtue of hanging—exactly two dozen presumed road agents, including Sheriff Henry Plummer, the gang's leader. This occurred between December 20, 1863, and February 5,

1864. It should surprise no one that organized robbery and murder in the district declined dramatically forthwith.

For more on the notorious Plummer Gang, extend your Alder Gulch visit to Robbers' Roost, a two-story roadside hostelry near Laurin (more on this in the next chapter) that often served as a gang hangout. *The Vigilantes of Montana,* written by Thomas J. Dimsdale in 1865 and republished in the University of Oklahoma Press's Frontier Library, offers a highly readable contemporary account of this stormy period in Virginia City's hectic youth.

THE ONE & ONLY TOMBSTONE

Still another lively ghost now enjoying a restoration boom, after many years of poor-but-proud existence as a worked-out mining camp, is Arizona's Tombstone. One of the most famous of all the rip-roaring silver camps, the storied "town too tough to die" almost did anyway. And why not? Its mines had long since been flooded. With miners gone, saloons began to close. Then the gay Bird Cage Theatre, the town's "cultural" showplace, dropped its curtain for the last time. But Tombstone still had its pride. And a surplus of fine old substantial buildings. And a little fracas known as the Earp-Clanton gunfight in the O.K. Corral, which, next to Custer's set-to with the Sioux on the Little Big Horn, is perhaps the frontier West's most refought battle.

They combined to keep the town alive even after it had suffered the ultimate indignity (in 1931) of losing the county seat. Curious, nostalgic tourists began to drift in. First the handsome old brick and stone courthouse was converted into a fine state-operated museum. Here and there a hold-out businessman, spotting the proverbial light at the end of the tunnel, fixed up a bit to attract some "ghost town" business. Then a few years ago a troup of Eastern history buffs formed

Historic Tombstone Adventures to continue the town's preservation and restoration and to make it—like Virginia City—something of a living museum. The results of all this concerted effort to re-create the past are impressive, and generally enjoyable, again overlooking such obviously distracting influences as automobiles, milling crowds, and huckstering a bit too persistent.

But you can often get around this with a little luck. So start off, if you will, by doing the things you're supposed to do. See the electronic dramatization of Tombstone's history in Schieffelin Hall, built in 1881 and nicely restored. Relive the Earp-Clanton shoot-out in the O.K. Corral's rebuilt blacksmith shop.

Visit the cluttered office of the *Tombstone Epitaph* and buy a copy of Arizona's oldest continuously published weekly newspaper, whose masthead perpetuates the story of the town's naming itself. When Ed Schieffelin set off prospecting the wild Apache country in 1877, a fellow soldier at nearby Fort Huachuca assured him, "Instead of a mine, you'll find a tombstone." When he found the ore he was looking for, he's supposed to have muttered, "Here's my tombstone." The town of Tombstone was laid out in 1879. When a newspaper appeared the following May—well, every Tombstone needs an Epitaph, doesn't it? As for Ed's mine, he let his brother name it. Al Schieffelin took one look, said "You're a lucky cuss." The Lucky Cuss proved to be one of Arizona's richest.

Browse the photographic studio of Camillus S. Fly, the glittering Crystal Palace Saloon, the cluttered Bird Cage Theatre, and the town's other "period pieces." Then—and here's where the luck comes in—try for the feel of the town by getting away from the popular places and, if possible, from the people who've come to see them.

We played a hunch, went for afternoon coffee to a cluttered hole-in-the-wall that obviously hadn't been restored. And just as obviously didn't need it. The place was virtually deserted and we had just begun to appreciate the old, dimly lit interior when the door opened and in strode an offduty bartender from the Crystal Palace up the street, boots clomping, open vest setting off colorful shirt and flowing tie, handlebar mustaches rampant over a weather-lined face. He sat down at the next table and, in approved best-Western style, presumably signaled the owner he'd have "the usual" (at least there was no audible order), and soon he was brought a piece of apple pie, a glass of milk—and a bowl. He dumped the pie in the bowl, poured the milk over it, and proceeded to eat the mixture with obvious relish and no little difficulty from the drooping mustaches. We chatted with him briefly. His soft, well-modulated voice didn't destroy the illusion. A gentlemanly bartender spooning in milk-soaked apple pie on a warm sunny afternoon struck us as a not-too-unlikely symbol for a town too tough to die . . . and really quite proud of it, thank you.

THE BOOMING GHOSTS OF COLORADO

Back in the 1860's and 1870's they were calling the section of Black Hawk Canyon west of Denver "the richest square mile on earth." And a century later it still is, in many ways. Colorado's first important gold discovery was made here on Black Hawk Creek between present-day Black Hawk and Central City on May 6, 1859, by John H. Gregory. Within a year the canyon contained a half-dozen settlements, as many as 15,000 people. And its many mines eventually produced some $85 million in gold alone.

CENTRAL CITY

But the strike that produced today's wealth was made in 1932, long after most of the mines had closed and the towns themselves— principally Central City, with Black Hawk and Nevadaville as struggling satellites—were largely empty shells. In the case of Central, however, that "shell" included one of the Western mining frontier's finest surviving monuments: the four-story Teller House (described in the next chapter) and, across a landscaped garden, the ornate Central City Opera House which, in its day, had hosted the likes of Edwin Booth and Emma Abbott. Two Denver women recognized what they could mean, not only to a depression-ridden mining area, but to the state and the nation. Miss Anne Evans, the daughter of Colorado's second Territorial governor, and Mrs. Ida Kruse McFarland, a Denver University professor and former resident of Central City, persuaded the town to refurbish the long-unused opera house and to gamble on a play festival. And on July 16, 1932, the ornate old theater reopened with Lillian Gish and Raymond Hackett in the Dumas tear-jerker, *Camille.*

The week-long festival was an immediate success. In 1940 the season was stretched to three weeks and operas began to appear, with singers from New York's Metropolitan. Expanded since then to include an almost summer-long program of opera and theater that attracts big-name performers from everywhere, it has helped spur a complete revival in the old town. As for how best to go about enjoying this now lively ghost, we'll leave that to you. It depends pretty much on your personal preferences and prejudices.

If you're a music and drama lover, then by all means plan a July or August visit, for as long as you can stay. Write the Central City Opera Association (910 16th Street, Denver, Colorado 80202) for program and ticket information, then get your reservations and you're all set. You'll enjoy every minute of it. The town literally hums during the season. Specialty shops flower in every available corner of the ornate old brick and stone buildings that line Eureka and Main streets. The museums are open. And there are always the people themselves—performers, spectators, and hangers-on—to hobnob with, or simply to observe.

If you like the excitement and gaiety but have no particular desire to attend a performance, then time your visit for the afternoon of an evening show. You can browse the shops, push your way (if you're lucky) into the Teller House, take a peek of sorts at the opera house, and otherwise sample the old camp's genuine charm. If you are more of a purist and want to see a prosperous Western gold camp that still manages to look like one, with almost no plastic surgery and precious little make-up, then visit Central City in the spring or fall when, with crowds gone, the natives go about the matter of working and playing pretty much as they do in any other small town. We suspect you'll be as delighted as you are surprised.

We wrote about Central for the first time almost twenty years ago:

> . . . But whatever you do, don't get the idea that Central City is a tourist trap, decked with artificial, history-scented finery to snatch a fast buck from you. It isn't. The town, with its narrow, twisting steep streets, its ornately corniced business blocks and gingerbreaded houses, its friendly open-spirited old-timers, is just as genuine as the towering mountains that rim it in every direction.

We're not at all unhappy with that assessment even today. Except for the reference to the old-timers, we wouldn't change it. Time has

Miss Helen Hayes in *Mrs. McThing* is billed as the attraction in the famed theater near Central City's Teller House.

taken its toll. And crowds get pretty thick in the summer. But last time we were there we drove to the very dead end of one of the upper-level residential streets, where we had a fine panoramic view not only of all the town itself but of much of the mine-scarred, mountain-locked district that produced it. We fell in love with the place all over again.

It all started for us almost twenty-five years ago. It was our first visit, and we were introduced not only to Colorado's No. 1 mining town, but to the *Mountain Nautilus,* and to Fritz de Mandel, the graying oldster who, after thirty years of trying, had finally pulled it from its ice-locked tomb. The *Nautilus,* or the rotting remains of it, just might be one of the first experimental submarines ever built and sailed in the United States.

Built by R. T. Owen, a Central City tinsmith, and launched nearly two miles above sea level in nearby Missouri Lake in 1898, the eighteen-foot craft is something of a mystery. After apparently sinking the sub deliberately, Owen drifted east where he is supposed to have pooled his know-how with Simon Lake, then at work on his own *Argonaut Jr*. Well, we chatted with de Mandel, encouraged him to reminisce, browsed his cluttered museum-antique shop, and came away with a simple brass candleholder. So much did we enjoy that first visit that we have since convinced ourselves the candleholder once graced the night stand of a lonely miner, throwing a feeble light on his scrap of writing paper as he scratched a letter to his wife in Vermont saying he'd already had a couple of good "shows" and tomorrow he felt he'd strike it rich for sure.

GEORGETOWN

Colorado has still more of these picturesque old mining towns that modern tourism helps to keep alive and, in some cases, prosperous. Georgetown, now almost underneath Interstate 70 about 25 miles south and west of Central City, is perhaps the finest. A Victorian masterpiece, it offers handsome old mansions, early mining-camp fire stations, ornate business blocks, and one of the West's most interesting old hotels (explored in the following chapter). Yet it is still active as a county seat, a popular ski center in winter, and a virtual mining-camp museum that is doubly enjoyable to visit because it has had to go to precious little effort to be one.

SILVERTON

From much the same mold is Silverton in southwestern Colorado. Its period hotel is the Grand Imperial and its principal attraction today is its status as turn-around point for the famed Silverton narrow-gauge railroad trip up from Durango. Yet the town is a county seat, too. And some of the nearby mines are still active, as is an impressive old mill a few miles up the Animas gorge. Obviously, the town has struck on a rather acceptable compromise between past and present. On false-fronted Blair Street, where the smoke-belching trains stop and Hollywood cameras grind out all their "western" footage, things have been left pretty much as they were when this was the rough tough section of Silverton. As for the town's main street, a block to the north, with the Grand Imperial and most of the town's other workaday stores and shops, it is hard-surfaced and, if not particularly modern, is at least not self-consciously antiqued.

So you can take your pick of streets. You're almost sure to like the town, except perhaps for a couple of summertime hours at noon when the train or trains (lately the Denver & Rio Grande Western Railroad has had to run a second section to accommodate the crowds) have disgorged their camera-toting passengers. Both streets then are almost as cluttered as back in the 1880's when the mining boom was at its peak.

CRIPPLE CREEK

Cripple Creek was a Johnny-come-lately among the mining camps. It exploded into feverish activity in 1891 when cowboy Bob Womack picked up gold in a pasture on the southwest slope of Pikes Peak and went on a spree—and woke up next morning to learn he'd told everyone where he found it and had sold his claim for $500. (This phenomenon of gold-discoverer-dies-in-poorhouse is, unfortunately, an all too familiar one.) Nearly $25 million in gold alone was taken out of the Cripple Creek district in 1901, its peak year.

But soon afterward the boom flattened out as water began to flood the deeper diggings of such famous mines as the Ajax, the Independence, the Vindicator, and the Portland. After World War II a 32,000-foot-long, 3,300-foot-deep tunnel was bored into the lower levels of some of the richer mines, and a more efficient gold mill built. Today there is still intermittent production. (Were the United States to give up its pegged $35 an ounce for gold, the town would experience an almost immediate mining boom.)

But the town is interesting to visit on other counts. Its "culture" isn't quite as serious as that of Aspen or Central City. But melodrama is still fun. And Cripple Creek as much as any other Western town helped create the current vogue for it. Similarly, while its Imperial hotel isn't in quite the same league with the Jerome and the Teller House, it provides the melodrama with a genuine stage. And the rail buff hits something of a jackpot here, for there is just no really practical way to get to Cripple Creek without driving on the abandoned right-of-way of one of the three railroads that once served it.

LEADVILLE

If Cripple Creek lives primarily on its hope for a comeback in gold, not so two other of Colorado's finest mining camps. Leadville, the state's biggest and most important camp, went through separate gold and silver booms before settling on the far less romantic but just as valuable molybdenum on which to build its prosperity. The mines at nearby Climax are the world's most important, and Leadville—whose almost breathtaking 10,152-foot altitude is still almost 1,200 feet below that of Climax—serves as its headquarters and base of operations. Perhaps its best-known citizens (after "the unsinkable" Molly Brown and her husband, Johnny, who have achieved considerable latter-day recognition) were Horace and Augusta Tabor.

Tabor was mayor and postmaster when Leadville was incorporated in 1878, almost twenty years after gold was first discovered in nearby California Gulch. He struck it rich there when a $17 grubstake to two German shoemakers gave him a one-third interest in the Little Pittsburg and $500,000 in gold in less than a year; after which he sold out for a million dollars. Thereafter he spent a good bit of his time and effort building hotels and opera houses and pursuing the lovely Elizabeth McCourt ("Baby") Doe. The essentially tragic bent of his life was thus set here. Despite subsequent moves to Central City and Denver, and even a brief try at being Colorado's senator in Washington—where he was finally able to give Baby Doe the spectacular wedding she wanted—his life was pretty much a failure. He died a few years later, in Denver, broken in spirit as well as in pocketbook.

Curiously enough, it is here in Leadville that you can fill in the final tragic details. A bit of inquiry will take you both to the unpainted house in town where the bitter Augusta spent her last years, and to the scarred mountainside east of town where Baby Doe died much later. Horace had always told her to "hold on to the Matchless." She did. And here, beside the decaying shaft of the Matchless Mine—all she had left as a tangible legacy—they found her one morning frozen to death, a lonely recluse who remained faithful to the end. (Like Molly Brown, Baby Doe too has achieved artistic recognition: *The Ballad of Baby Doe* has been performed by the Santa Fe Opera, at the Central City Opera House, and elsewhere.)

CREEDE

The list of lively ghosts is nearly endless, but we can't stop without recommending Creede, on the extreme upper stretches of the Rio Grande in south-central Colorado. Like Leadville, it is cheating death on the strength of recent mining activity. Not too long ago we drove up on the ledge overlooking the town to examine its picturesquely set old cemetery, and found the high grassy plateau alive with signs of renewed prospecting activity—tiny claim flags amid the wildflowers, jeep roads disappearing beyond businesslike mining-company signs urging the "unauthorized motorist" to keep out, and an unmistakable buzz of activity down in the town itself.

Like Leadville too, Creede is just prosperous enough as a town so that it doesn't feel compelled to make a conscious effort to preserve or restore its relics in order to appeal to the visitor. If it appears pretty much as a small town living on miners, fishermen, and a handful of nearby ranchers, it's because that's pretty much what it is. It is, for our money, all the more charming for it.

Creede is unique among Colorado mining camps for having its own poet. In the celebrated words penned by Cy Warman in the early 1890's, this was the town where

> The cliffs are solid silver,
>   With wond'rous wealth untold,
> And the beds of the running rivers
>   Are lined with the purest gold.
>
> While the world is filled with sorrow,
>   And hearts must break and bleed—
> It's day all day in the daytime,
>   And there is no night in Creede.

Well, Warman was a newspaperman, so perhaps he can be forgiven. But the town *was* a lively one, reaching a population of some 8,000 by 1893, when the bottom fell out of the silver market everywhere.

And it has had the usual number of unusual characters. One was Bob Ford, reputed slayer ("the dirty little coward" in the well-known ballad) of Jesse James. Ford, also from Missouri and the owner of a saloon/gambling house, was himself slain here in 1892.

(His body has been moved back to Missouri; and the bar behind which he was standing when shot was, last time we heard, in the Elks Club.) A favorite of the town's sporting element, Ford was accorded what newspaper accounts hailed as one of Creede's biggest and gayest funerals, no little credit for which was due to the fact that, flowers being in understandably short supply, his mourning friends made do with what was nearly always plentiful in even the poorest mining camps: wine, champagne, and other assorted spirits.

Times have changed, of course, since then. There's night in Creede now. And even the days are no longer *that* lively. But they're still fun. And the surrounding countryside—mostly sheer-walled cliffs with snowy mountains beyond—is fully as spectacular as when "Soapy" Smith was around to make his silver-tongued pitch . . . and to prove the hand is quicker than the eye by selling cakes of scented soap wrapped in a dollar bill. Those were indeed the good old days, at least for the fast-talking con man. And one can still capture much of the feel of it in the rakish, offhand atmosphere of a town like Creede.

"THE BEST
DAMNED HOTEL"

By early 1869 Central City had a problem. And the *Daily Register* wasn't about to let folks forget it. "We are the wealthiest community in Colorado Territory," the paper asserted, with that calm self-assurance so typical of frontier journalism, "yet we have no hotel fit to stop in."

True, Charles Wentworth had done his best. He'd sent to Chicago for new mattresses so his Connor House could boast of being "the only hotel in the city having anything but hay beds." Still, this was hardly good enough for a nine-year-old mining metropolis that was getting bigger and better every day. And richer too. Everyone agreed that "The Little Kingdom of Gilpin," as the district liked to call itself, could hardly afford to settle for anything less than the best to be had.

And so it was Henry M. Teller, one of Central's more substantial citizens, who agreed finally to take the money contributed by civic boosters (one of whom was Charles Wentworth himself, which tells much about the lusty esprit de corps to be found in these mining towns) and put up a hotel to cost not less than $30,000. That was in May 1871. He set to work on it in July. And on June 24, 1872, it was open for business, with total construction costs having come to something better than $100,000. But no one, apparently, was unduly upset.

NOTHING BUT THE BEST

The Teller House, all agreed, was something special. (A lone detractor did pounce on its admittedly plain exterior, sniffing that it could "easily be taken for a New England factory.") For one thing, it boasted running water, brought down from Teller Springs in nearby Prosser Gulch. For another, its rooms, as an admirer pointed out, were constructed "without transoms." Each door, that is, was provided with "a patent safety lock. . . . Guests may therefore lie down to peaceful slumbers, undisturbed by apprehension of getting their heads blown off or valuables lifted by burglars."

Naturally such a remarkable hostelry demanded an equally remarkable dedicatory gala. And if contemporary accounts are to be credited, it was all of that. Seventy-five couples attended the June 27 grand inauguration ball. And festivities, one observer reported next day with obvious pride and satisfaction, "continued until daylight, when the large assembly retired in good order (sic) to their respective homes. This notice ought now to conclude with a grand display of rhetorical pyrotechnics, but charity toward our readers forbids. We have said the ball was a triumph, we now reiterate the declaration."

If the ball was a triumph, so was the Teller House. And it is a triumph today. But, like Central City itself, it's had its ups and downs. Today's success dates back to 1932 when, as noted in the previous chapter, the Central City Opera House Association took over the hostelry and extensively renovated it. Layers of old paint were removed to bring back some of the hotel's former elegance. Old furniture was restored or period replacements located. The chickens, needless to say, were chased from the second-floor dining room before it was reopened. And a local artist restored the murals (Venus, Diana, Aphrodite, and the rest) in the bar.

The bar, according to a fine story in Sandra Dallas's fascinating *No More Than Five in a Bed,* was known for a time as "The Elevator." A wag, it seems, had once taken a sign reading "To the Elevator" and hung it next to the barroom door, which opened off the lobby. In an age when "ladies" did not frequent bars—and only guessed at the kind of lewd art their menfolk favored while enjoying a friendly glass—the embarrassment of elevator-seeking womenfolk must have, while it lasted, created a good bit of masculine hilarity. (This is as good a place as any to urge the reader to invest in Miss Dallas's book. She covers all of Colorado's famous Rocky Mountain "Waldorfs" in considerable detail and with obvious affection.)

Restoration, as it progressed, even included what would today be called instant legend. In 1936 an artist painted a picture of his wife on the worn floorboards of the bar, under circumstances we are still not too sure about (but can guess, its having occurred in a bar and presumably late at night). Anyway, the painting was soon associated with the old ballad "The Face on the Barroom Floor," and

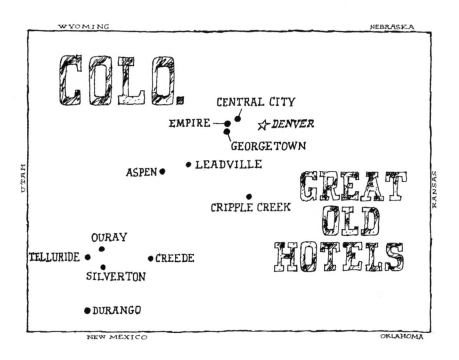

COLO.

CENTRAL CITY

EMPIRE ☆ DENVER

GEORGETOWN

● LEADVILLE

ASPEN ●

CRIPPLE CREEK

GREAT OLD HOTELS

OURAY

TELLURIDE ●   ● CREEDE

SILVERTON

● DURANGO

UTAH

KANSAS

promptly became a rival to the nudes on the wall as a tourist attraction. We confess the pouting brunette was one of the first "ladies" we saw in Central City, not too many years after she had so "mysteriously" appeared. And even then, carefully protected by a table from the bumbling footsteps of the irreverent and the witless, her Mona Lisa-like expression struck us as delightfully titillating and she seemed as ancient—and as alluring—as sin itself.

But the Teller House story, from hardscrabble origins to latter-day revival, is not unique. It is paralleled by that of a dozen or more other early mining camp hostelries. Some were larger, others more modest in size; they varied in elegance, too, with the affluence and taste of their owners. But considered together, they tell much about the mining camps they served, and about the men who built those camps.

They were strong men, for the most part, impatient, proud, supremely self-confident. To recognize a need was to start tackling it forthwith. Fortunes were made and lost overnight; towns were built—

and often abandoned—almost as quickly. So whatever was to be done, they apparently figured, was to be done at once. And nowhere does this show up more dramatically than in the speed with which the building of "the best hotel west of Denver" (substitute at will "the finest hostelry between Kansas City and San Francisco" or "the best damned hotel west of the Missouri River") became the *sine qua non* of almost every bustling gold or silver camp.

Once enough underground wealth had been found to assure some permanence to the district, civic boosters began clamoring for the amenities they'd left in the East. Only they wanted it to be better than what they'd had back home, because they were richer now. And not only did they demand improved creature comforts (finer than merely adequate bed and board, though often they lacked even that), but they also insisted on cultural enrichment—drama and music, that is, rather than the rough saloon/dancehall/brothel fare that somehow seemed to appear in plentiful supply almost simultaneously with the first show of "color" in the prospector's pan.

So Central City wasn't alone in demanding and getting a fine hotel. It was merely one of the first to move in and satisfy this hunger for the "better things." Several other rich and would-be-rich Rocky Mountain mining camps followed her lead. The result is a rather notable collection of substantial hotels and impressive opera houses that often contrasted quite strikingly with the tent-buildings, false-fronted stores, ramshackle log cabins, and rough clapboarded houses that surrounded them. Even today the contrast is often surprisingly sharp. And this of course merely adds to one's pleasure in hunting them up and collecting the fine old stories that have settled over them like an early fall snow, covering unsightly cracks and crevices and creating in their place loveliness, excitement, and a certain air of mystery.

We started with the Teller House—and the Face on the Barroom Floor—many years ago. We might as well do so again, here. We'll drift on from it to the Hotel de Paris in Georgetown and the Vendome at Leadville, to the Imperial at Cripple Creek and the Grand Imperial at Silverton, to the Beaumont at Ouray, the Jerome at Aspen and the Strater at Durango. Along the way we'll look, too, at the opera houses.

From books one can ferret out the historical details and even the stories and legends that surround them. But the essential ingredient is still imagination, the ability to re-create the scene as it was then and to relive something of its drama and excitement. Supply that imagination and you have filled a vacation trip with unforgettable impressions. Nor is it as difficult as you might suppose, for in most cases the rugged mountain setting, the ugly mining scars and moldering mine structures, the dated, often decaying homes and stores and other public buildings all help to visualize these old hostelries as they were in their heyday.

GLAMOUR GALORE FOR CENTRAL CITY

Of course, it would make re-creating the past even simpler if the Teller House lobby, with its collection of ores, could proudly exhibit President Grant's own private chamber pot.

(It was back in 1873 that the doughty General, a great admirer of the West, was making his triumphal inspection tour of the Rocky Mountain mining towns. And Central City was determined to put its best foot forward. The boardwalk in front of the Teller House would obviously need covering before the Presidential foot descended from the carriage. But gold was so common. Finally it was decided to bring silver bricks over the trail from Caribou, off to the north. Some $12,000 worth of them subsequently smoothed President Grant's way to the hotel. And meanwhile, upstairs in the Presidential suite, there waited—presumably—what may very well have been Colorado's first custom-crafted chamber pot. For the Teller House, anxious that everything be first class-plus for its most distinguished visitor, had reportedly written the White House for a mold of the chief executive's posterior in order to assure complete satisfaction.)

Browse the establishment as you will. It too has a "Baby Doe" suite, a cozy, well-appointed rendezvous where H. A. W. Tabor, the Silver King, kept his beautiful young companion while still encumbered with the stern and admittedly plain Augusta.

(This is one of the Rocky Mountain West's most celebrated triangles [we touched on it in the preceding chapter]. Horace and Augusta spent eighteen years together in the Colorado gold camps, he storekeeping and dreaming of wealth, she taking in laundry and boarding miners to keep them going. Then suddenly a lucky strike made Tabor a millionaire. The pert, vivacious "Baby" Doe soon appeared on the scene, and Horace and Augusta drifted apart. Tabor played an important role in the promoting and building of several Colorado hotels and opera houses. But when he died in Denver in 1899, he was penniless. Ironically, the two women who loved him both died in Leadville, only a few miles apart: Baby Doe in abject poverty, Augusta—the only one of the three to whom wealth meant nothing—a millionairess.)

Wander through the landscaped garden to the Central City Opera House, a handsome companion piece to the Teller House. Excellently proportioned, with four-foot-thick stone walls and a simple Empire-style decor inside, it was opened on March 4, 1878. And for ten years or so it drew to its stage such fine actors as Edwin Booth, Lotta Crabtree, Emma Abbott, and many others. You'll enjoy the frescoes, the crystal chandeliers, and the original hickory chairs.

FRENCH LOUIE'S MASTERPIECE IN GEORGETOWN

We've started off with the Teller House because it is, after all, *still* a Rocky Mountain Waldorf. But Georgetown's *Hotel de Paris* (called dee-*pair*-us by nearly everyone but its builder) is our sentimental favorite. Of all Colorado's famed early-day hostelries, it probably came the closest to fitting the name. We saw it for the first time while it was still a hotel, just a few years before it began its gradual metamorphosis into state historical monument. While it admittedly lacked the spit and polish, not to say convenience, of a Hilton, it possessed something of at least equal importance: an almost unique personality. With a builder like Louis Dupuy, it could hardly be otherwise.

"French Louie" drifted into Georgetown around 1870 and worked just long enough to be seriously injured in an accident. His subsequent entry into the bakery business is probably the best thing that could possibly have happened to Georgetown and Colorado. Steadily he progressed from prosperous baker to popular restaurateur to famed (and eccentric) hotelkeeper. Only after he died in 1900 were enough facts learned about him to explain his success at least partially.

Born Adolphe François Gérard, he followed the almost classic pattern of the restless, young, wealthy and/or titled European ne'er-do-well of the 19th century. Well educated but unable, or unwilling, to settle down, he squandered a sizable inheritance, then came to the United States to seek a new fortune. If he was more successful than

Here in Georgetown, French Louie gave the Silver Kings of Colorado
their first taste of all the elegance money could buy.

most, it's probably because he worked harder than most. Still, he
worked on his own terms, according to his own tastes. And the
miners, whether rich or poor, had to accept him on his own terms,
too.

Dupuy has been described as "an innkeeper who hated his guests,
a philosopher, a poet who left no written record of his thoughts, a
despiser of women who gave all he had to one, an aristocrat, a prole-
tarian, a pagan, an arcadian, an atheist, a lover of beauty . . ." and a
number of other things. Perhaps he didn't actually hate his guests, but
his attitude toward them was admittedly cavalier. He cheerfully accepted those who pleased him. But visitors he did not like the looks
of were not permitted to register. And guests who displeased him
were ordered to pack and leave forthwith. "If you are a college man,"
he once explained to a friend, "surely you know that no gentleman

invites himself to be the guest of a stranger. This house is my own, and if I want guests, I invite them."

He had a legitimate point. His was no joint venture of civic boosters ashamed, like those in Central City, that they had no decent place to bed down a visitor. He financed the Hotel de Paris himself, and apparently built a good part of it with his own hands. Certainly his elegant, patrician hand is apparent wherever you look. Outside the two-story brick and stone rectangle, set flush against the

street, there's the crowning *cheval-de-frise* of gilded spikes, the gate guarded by royal lions, the enclosed rear courtyard. Inside, indications of his genteel tastes were even more impressive. On that first visit we marveled at the carved furnishings, flowered carpets, diamond-dust mirrors (a particularly handsome one at the turn in the stairway permitted the guest descending to dinner to make a last-minute check of his or her dress), fine sculptures and paintings, the silver casters on the dining-room tables, and a magnificent china closet of fine Haviland.

In his own apartment just off the dining room we browsed through his books, many in French (there were some three thousand of them in the hotel when he died), and admired the heavy leather chairs with their carved arms. In the sitting room frequented by "drummers" we were more than a little impressed by the walnut woodwork, made by a French craftsman, and the extra bed designed to fold up and resemble a writing desk when not in use. The ten 12-by-20-foot bedrooms upstairs were just as meticulously appointed: fine period furniture, carpets, marble corner lavatories, and beautiful gaslights (although by then there was also electricity). It was a modest little masterpiece, from wrought-iron grill on the roof to basement wine cellar. And it still is, as an historical monument, though wine and gourmet meals are no longer available. The atmosphere persists.

"If this were my place," Miss Dallas quotes a Frenchman as saying to Louis Dupuy as he surveyed the splendid dining room, "Oh, I would have slave girls and music at dessert; with my wines I would have the ceiling to open and orange blossoms and roses to fall upon the table." His host rose to the occasion. "I make one smell the roses and imagine the slave girls," he replied, "by my wine."

Even now, almost a century later, he can still do it, if you give your imagination a bit of a nudge.

LODGING & AN OPERA FOR ASPEN

The Jerome at Aspen, while twenty years younger than Central City's Teller House, has enjoyed—or endured—a checkered career that is remarkably similar to it, even to a newspaper-prodded conception. After detailing for months the need for a decent hotel and extolling "the unexcelled business opportunity" it represented, the *Aspen Times Weekly* finally helped persuade mine-owner Jerome B. Wheeler to take the plunge.

The three-story Jerome (inevitably hailed as "the handsomest hotel on the Western Slope" and "Aspen's Greatest Monument") was opened in November 1889 with a banquet and ball "rivalling in luxurious splendour some of the festivals of the capitol of ancient Rome." Helping to buttress its claim to "architectural extravagance" were such features as a three-story skylighted lobby, electricity, and steam heat, and a remarkable water-powered elevator, operated by ropes tugged by the apparently delighted passengers.

With the collapse of the silver boom in the 1890's, the Jerome went into a decline, though like the Teller House it continued to serve the thinning ranks of the faithful. Then with the arrival of Walter Paepcke (whom we met earlier), it, with that other monument to Mr. Wheeler, the three-story *Wheeler Opera House,* provided a kind of hub for the boom that has transformed the old silver camp. The Jerome was refurbished inside and out; many of its original ninety rooms were given furnishings from the Palmer House in Chicago, and its fifteen bathrooms substantially complemented. As for the fire-gutted Wheeler, for a time one of Colorado's most celebrated, it too was reconditioned and allowed to present plays, concerts, and folk-song events to an increasing number of culture-conscious visitors.

Alas, as this is written the Jerome is closed while it writhes through one of its periodic financial crises. We relegate notice of its closing to problematical status because a knowledgeable friend on the scene assures us this is but another Perils-of-Pauline episode, that by the time this is in print and being read the proud old hostelry is likely once again to be registering the great, near-great, would-be great, and plain everyday traveler who enjoys seeing, if only for a night, just how the Silver Kings lived.

THREE ON THE MILLION DOLLAR HIGHWAY

A hundred-mile-long stretch of highway in southwestern Colorado is strung with three more interesting "Waldorfs," two of them open for business as usual. The Million Dollar Highway—U.S. 550 from Durango north to Montrose—is one of the West's most exciting roads. Its name derives in part from its costliness (traversing as it does Colorado's most rugged mountain ranges) and in part from the quantities of low-grade gold ore worked into its cliff-hanging roadbed. Combining this scenery with the historic richness of Durango, Silverton, and Ouray, and their hotels, helps to make it one of the West's most interesting highways as well.

The *Strater* in Durango is today actually two hotels in one, both of them built by Henry Strater. He opened the original Strater in 1882, a handsome four-story Victorian affair of red brick trimmed in white stone and topped with a cupola. Then, having leased it and promptly fallen out with the lessee over how it was being run, he proceeded to build the three-story *Columbian* adjacent to it! The two hotels are combined now, and operate as one. But for the cupola, they appear today from the outside much as they did in the booming 1880's. At least from the front.

Inside, however, they have been vastly improved. Although guest rooms had velvet curtains, a wood stove, and an occasional piano, comfort facilities were limited to the traditional washstand and crockery set. And this dictated a back-of-the-hotel architectural configuration that featured a three-story privy. . . . Unknown—to us, at any rate—is what comparable facility was made available to the chambermaids who lived on the fourth floor and were, according to Miss Dallas, "well known for their amiability toward male guests." This laudable congeniality no doubt helped account for the "Monkey Hall" tag the upper floor promptly acquired.

The postwar travel boom, and the increasing popularity of the narrow-gauge steam train trip to Silverton that originates within sight and sound of the Strater, has triggered a gradual refurbishing and upgrading. From the lobby with its crystal chandeliers and plush to the guest rooms with their antiques, from charming gazebo restaurant to gay melodrama theater, the Strater-Columbian is pure Victorian. And altogether satisfying.

The Grand Hotel in Silverton, later the Imperial and now the *Grand Imperial,* opened in 1883. It promptly became "the home of the silver kings" and the overnight stopping place for notables like Diamond Jim Brady and Lillian Russell, whose life-size oil looks down imperiously on guests as they hit the first landing of the grand staircase. Its decline was more severe than most; its restoration, which came in 1950, more lavish. It was ordered by a wealthy businessman who probably allowed nostalgia to outweigh the shrewd commercial acumen which makes possible such impulsive indulgence. In any case, what *he* lost in dollars, today's traveler more than recoups in charm and comfort (modern baths were added generously).

In our opinion, and we make no claim whatsoever to being an authority on the subject, the Grand Imperial bar is the most beautiful in Colorado. Its cherrywood is magnificently crafted, its three giant horseshoe mirrors tremendously impressive—especially when one tries to visualize their being transported intact from Paris to Silverton, the last hundred miles or so of the trek over rugged mountains via narrow-gauge train.

The third Million Dollar Highway hotel is the *Beaumont* at Ouray. And perhaps it's the ghost of that pretty Chicago maid—her throat

cut following a gay party soon after the hotel was opened in 1887—
who's to blame. But the hostelry ("for its size, the prettiest and most
artistically arranged hotel in Colorado," according to one of its early
partisans) is now closed. And it's really a shame.

Only a few years ago we thought it was well on its way to staging
a comeback. An energetic young melodrama company was in operation. The central lobby with its vaulted ceiling had been sufficiently
restored that one could picture Lily Langtry, Sarah Bernhardt, or
Madame Schumann-Heink sweeping up the Y-shaped staircase. Or
imagine the excitement created by Belgium's King Leopold when,
while presumably demonstrating his mountain-climbing technique on
the balustrade around the circling secondary-story balcony, he tum-
bled over it. (He dropped to the lobby level unhurt, landing on a
well-stuffed sofa.) Also, a cheerful Victorian bar had been installed
in the space once occupied by one of the building's two banks (which
just could be a record in itself).

The Beaumont had several other claims to fame. It was wired
for electricity by George Westinghouse and Miss Dallas suggests that
it may have been the first hotel in the country to boast alternating
current. Unusual, too, was the hot water supplied to the hotel bathrooms—courtesy of Ouray's nearby mineral springs. But whether
or not you're allowed to enjoy the Beaumont as a guest, you can always appreciate the imposing exterior. Its castle-like square tower,
with tiny dormers breaking the steep pitch of its slate roof, dominates
the mountain-locked little town. And even from the street you can
shiver deliciously with thoughts of that poor maid as she patrols the
third-floor balcony where she was slain by her jealous lover.

In a letter the owner, a woman living in nearby Ridgway, indicates that the Beaumont is to become a private club. However, we
suspect that anyone seriously interested could obtain permission to
inspect it by making local inquiry.

VICTORIAN COMFORT AT EMPIRE

Far happier is the story of the (now) *Splendide* at Empire, on
U.S. 40 some 45 miles west of Denver, near both Central City and
Georgetown. A two-story frame affair with a comfortably inviting
front porch, the Splendide looks more like a rambling private home
than a commercial hotel, probably because that is what it originally

was. James Peck struck gold in the area in the early 1860's, built the Peck House for his family and a steady stream of friends, relatives, and travelers in need of a place to stay. Perhaps the most notable feature of the house, aside from its expensive furnishings, was its initial water system—spring water brought a quarter of a mile in pipe made of countless small sections of aspen hollowed out with a hot poker. With the decline of mines in the area, the Pecks added to their home and turned it into an excellent small hotel that boasted one of the finest cuisines in the mountains.

By the 1950's, however, the Peck House was a pretty dilapidated affair. Then fortunately two energetic women with an appreciation for history and a love for antiques took it over. And they have now restored it to pretty much what it must have seemed to begin with— a warm, friendly, family-type hostelry. Bathrooms and closets have been added, of course. But the tiny, cluttered lobby with its old lamps and bookcases, the guest room with its rare twin "sled beds," the ice cream parlor with its coiled wire chairs and candy-striped walls, the old desk with its ancient guest books—all these evoke the best of restored Victorianism.

MEMENTOS OF MR. TABOR

The roster goes on and on. Leadville's entries are the *Vendome Hotel,* now but a pathetic shadow of its former glory as the Tabor Grand, and the *Tabor Opera House,* not too much better off but at least enjoying something of a restoration. First fruit of this refurbishing is Tabor's elegant suite—an altogether fitting start. For while his career was more than a bit checkered, he was an untiring booster of whatever he thought best for his beloved Colorado.

And his most impressive contribution to the state's cultural scene— the Tabor Grand Opera House in Denver—is no more. When completed in 1881, the five-story, red-brick structure, trimmed smartly in white stone, was hailed as one of the most lavishly appointed theaters in the country. As it should have been. For Tabor told the opening-night audience: "I said, 'If Denver was to have an opera house, it should have one worthy of the city.' Here is the opera house. I shall leave it to your judgment if I have done my duty in this respect." And he had. (But to be perfectly candid about it, he was not opposed to boosting Horace Tabor while doing his duty to Denver. This was revealed a bit earlier that same opening night when he spotted an oil por-

trait in the ornate theater lobby. "Who's that?" he demanded of Bill Bush, his partner. "That's Shakespeare," Bush replied, going on to explain he was the world's most famous playwright. But Tabor cut him off with flawless gold-camp logic: "Well, what the hell has he ever done for Colorado? Take it down and put my picture up there.")

Denver, to her shame, failed him, and recently permitted the historic building to be razed in the name of "progress." Curiously enough, the salvager's iron ball merely fulfilled Charles Kingsley's lugubrious lines inscribed on the theater's handsome curtain beneath the painting of some extensive Roman ruins:

> So fleet the works of man, back to the earth again,
> Ancient and holy things fade like a dream.

Leadville's theatrical monument to Tabor still stands, though, after a career almost as hectic as that of its builder.

It opened November 20–21, 1879, with an ambitious double feature: *The Serious Family* and *Who's Who*. But attendance at the inaugural gala was unfortunately depressed by an awkward inadvertence. Vigilantes had chosen this festive occasion to damp down the town's always sizable lawless element with a pair of hangings. Thoughtlessly, they had left the bodies to dangle from the rafters of the nearby courthouse, then nearing completion. The event tended to preoccupy the populace, keep it from responding to the arrival of culture as it might otherwise have done. It is reported, however, that the arrival in 1882 of the Abbott English Opera Company, presumably with no Vigilante distraction, created the proper mining camp frenzy. To honor the occasion suitably, the *Chronicle* records that "plug hats, heretofore a rarity, suddenly appeared on the heads of male bipeds," while the ladies appeared "in full bloom; flashy dresses, white opera hats, and colors flying." And something of a record for contrasts must surely have been set later that same year when Oscar Wilde appeared, dressed in black velvet, with knee breeches and black stockings. The topic of his lecture: "The Practical Application of the Aesthetic Theory to Exterior and Interior House Decoration, with Observations on Dress and Personal Ornament." The lecture probably did little to establish a meaningful rapport between the practicing aesthete from Britain and his rough-and-tumble audience. But the miners had their own practical criterion for measuring the worth of a man: by the time Wilde left Leadville they were frankly impressed by his capacity for holding hard liquor.

The fortunes of the Tabor Opera House, like that of Tabor, reached a peak in the 1880's. That's when the proud theater welcomed such great names as Maude Adams, Anna Held, Richard Mansfield, Helena Modjeska (in *As You Like It*) and Robert Mantell. John Philip Sousa appeared with his band, as did the Metropolitan Opera Company and the Chicago Symphony Orchestra. Many of the photographs, playbills, and original sets have been preserved. The partially restored opera house is privately owned and a modest tour fee is charged. Only the 99.44% *un*romantic could possibly feel he hadn't got his money's worth.

GOOD LUCK & HARD TIMES

As for the "Waldorfs," there are many more. Cripple Creek boasts a pair: the *Palace* and the *Imperial* (built in 1896, now restored and home of the state's best-known melodrama company).

Telluride, in far southwestern Colorado, offers the three-story *Sheridan,* which has seen better days.

And some of the most famous are of course gone now. Recent razing of the Denver's venerable *Windsor* (built in 1880) destroyed a picturesque reminder of much that was important in the capital city's early social, cultural, and political life. The impressive six-story stone affair, that may or may not have been patterned after Windsor Castle, played host to the Colorado legislature while the gold-domed Capitol was being built. Thereafter it served as rallying point—and, upon occasion, trysting place—for the city's great and near-great. It, too, had its memento of Horace Tabor and Baby Doe: their lavishly furnished honeymoon suite, complete with hand-carved walnut bed, square piano, and gold-encrusted high bathtub in which the second Mrs. Tabor allegedly bathed while servants poured water from gold-plated pitchers.

Another magnificent hostelry that is gone now (or nearly so) is the ornate, four-story *La Veta* in Gunnison. Each of its one hundred rooms had its own fireplace, fine chandelier, and walnut furniture. And a guest occupied his room free any day the sun failed to shine—a proud booster-ish promotion which the management was forced to make good on only seventeen times over one twenty-five-year period. But don't bother to look up this once proud relic unless you enjoy pain. Having fallen on hard times, it was bought by a contractor who tore off the top floors and roofed the truncated remainder with sheet iron to make living quarters and a garage. Even the Windsor's fate as an asphalted parking lot is less humilating than the La Veta's status as a living-death reminder of erstwhile opulence.

FOR AN ELEMENT LESS REFINED

There are also many notable Rocky Mountain Waldorfs outside Colorado. Plus waldorfs with a decidedly little *w*—like *Robbers' Roost* in southwestern Montana. This two-story log building, with full-length porch and upstairs veranda, was built in 1863 as a roadhouse to serve the busy stage route between Virginia City and Bannack, the Territory's principal gold camps.

Besides being a rather remarkable structure in its own right, Robbers' Roost owes its place in history to the fact that it served as a rendezvous for Henry Plummer and his notorious band of road agents. They took over almost from the day it opened and held on until the Vigilantes stepped in and liquidated the gang. And Plummer, ironically, had just succeeded in getting himself elected sheriff!

Finally, for one last little-*w* waldorf, this one back in Colorado, we would suggest the *Creede,* named for the town it is in.

Neither old (it was built in the 1890's to replace an earlier hotel destroyed by fire) nor pretentious (it's a two-story, tacked-onto, nondescript frame structure), the Creede somehow manages to evoke—for us, at any rate—the appearance and mood of the legendary old gold-camp hostelry even better than most of the painstakingly restored capital-*W* Waldorfs. The porch over the sidewalk, the worn wooden floors, the out-back cribs, the old bar, the casually displayed pictures and clippings and unassorted relics, the plain tables and plain food . . . it's all there to give you the unadorned, this-is-the-way-it-was glimpse of the Rocky Mountain mining frontier you wanted when you started this particular tour.

One aspect of the Creede tells much about the early-day West as a whole. While it maintained—and didn't try to hide—its row of small brick cribs, the Zang, as the hotel was known as then, considered itself a respectably upright institution, and proved it by hiring a bouncer to keep its bar free of rowdies. No ambivalence here at all: That's the way life was.

And happily you can rediscover it for yourself, just by driving around some exceedingly beautiful mountain countryside "collecting" old hotels.

WHERE THE MARKER-LIGHTS GLOWED

The afternoon was bright and sunny, strictly routine for the Rockies. It was the kind of day when you're grateful just to be alive and able to enjoy the peace and beauty of the mountains.

We were driving, leisurely, somewhere below the Colorado-New Mexico line. Durango was an hour or so behind us. Another few minutes and we'd be in Chama. Then suddenly we saw it on the side of the mountain to our left, a string of black beads snaking slowly through the pine and piñon behind a panting, smoke-belching little teakettle with "197" painted in white on her black side. It was the *San Juan* of the Denver & Rio Grande Western Railroad, the nation's last regularly scheduled narrow-gauge passenger train.

We slowed down to watch the toylike train drop down off the mountainside in deliberate, twisting curves to the level of the Chama River valley. Even then we realized that in our overpowered automobile we were drawing away. Again we reduced our speed until we seemed barely to be moving. We loved every moment of it. But perhaps only a fellow rail fan can appreciate fully the bittersweet ambivalence of our mood. There was pure joy in stumbling on a passenger train in such an idyllic setting—and not just any passenger, but a curious, last-of-its-breed, narrow-gauge passenger, train. Yet there was simultaneous sadness, too, that came with the awareness that we were watching not so much a common carrier, a facility for public transportation, as an animated museum piece.

At the station in Chama, itself a museum piece, actually, we stopped for a closer look. Only a passenger or two was visible. But D&RGW men bustled about the train, servicing it as if it were the sleek *California Zephyr*. Even then, of course, and this was not too many years ago, the *San Juan* was dying on its tiny wheels. But like many a noble institution before it, it was determined to die

102

proudly, maintaining a fine tradition of service, keeping up appearances to the end. No matter how abbreviated the passenger list, she ran complete with parlor car and full dining facilities.

Later we opened our copy of the D&RGW's *Green Light* and there it was—the picture-and-text obituary.

> A colorful part of the old West which had lived on long past its time died officially on the last day of January. On that day, the San Juan . . . joined the handcart, the covered wagon and the Concord coach on the pages of history.

Why did it have to go? Why, our heart argued with our head, couldn't the Rio Grande have preserved this final picturesque symbol of that golden age when the West, meeting the challenge of incalculable wealth in gold and silver, did indeed produce men to match the stature of her mountains?

> The last westbound San Juan pulled out of Alamosa . . . in early morning below-zero cold with 16 "through" revenue passengers . . . the heaviest load in many long months. . . . Elementary economics had taken its toll. Modern highways had shortened the distance between Alamosa and Durango by one-fourth and cut traveling time more than one-half.

There it was. Romance giving way to miles-per-hour statistics. Picturesque scenery and adventure-packed history breaking up before the hard dollar-and-cents facts of life:

> The 70-year-old 200-mile line had been a heavy money-loser for years, with the heaviest losses directly attributable to the unpatronized passenger train.

Sic transit gloria mundi. And the end is not yet. As we write this we await, fearfully, the next issue of *Green Light.*

THE D&RGW HANGS ON

Several years have passed since the *San Juan*'s demise and those "elementary economics" continue to take their toll. With its passenger traffic, the scenic narrow-gauge has now lost its freight business. Or most of it. And abandonment of the line now seems inevitable. *"Going . . . going . . ."*—we wrote in a *Denver Post* article not too long ago—"And in a few more years most of Colorado's romantic narrow-gauges will be gone."

And now—*Gone!* As this was being readied for the printer, the Interstate Commerce Commission gave its final permission for abandonment of all but the Durango–Silverton run. Now Colorado and New Mexico have authorized legal state agencies to purchase from the D&RGW the equally scenic Antonito–Chama section. Plans for use of this Toltec Gorge/Cumbres Pass run are still tenuous, but it is virtually assured now that summertime passenger service will once again be available to the sentimentalist.

Meanwhile the mountainous western two thirds of Colorado, beyond the Denver/Colorado Springs/Pueblo gateways, may soon be limited to a pair of prosperous freight-only routes. (Today the future is clouded even for the now greatly downgraded *Zephyr,* which pioneered the glass-domed passenger cars that gave arm's-length immediacy to the scenery that the early rail passengers came West to see.) Nevertheless the legacy of the gallant narrow-gauges—along with a few contemporary standard-gauge lines—is not so easily erased from sight. Those old-time railroad builders were a hardy breed. They built well; and for that we can be humbly grateful today.

A century ago Colorado was a sparsely settled Territory with a population of about 40,000, this despite a couple of "Pikes Peak or Bust" gold rushes and the establishment of several scores of mining camps in the hills beyond Denver. Then came the railroads, and during the 1870's and 1880's a clutch of adventurous lines—the Colorado Central, the Denver & Rio Grande, the South Park, the "Switzerland Trail," the Colorado Midland, and many others—met the challenge of every new gold and silver strike. With unflagging zeal, boundless optimism, artful ingenuity often bordering on genius, and—all else failing—sheer guts, they created an expanding network of steel rails that probed deep canyons, crossed and recrossed rocky streambeds, and vaulted virtually impassable mountain passes.

The railroad was the lifeline of every mining camp in the hills that boasted any wealth at all. (As for such a fantastically rich area as Cripple Creek—actually a district embracing a dozen or more separate, competing towns with a combined population that may have reached 60,000 or more in the early 1880's—it was served for a time by no less than three railroads, plus a pair of interurban-type electric systems.) No physical challenge was too great as ingenious railroad men laid out giant switchbacks, bored tunnels above the timberline, scratched shelf roads from naked mountainsides, and outwitted dead-end canyons. ("Mears's Maze" was unique. Named for its creator, Otto Mears—who was president of the Rio Grande Southern Railroad, and a near-genius—it combined the use of a turntable for the locomotive, and gravity for the train, to negotiate Corkscrew Gulch and thus serve the Red Mountain Pass district above Durango.)

Construction perforce was in rock. And, fortunately, a rocky roadbed is not something one pulls up and sells for scrap when the line is abandoned. The happy result, then, is a series of adventure roads, most of them offtrail and relatively undertraveled, that give the hardy motorist (1) an unsurpassed view of some of Colo-

---

Before We Start . . .

A few parenthetical disclaimers may be in order here. In the first place, we do not wish to imply that rail-into-auto roads are limited to Colorado: we've found, and enjoyed, them in other states. And their number, alas, is increasing as abandonment of money-losing branch lines continues.

Too, we would not want to give the impression that we consider this a complete list even for Colorado. There are some promising ones we know about and haven't yet got around to logging. We're sure there are others we'll learn about next week or next year. (There's even one particularly exciting pass route we haven't added to our collection—and just may not, ever: right now we're inclined to hold it back like a "see Naples and die" life insurance policy!)

Then, finally, there's the quality of the roads themselves and what we might call the effort-to-enjoyment ratio. Now obviously none of these roads are superhighways, although one, substantially upgraded, helps fill in a section of an Interstate. Most are secondary roads and some, at least to many a flatlander, would rate more as a goat trail than a road. Obviously, too, we haven't driven all these roads in the past two weeks—and it wouldn't always help too much if we had, for a mountain storm can change the condition of almost any road overnight.

So inquire locally to be on the safe side. And if mountain driving, even on major highways, does not particularly exhilarate you, then perhaps you'd better pass up rail-into-road collecting altogether. The rewards are more than generous. But you have to work for them.

rado's finest scenery, and (2) an interesting insight, as an extra, into Rocky Mountain railroad building as it served the region's succession of gold and silver camps. For almost a score of years now we've hunted out these rail-into-auto roads. Here are some of those we've found to be the most rewarding.

CLEAR CREEK CANYON HIGHWAY

If the qualifiers above didn't completely discourage you, perhaps you'd like to start with Clear Creek Canyon. And then quit. Once hailed as "the most wonderful piece of railroad engineering in America," it is now, as U.S. 6, a top-drawer example of highway engineering. The old *Colorado Central* pushed west from Denver up between the sheer walls of Clear Creek Canyon to serve such rich mining areas as Central City/Black Hawk, Idaho Springs/Empire, and Georgetown/ Silver Plume. Along with gold and silver, the line hauled Presidents, other visiting dignitaries, and special trainloads of ordinary tourists. For these, as a fitting climax to the exciting canyon route, there was the world-famous *Georgetown Loop,* only a few physical traces of which have survived construction of Interstate 70 through this steep and narrow notch. Currently there's talk of some kind of a reconstruction of this altitude-gaining loop. And this would indeed be as fitting a tribute to the genius of the early railroad builders as a rejuvenated Mears's Maze.

Today from Golden west to its junction with Interstate 70 near Idaho Springs, U.S. 6 utilizes most of the Colorado Central's spectacular right-of-way—a smooth, easy-climbing route highlighted by a half-dozen tunnels, colorful canyon walls, and mile upon mile of tumbling white water. For extras there's an old engine at Central City (up Colorado 119), a stub train at Idaho Springs, and a former depot-turned-restaurant at Silver Plume.

LEAVENWORTH MOUNTAIN ROAD

The *Georgetown & Gray's Peak* was perhaps the most "far out" of all Colorado narrow-gauges when it came to altitude. After switchbacking its way up Leavenworth south of Georgetown, it followed the creek of the same name to the present ghost town of Waldorf. Beyond, far above timberline on rugged Mt. McClellan, it finally ex-

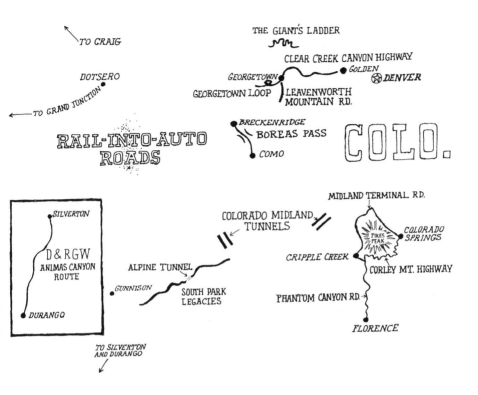

pired. But not before it had seesawed to a dizzy 13,100 feet above sea level, the highest point ever reached in the United States by an adhesion railroad. Today the auto road up Leavenworth to Waldorf uses most of the G&GP right-of-way. And much of it slices through unmarred forest, thus giving the motorist some of the feel and thrill of expectancy we suspect the Mt. McClellan-bound excursionists experienced three quarters of a century ago. Try it, too, for a new look at Georgetown, Colorado's Victorian masterpiece (which we visited earlier).

CORLEY MOUNTAIN HIGHWAY

This could be the highlight of your next Colorado Springs vacation. The *Cripple Creek Short Line,* a 45-mile standard-gauge affair, was blasted and hacked from the pink granite of Pikes Peak's eastern and southern flanks in 1900. And what it lacked in economic justification (the Cripple Creek mining district already had two other well-established railroads), it clearly made up for in scenery. It even elicited a famous "Bully!" from Teddy Roosevelt. "This is the ride," he added for good measure, "that bankrupts the English language!"

But scenery, alas, failed to pay off the bonds. The Short Line went into receivership in 1919. In 1922 one W. D. Corley bought it—lock, stock, and nine tunnels—and converted its easy grades and gentle curves into the spectacularly beautiful Colorado Springs–Cripple Creek toll road. It's free today, as the Gold Camp Road, and a road no rail fan should miss.

PHANTOM CANYON ROAD

Even the name of this one has a kind of shivery appeal. And it's likely to deliver on the shivers, too, especially on a sunny summer weekend when the Colorado Springs sightseeing buses are whipping over it as if bent on getting out of the canyon before the 3:24 cloudburst. All this notwithstanding, the road is eminently worth the effort.

The 40-mile *Florence & Cripple Creek Railroad,* a narrow-gauge, was built up the canyon in the early 1890's. And at tremendous expense, for it had to climb from 5,187 feet at Florence to 10,300 feet at Cripple Creek. Grades were so bad in Eight Mile Canyon that only eight loaded freight cars could be taken up at a time. Deficits mounted, understandably, and the line received its financial comeuppance in 1912 following a disastrous washout. In 1916 it became an auto road.

As Colorado 67 today, Phantom Canyon contrasts sharply with the Corley road, following the bottom of a beautiful gorge rather than riding the high flank of a mountain. Taken together, the roads give one a nice cross section of back-country Colorado mountain driving. Our suggestion: Next time you're driving Interstate 25 between Colorado Springs and Pueblo, and have an extra half-day or so to spend, invest it here. Take the Corley road to Cripple Creek (fascinating in its own right), then drop leisurely down Phantom Canyon to Florence. U.S. 50 will quickly return you to Pueblo.

That is, if you don't decide to explore famed Royal Gorge. "Rail" attractions here include an incline railroad ride to the bottom of the 1200-foot-deep canyon and a miniature railroad ride along its northern rim. From top and bottom the deep-clefted canyon is eminently worth seeing, despite congestion and commercialization. To avoid this, and still enjoy the awesome gorge, inquire in Canyon City about the road to the old tunnels at the east entrance to the gorge. Perhaps it's only because we first stumbled on these tunnels ourselves, giving us a kind of proprietary interest in them, and had them to ourselves all the time we were there, that we can still feel the excitement of viewing the gorge from this isolated notch in the canyon wall.

MIDLAND TERMINAL ROAD

If you must forgo Phantom Canyon, swing north from Cripple Creek (on Colorado 67) on the abandoned right-of-way of the third line serving the district. The *Midland Terminal Railway* was the first to be built, the last to be abandoned. From the Springs to Divide it was once part of the Colorado Midland (see below). Today Colorado 67 follows much of its old route and actually uses the original grade for some ten miles. Be sure to notice the smoke that still stains the entrance portals to the tunnels, a satisfying extra touch of realism.

MIDLAND TUNNELS

The *Colorado Midland* is one of the hundreds of ambitious 19th-century lines that *almost* lived up to their promise. Built in the late 1880's as a standard-gauge, it pushed westward from Colorado Springs to beyond Glenwood Springs, promising for a time to give the Denver & Rio Grande a run for its money. But it could never quite make it to Salt Lake City. The result: the CM is best known now as one of the largest railroad abandonments in the world. World War I brought the evil day. In 1922, that part of the right-of-way piercing the Continental Divide, at the 11,528-foot level, via two-mile-long Carleton Tunnel, became a toll road. Today much of the magnificent grade on either side of the Divide can still be driven. But seepage has, alas, now closed the tunnel itself.

Midland relics remain, however. Just off U.S. 24 at Lake George (some 35 miles west of the Springs), Eleven Mile Canyon offers a pleasant stretch of roadbed, a clutch of abandoned tunnels—and car-window trout fishing. Out of Buena Vista, on to the west, are even more exciting grades. And more smoke-smudged tunnels. Watch for the turnoff as you near the Arkansas River just south of Buena Vista.

While still on joint U.S. 24–285 just east of the river you'll see the sign, "Midland Scenic Road." Highlight of this leg is the old Colorado Midland depot site on a ledge some 300 feet above the river and directly opposite Buena Vista. Faced with climbing that hill or riding the buckboard, before ski lifts, most people promptly gave their passenger business to the Denver & Rio Grande. The second section, detached from the first now by the collapse of a high trestle, must be reached from downtown Buena Vista. Cross the river, and once you've climbed onto the old right-of-way, with its tunnels and superlative view of the entire Arkansas valley, you can follow it for miles.

SOUTH PARK LEGACIES

These rail-into-auto-road treasures come to us courtesy of the storied *Denver, South Park & Pacific,* another ambitious D&RG rival that didn't get even as close to the Pacific as the Colorado Midland did. But it did manage finally to reach Leadville and Gunnison. And these two branches, upon abandonment, add a pair of spectacular auto roads to our list. The first is the quietly beautiful Boreas Pass route. It leaves U.S. 285 at Como, crosses the Continental Divide at an altitude of 11,492 feet, and comes out at Breckenridge.

The Alpine Tunnel section lies west of the Arkansas River where the DSP&P main line drew a deep breath and then plunged straight into the mountains for Gunnison. Well, it finally made it. But after you've driven to Hancock (some six miles above St. Elmo and the end of the line for your car), you understand why the feat of building the road—and then trying to keep it open in winter—contributed to the line's premature demise.

But the route up and back is beautiful, offering scenery, history, relic hunting, and dramatic photo possibilities. You leave U.S. 285 at Nathrop, on Colorado 162. The route ascends beautiful Chalk Creek Canyon, to serve Montezuma Hot Springs (a shadowy relic of a more leisurely age when "taking the waters" was both fashionable and great fun), then crawls out on a narrow ledge along the south bank of Chalk Creek.

The roadbed is narrow, but quite safe (it's one way up as far as St. Elmo) and offers superb scenery all the way. Stop occasionally to appreciate the almost sheer Chalk Cliffs themselves, on the opposite side of the canyon—the holes, caves and ledges, the scattered pines that stand starkly tall and green against them—and the mass of Mt. Princeton itself, with the old Hortense Mine wagon road still visible as a thin slash across its rock face above the timberline. Just to stare up at it is to begin to appreciate the awesome courage and determination of yesterday's road builders. And the gutsy fortitude (or was it numbed resignation?) that must have characterized those who traveled these primitive roads!

St. Elmo itself is a picturesque near-ghost surrounded by nearly a dozen true ghosts. For the most spectacular scenery and most picturesque mine relics follow the DSP&P right-of-way past the ruins of Ohio Mills, through abandoned Romley and the rusted remains of the Mary Murphy Mine to Hancock, from whence all life has long since sped. This is where you park your car and walk the mile or so to the east portal of Alpine Tunnel. The wildflowers here, incidentally, are spectacular, too—in size, color, and variety.

THE GIANT'S LADDER

We'll stop with this one, the nonpareil of rail-into-auto roads. There are many, many more for you to discover and enjoy, but if you've gone along with us this far, you're well able to go on alone. Finding them yourself, after all, is often half the enjoyment. But this one— Well, we'll supply the routine dates and statistics. You can fill in the superlatives as you will.

Until the six-mile-long Moffat Tunnel was completed in 1927, the *Denver & Salt Lake* (now the D&RGW) twisted up and over

The view from the Pacific side of Corona Pass makes this rail-into-auto road ideal for the leisurely tourer in Colorado.

James Peak and the Continental Divide via Corona Pass. At 11,680 feet, this was the highest point ever reached by any *standard-gauge* adhesion railroad in the world. (The Georgetown & Gray's Peak was narrow-gauge.) And today virtually every foot of the 34-mile rail section retired because of the tunnel—from Tolland on the East Slope to Winter Park on the West Slope—is open to the cautiously adventurous motorist. It features Yankee Doodle and several other trout-filled lakes, the exciting Needle's Eye tunnel, a couple of long trestles, the remains of a novel trestle/tunnel corkscrew, stretches of breathtaking above-timberline shelf road, and tremendous vistas of the North American continent's rocky spine from a beautiful alpine meadow. *Nonpareil?* Well, it's both an impressive example of railroad engineering and a dazzling potpourri of magnificent high-country scenery. It's the Colorado the full-color travel brochures promise you. Just that.

"IRON HORSE MANURE"

Many other railroading mementos are to be found throughout Colorado and the West. Most common perhaps is the now-retired, cold-boilered steam engine, resting proudly in parks in big cities and small towns alike all across the land. In Colorado you find them at Gunnison, Montrose, Colorado Springs, Idaho Springs, Central City, and Boulder. Passenger cars are attached to "teakettles" at Boulder and Alamosa. Durango has a handsome 1882 business-observation car on display. Vintage cabooses can be inspected at Montrose, Lake City, and Alamosa: an 1886 "crummy" even serves as Chamber of Commerce office in Ouray. And Craig, terminus of David Moffat's Denver & Salt Lake, honors the railroad builder with the state's most remarkable Chamber office—his plushly appointed business car, the *Marcia.*

The state's finest concentration of railroadiana, however, and one of the best collections in the country, is at Golden, just off Interstate 70 some 15 miles west of Denver. The Colorado Railroad Museum, housed in an authentic replica of an early-day depot, is a growing, study-and-research-minded institution. It offers outside tracks clogged with old engines, vintage freight and passenger cars, interurbans, and all pertinent track and signal equipment. Interior displays include historic signposts, old timetables, ancient newsclips, photographs, orders, and papers. To spend an hour or a day browsing the museum inside and out is to relive, as best one can in these latter years, one of the most dramatic aspects of all in the multifaceted winning of the West.

DURANGO–SILVERTON ON THE D&RGW

All is not lost, of course. Not entirely. In southwest Colorado the nation's last "legitimate" (as of this writing) narrow-gauge passenger train still rambles a 45-mile-long summertime course up the deep cleft of Animas River Canyon from Durango to Silverton and back. Nostalgia has combined with exciting scenery to bring bustling popularity to this canyon route. During the busiest weeks of the summer the *Denver & Rio Grande Western* must now run a second section most days to handle the demand for seats. A letter to the D&RGW agent at Durango will bring details on schedules and tariffs.

But if you fail to get a seat at the last minute, don't feel too bad about it. For rail-into-auto roads, you don't need a ticket. And we've found touring them—they're in and around Durango and Silverton, too—as enjoyable as any travel hobby we've ever pursued.

MOUNTAINS AND MOUNTAIN PASSES

Driving in the mountains—and we're thinking here of the high mountains of the West—is much like eating olives. More often than not, there is no middle ground: one either enjoys it immensely or finds it extremely distasteful. Remember the story of the old man, asked by the young reporter how he stood on some burning issue of the day? "Son, I haven't decided yet," he said. "But when I do take a stand, it'll be a strong one." Many a motorist is like that, though often it takes but a single mountain drive to decide the issue.

I can still see the tight lips and hear the quivery voice of a very dear friend as she told of driving the old Cody (east) entrance to Yellowstone National Park. Then and there, she said, she and her husband had taken the pledge: they promised the Good Lord that if He forgave them this one innocent indiscretion, they'd never let it happen again. Similarly, I remember running into a vacationing newspaper colleague at a restaurant in Gunnison and hearing him say of the Million Dollar Highway, "Never again! I regret that I have but one wife and two sons to give to the exploration of Colorado." And so it goes with the non-olive lovers.

The opposite response can be just as strong, of course. And just as immediate. I recall vividly my own first mountain pass—old *Raton Pass* on the New Mexico-Colorado boundary. And it was love at first sight, not just for Raton itself but, as we suspected then and confirmed subsequently, all mountain passes. Every element was there in that first experience, caught in a single eight- or ten-mile stretch of narrow, twisting asphalt. There was the rapid exhilaration of the physical ascent itself . . . the tingling excitement of broadening, ever changing panoramas . . . the not-unpleasant popping of eardrums . . . the breath-quickening inner tension of awesome chasms just beyond the car window . . . the almost godlike thrill of looking down on lofty treetops . . . and, finally, the soul-stretching experience—inspiring, yet at the same time humbling—of mountains-beyond-mountains beauty, limitless and ageless. I felt it then, over thirty years ago, on Raton Pass. I have never failed to feel it since, in varying ways and with varying intensities, on every mountain road I've been on.

Needless to say, after this the more of these passes Helen and I have logged, the more we've enjoyed them and the more avidly we've hunted out new ones not yet driven. Needless to say, too, the reader of this chapter should also be an "olive-eater." So before we get onto

the passes themselves, a few cautionary words. If you don't thoroughly *enjoy* mountain driving, or don't find yourself relaxed and anticipatory while doing so, let us suggest you pass on to the next chapter. Even superb scenery is not worth the effort, for driver or passenger, if one must concentrate apprehensively on the sheer mechanics of driving. In any case (and if you're still reading we'll assume you plan to stay with us), mountain driving calls for a few commonsense rules and guidelines. Follow them and your driving will be not only safe but enjoyable as well.

Guidelines for the Mountains

◀ Most mountain roads are twisting and relatively narrow. *Always* keep to the righthand lane, especially on curves, no matter how precipitous the dropoff beyond the car fender.

◀ Never stop or pass on a blind curve, no matter how beautiful the view or how slow-moving the vehicle ahead. Incidentally, truck drivers in the mountains are uniformly helpful; they'll signal if and when they figure it's safe for you to pass.

◀ In slide areas—and that's most of the time—watch for rocks in the road.

◀ On downgrades (always difficult to gauge because of the prevalence of optical illusions), take another tip from the truck drivers: *gear down* to let engine compression do as much as possible of your braking. Coasting downhill, though made possible in some instances by modern highway engineering, is both foolish *and* illegal.

FOLLOWING THE GREAT PASS FINDERS

With all this in mind, then, a last note of assurance. The rewards of touring mountain passes are not limited by any means to the thrill of beauty or the tingle of excitement and potential danger. There is the satisfaction of discovery, too. No mountain pass road—whether for stage coach, ore wagon, railroad, or automobile—was constructed without human heroics. And often the heroics extended even to the using of the road.

Consider, for example, the story they tell of Otto Mears and his "Rio Grande Impossible" (Rio Grande Southern RR), the tortuous narrow-gauge railroad he built between Durango and Telluride to serve the booming mines in this extremely rugged southwestern corner of Colorado. The line had just been completed and a special train was carrying Mears and his official party over the route to highlight special celebrations under way at every mining camp along the way. But by the time they reached Rico, then the largest silver camp in the state, Mears had apparently had enough. Called upon to say a few words, he said them, bluntly and to the point. Anybody that would ride the rail line he'd just built, he allegedly told the happy crowd of well-wishers, was ready to be put away. Personally, he wasn't leaving Rico until they brought him a horse and buggy!

(A few years ago, a high school football coach proved such coastability on the excellent new Monarch Pass road—U.S. 50—west of Salida, Colorado. When his brakes failed at the start of the descent he cool-headedly organized his passengers, and sent them scurrying from side to side, on signal, to counterbalance the centrifugal force on curves. He and his team rode out the hair-raising 23-mile descent successfully—and, with speeds up to 100 mph, in what must surely have been record time.)

◀ Remember, in the mountains the car going *up* a grade always has the right-of-way. This is particularly important to remember on narrow and one-way roads (of which there are still a few, though their numbers decline steadily). Then it is your responsibility, if descending, to watch for the approaching car, locate a turnout and, if possible, be in it by the time the oncoming car meets you.

◀ Finally, be patient and courteous. When in doubt, you'll find these attitudes hard to beat as safety measures.

Well, discovering these heroics and, where possible, reliving them, makes each pass road different, distinctive, and that much more meaningful. We touched on this in the chapter on the great Trails, when we talked of the importance of *South Pass,* not merely as a physical crossing of the Continental Divide for the Oregon and California trails, but for the role it played, because of its relative ease of travel, in the development of much of the West. Had not such an easy pass through the mountains existed, or had it existed somewhere else, the entire "course of empire" could well have been altered.

Western geography is not Eastern geography. Often as not travelers beyond the Mississippi and the Missouri went not where they wanted to, but where they could. This is true of the first travelers; it is also true of those that came after them, for by then patterns had been set. Vardis Fisher brought this out recently in an eloquent tribute to "The Lingering Frontier." Tracing the development of his beloved West, he pays homage to the early explorers, men like Simon Fraser and David Thompson, who traced out the first routes in Canada. To the Mountain Men of America like Andrew Henry, John Colter, Jim Bridger, and Jedediah Smith. And to army officers like Captain John Charles ("The Pathfinder") Frémont. They were, "pathfinders," all right. But Fisher adds, ". . . It might be more appropriate to call them pass finders, because passes across the Divide are what many of them were looking for."

They found them, these pass finders. And those who came afterwards used their passes, thus setting the pattern for settlement and development of the Rocky Mountain states. And those of us who follow today get yet another lesson in history. We've mentioned old *Donner Pass,* in California, and how easily it can evoke for the visitor the unhappy plight of the inexperienced Donner Party, faced with crossing the fearsome Sierra Nevadas in the face of an early fall blizzard. Lewis and Clark, too, were pass finders, and we've said how meaningful it is to retrace in a car the mountain-topping section of their route along the Montana-Idaho boundary.

For a single pass that perhaps best sums up what we're trying to say, consider *Togwotee* in northwestern Wyoming. It crosses the Continental Divide on U.S. 26–287, a modern highway that probably carries more motorists to the Yellowstone/Teton Mountains wonderland than any other road. Yet it is also one of the truly historic passes in the West. John Colter, the wily, lone-wolf Mountain Man who made a name for himself trapping beaver and telling tall tales, was the first non-Indian to traverse the route. He was also the first non-Indian to see the geysers, mud pots, hot springs, and other natural wonders of Yellowstone, all of which helped to mold his early reputation as the greatest truth-stretcher of them all.

And I think I know now the frustration he must have felt. It was on Togwotee Pass that I discovered the Tetons . . . saw them for the first time and realized (as at different times I have at Grand Canyon, Yosemite, Dead Horse Point, Monument Valley, and several other places of almost overpowering emotional impact) that no matter how many pictures you see beforehand, no matter how hard you try to imagine it, there are certain scenes you simply cannot get ready for. You think you know what to expect—until you see it. Then the scene is there before you—stark, unreal, something you're seeing, as it were, for the first time. The Tetons were like that to us. And because they were, we've always felt just a bit akin to Colter. We know that no one else can really appreciate anything we say or write about them until he sees them for himself.

COLORADO, IN GENERAL

But enough for the scatter-gun approach to mountain passes. Let's get down to specifics on a more manageable area—like Colorado. To range too far afield in collecting passes would spread our efforts pretty thin. Old Colorado hand Marshall Sprague, who has written a book on the subject and has probably as much or more firsthand experience with it than any writer around, estimates that there are more than 350 high passes along the Continental Divide and spur ranges of the Rockies in the 1,200-mile-long slash of mountains from the Canadian border to northern New Mexico. Many of these can be negotiated only on foot, horseback, or, with increasing frequency, by four-wheel-drive vehicle. Still, at least half can be reached on asphalted or graveled roads, quite safe when subject to the criteria previously listed. And most of the high ones are pretty well confined to Colorado, simply because the Centennial State is also "the highest state" to begin with, with a mean elevation of 6,800 feet. (Actually, the vertical ascent from valley floor to mountain pass, as Sprague points out, is usually around 3,000 feet, whether you're in Colorado,

Wyoming, Idaho or Montana. And it's this climb—and subsequent descent—that provides the fun of pass collecting.)

How many Colorado passes, then, are there that we're supposed to visit? Well, no one knows for sure. Much depends on whether or not you include all the so-called jeep roads. These have proliferated mightily in the past few years, which makes it risky to draw up any hard-and-fast list. Too, weather can change the roster with a single good mountain shower. So the following chart is a suggested starter list of "collectible" Colorado passes, as of the time of writing. Those with either federal or state highway status are from the official Colorado highway department map. A few are closed in winter; otherwise their year-round accessibility is more or less guaranteed. "U.S.F.S." indicates a Forest Service road.

A STARTER COLLECTION OF COLORADO MOUNTAIN PASSES

Pass	*Altitude*	*Highway & Location*
Berthoud	11,314 ft.	U.S. 40, W of Denver
Boreas	11,482	U.S.F.S., SE of Breckenridge
Buffalo	10,180	U.S.F.S., E of Steamboat Springs
Cameron	10,285	Colo. 14, W of Fort Collins
Corona	11,680	U.S.F.S., W of Rollinsville
Cottonwood	12,126	U.S.F.S., W of Buena Vista
Cumberland	12,015	NE of Gunnison
Cumbres	10,022	Colo. 17, W of Antonito
Douglas	8,268	Colo. 139, S of Rangely
Fremont	11,318	Colo. 91, N of Leadville
Gore	9,524	Colo. 134, NW of Kremmling
Hoosier	11,541	Colo. 9, N of Fairplay
Independence	12,095	Colo. 82, E of Aspen
Kenosha	10,001	U.S. 285, SW of Denver
La Veta	9,413	U.S. 160, W of Walsenburg
Lizard Head	10,222	Colo. 145, S of Telluride
Loveland	11,992	U.S. 6, W of Denver
Marshall	10,856	SW of Salida
McClure	8,755	Colo. 133, S of Glenwood Springs
Milner	10,759	U.S. 34, W of Estes Park
Monarch	11,312	U.S. 50, W of Salida
Poncha	9,010	U.S. 285, S of Salida
Rabbit Ears	9,426	U.S. 40, NW of Kremmling
Raton	7,834	U.S. 85–87, S of Trinidad

Those passes on the second list are, for the most part, recommended for the tourer who has already served his apprenticeship on the state and federal routes.

DOWN THE CONTINENTAL DIVIDE

Our love for the mountains, as we've said, started on top of Raton Pass. But our collecting of mountain passes didn't start until a couple of years later, and a couple of hundred miles to the north. Friends in Denver with whom we were visiting took us on what seems to be the perfect introduction to the Colorado Rockies for a first-time visitor. The circle trip contains a smattering of everything one comes to Colorado to see—snowy peaks, noisy white-water

Red Mountain	11,018	U.S. 550, S of Silverton
Shrine	11,075	N of Leadville
Slumgullion	11,361	SE of Lake City
Spring Creek	10,901	SE of Lake City
Tennessee	10,424	U.S. 24, N of Leadville
Trail Ridge Crest	12,183	U.S. 34, W of Estes Park
Vail	10,603	U.S. 6, W of Dillon
Willow Creek	9,683	Colo. 125, N of Granby
Wolf Creek	10,850	U.S. 160, NE of Pagosa Springs

A SELECTION OF INQUIRE-FIRST PASSES
(Mostly Four-Wheel-Drive Roads)

Pass	Altitude	Highway & Location
Argentine	13,132 ft.	SW of Georgetown
Cinnamon	13,009	W of Lake City, SE of Ouray
Engineer	13,175	W of Lake City, SE of Ouray
Georgia	11,598	NE of Fairplay
Mosquito	13,180	Between Fairplay & Leadville
Ophir	11,789	NW of Silverton
Schofield	10,000	N of Crested Butte
Taylor	11,950	S of Aspen
Tincup	12,154	W of Buena Vista
Webster	12,108	NE of Fairplay
Whiskey	12,802	W of Trinidad

streams, sparkling lakes, crumbling ghost towns, exciting shelf roads, rocky canyons, magnificent forests, colorful wildflowers, and awesome stretches of above-timberline wasteland. This loop contains it all, and more, and we have considered it ever since to be Colorado's ideal, One-day Grand Tour. If by chance you're considering a similar first visit, we urge you to let this all-day loop be your introduction to the Rockies, too.

DENVER AREA

They drove us west on U.S. 40 over snowy *Berthoud* Pass to Granby. Striking north on U.S. 34, we picnicked beside beautiful Grand Lake, the self-proclaimed highest yacht anchorage in the country. From here we entered Rocky Mountain National Park, thrilling to *Milner* Pass and the superlative *Trail Ridge* Road before dropping down onto the plains again, through Estes Park and rock-strewn Big Thompson Canyon. We'd logged our first three Colorado passes. And we've been working on the rest of them ever since.

Trail Ridge is not just a "road"—it's a magnificent engineering feat, a staggering emotional experience, a vacation "happening" in the finest sense of the word. Nor, technically, is it really a pass. It seeks out no utilitarian notch, but deliberately traces its breath-taking course along the very crest of the mountains. And it makes a 15-mile-long labor of love out of the project. These are its 15 above-timberline miles, no less than four of which are above 12,000 feet. The "pass" point is 12,183 feet above sea level, making this road the highest through highway in the United States.

Loveland was perhaps our next pass, when it was still gravel-sur-faced and made doubly exciting by its tight hairpin curves. Over the years it has remained a favorite, and we're far from alone in believing that its vast panorama of snowy peaks is probably the finest one to be found anywhere. Upgrading and hard-surfacing of the pass has destroyed none of this soaring beauty—just made it a bit easier for one to absorb and appreciate while still driving in complete safety. Currently, work is under way on the twin tunnels by which Interstate 70 will burrow under the Continental Divide and thus es-cape the September-to-May threat of ice and snow that plagues the 11,992-foot-high pass. Once it is open, the status of Loveland is somewhat in doubt. But that is still several years away. In the mean-

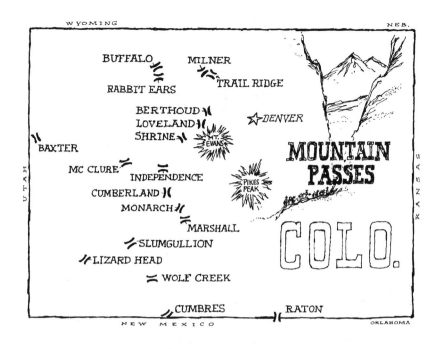

time, put this route above the timberline well up on your collecting list.

DOWN FROM LEADVILLE

Even higher—at 12,095 feet high—is *Independence* Pass, the "short cut" in to Aspen from U.S. 24 below Leadville. At long last this lofty breathtaker is being upgraded. In a matter of time, presumably, it too will be hard-surfaced. And we'll admit to a slight feeling of regret on this improvement. Perhaps we're remembering the time we were caught in a rain while still a quarter-mile or so from the crest on the west approach where, from an unrailed road (but with a decent shelf), you look down into the headwaters of the Roaring Fork, an incredibly lush, green valley that surely not even the Garden of Eden could have surpassed in beauty.

True, rocks, loosened by the storm, were beginning to roll down onto the roadway. But none threatened to topple us off into our Eden. They were relatively small and we detoured easily around those our Plymouth couldn't straddle. But the firsthand reminder of what this one-time stage road could have done, had it chosen to shrug us off her shoulder, has stayed with us ever since, to make us feel that we and the mountains are now partners. Pavement won't destroy this beauty, of course. But it will increase traffic to the point where stopping to enjoy it will be a bit more difficult. Our suggestion: Log this one as soon as you can!

Confirming what Old Colorado Hands have long known, that the alpine tundra on the crest of Independence is the most representative to be found anywhere, the U.S. Forest Service has laid out paths and erected informational signs to help the visitor understand better what he is seeing. Similarly interesting and instructive exhibits on the area geology and ecology have been erected on the east slope.

Monarch Pass is the next major crossing of the Continental Divide to the south (below *Cumberland*). Its engineering, as we've noted, is impeccable. If you would experience the "before" and "after" of mountain driving in a single circle tour, this is an ideal place to do it. Try *old* Monarch from the top down, then swing around to the south (left) and complete your loop with the *new* Monarch. There's a small sign for the old pass near the crest of the present one. You swing west into the forest, climb briefly, then descend the west side of the divide on a fairly steep shelf road, narrow but quite safe when dry, that opens up vistas of an isolated old mining country many Colorado residents have never seen.

This is particularly true if you should decide to go gung-ho on your exploring here and, instead of swinging south to make your circle, loop north to make a *clockwise* circle. The Old Monarch Pass Road is virtually the same as the stage road built in 1880 to serve the mining booms that created White Pine, Ohio City, Pitkin, and several other ghosts and near-ghosts. These places are interesting to poke into. Then from Pitkin, where you drive occasionally on the abandoned right-of-way of the colorful Denver & South Park narrow-gauge, you begin climbing again toward another pair of 12,000-foot passes. Both are unpaved but otherwise totally unalike. At Quartz, now almost totally reclaimed by the forest, you start zigzagging toward the treeless crest of 12,015-foot *Cumberland*. And somehow the view from here strikes us as different from any other Colorado pass we've been on. Spiny ridges of individual mountain ranges stretch off to the north, south, and west, seemingly to infinity. And

despite the fact they range upwards to 14,000 feet and higher, you seem for some reason to be looking *down* on all of them. It's an exhilarating, and at the same time a rather awesome, experience.

Only after adjusting to this do you begin to notice the mine scars, the remains of sheds and other mining structures, even the ruins of a mill, all dotting this up-ended mountain top rising above the timberline. It's a vivid reminder of the courage and perseverance it took to discover, much less to dig out and transport, the silver that boomed this area in the 1880's and 1890's. Then Cumberland served as a stage and freighter route too, extending north to Tincup, where you complete your circle with yet another stage-road crossing of the Continental Divide.

Until 1905, *Cottonwood* Pass was the 12,126-foot link between the western-slope mining districts and the older Leadville area mines. Long abandoned to all travel, the Cottonwood route was only recently opened by the U.S. Forest Service. Now it offers relatively easy access to the Taylor Park region, from Buena Vista on the Arkansas River.

The next Continental Divide crossing below Monarch (the U.S. 50 Monarch) is *Marshall* Pass, the abandoned right-of-way of the Denver & Rio Grande narrow-gauge line to Gunnison. Before that, it too was a stage road. Opened in 1877, it was taken over by the D&RG in 1881 and for a time it enjoyed main-line status on the route between Denver and Salt Lake City. Even when standard-gauging moved main tracks northward, however, the rich Gunnison valley kept the narrow-gauge busy, and little steam trains belching smoke continued to toil over Marshall until the mid-1950's.

Other well-known passes once serving as railroad grades include *Corona* (west of Denver and perhaps the most spectacular of the lot), *Boreas* (above Fairplay and quietly beautiful all the way), and *Baxter* (on the Utah line northwest of Grand Junction). This is the "railroad division" of our mountain pass collection and it contains some of the best.

MISCELLANEOUS & WONDERFUL

But there's really no completely satisfactory way to group most of the others. Many were stage roads, as we've seen; but often they were taken over by the railroad builders. It is generally agreed that *Wolf Creek* in the southwest, though only 10,850 feet high, is one of the state's most beautiful, both from an engineering standpoint and because of its magnificent forest scenery. We hadn't fully agreed until a crisp June morning a few years ago. We drove it early that day, before a bright sun could knock off the soft wet snow that had blanketed the evergreens during the night. The montage of green branches, white snow and cloudless blue sky was overwhelming and we've been a Wolf Creek booster ever since. (But for best results you *still* need a night-before snow!)

For beauty, spiced with the added tingle of excitement that comes from driving a lightly traveled route, we favor *Spring Creek* and *Slumgullion*. Both are on Colorado 149 between Lake City and Creede, and quite close together. This entire route is a well-nigh perfect byway. Its gravel surface tends to discourage the nonfishermen, and the trout men spend their time on the water, not driving up and down the road. There are lakes and waterfalls within view of the highway, plus some of the state's finest cattle ranches. Just off the road are trails leading to many once active mining towns, now picturesque ghosts.

MORE FOR THE RAIL BUFFS

A strong contender for isolated-beauty honors would be *Cumbres* on the New Mexico boundary. Colorado 17 is being upgraded, but it is not likely to become a busy highway in the foreseeable future. One of its nicest features, especially for rail fans, is its proximity to the Denver & Rio Grande Western's narrow-gauge tracks of the Antonito–Durango line much of the way. As this is being written, the fate of the line is very much in the lap of the gods, particularly those gods whose bureaucratic responsibility it is to determine when a railroad line has paid its debt to society and may be permitted to fold its tents and steal away. The D&RGW insists that the time for tent-folding is at hand. (As this goes to press, the I.C.C. agrees; but Colorado and New Mexico are taking steps to forestall closing, as was mentioned in the preceding chapter.) At any rate, citizens of the two-state area, few of whom use the line for anything but a jogger of nostalgic memories, insist that it be maintained, somehow, by someone, as an historical monument. For the moment, at least, the line is still spiked down. And occasionally there is even a train on it. If so, it provides a definite extra for a road that is already one of the state's prettiest.

Perhaps one reason we've always liked Cumbres is just because of all that railroad publicity it used to get. We saw it for the first time only a few months after an unusually severe winter storm had blanketed the area with snow, and seventy-one crewmen, several locomotives, and a whole work train had been "lost" for a couple of weeks on or near the top of the pass. They'd had to wait for a snowplow train to dig through the mountainous drifts that had buried the first snowplow train that had been sent in originally to find the "missing" work train! It was all quite interesting, except perhaps for the seventy-one D&RGW crewmen themselves—none of whom, we suspect, enjoy driving Cumbres now, even on the Fourth of July.

LANDMARK PASSES

So it goes. Each pass has its own characteristic charm. Each opens up another fertile valley, another once important mining district, another interesting piece of scenery or bit of history. There's lovely *Shrine* Pass, for example, out of Redcliff. It isn't even marked on many maps now. But we'll always remember it with pleasure for the rare view it once afforded of majestic Mount of the Holy Cross some fifteen miles to the west. Even then, years ago, natural and continuing erosion had destroyed much of the once nearly perfect symmetry of the snowy cross, and deprived it of its National Park Service status as one of our scenic wonders.

However, when famed frontier photographer William Henry Jackson exposed the glass plate that made the cross familiar around the world, snow packed into deep rock crevices emblazoned the Christian symbol against the side of the mountain on a truly heroic scale. Though much of that former impressiveness is gone now, the narrow, twisting, lightly traveled road still opens up a vast expanse of fine Colorado mountain real estate—more than enough to justify its inclusion on anyone's tour.

Similarly, passes are often especially interesting for a single feature. For example, attention is called to two striking physical landmarks by *Lizard Head* and *Rabbit Ears* (this one not to be confused with the Santa Fe Trail's great sign seen from the Cimarron Cutoff).

Vail, a gentle and relatively obscure little pass despite service on busy U.S. 6, is now known far and wide for the handsome ski facility that sprang from a sheep pasture on its western flank only a few years ago.

Buffalo Pass, another mountain crossing opened up by the Forest Service in the interest of improved mobility in fighting fires, is an altogether satisfactory byway that receives added interest for its having been used by buffalo to cross the Continental Divide. Of course buffalo traffic is a bit difficult to encounter these days, but the early morning we crossed it a few years back we were happy to settle for a couple of deer. So light is the traffic on this route (or was then) that they seemed almost as pleased to see us as we were them.

Each pass, then, is just enough different from its fellows—if not in topography or history, then in the details of one's own particular driving experience—to make logging it worthwhile.

One pass we had hoped to put at the top of its own specialized category was *McClure,* off westerly from Aspen. The category: One-Lane, Shelf Road with Switchbacks. We were still rather new at passes when we got to this one. It looked narrow, admittedly. Plus steep. But it was clearly marked on our Gousha maps, which we

Trout Lake, near Colorado's Lizard Head Pass, is one of the rewards for driving from Telluride to Rico.

trust implicity. And the road over it led in the direction we wanted to go. So we started up, as confident, as historian E. E. Dale likes to put it, as a Christian with four aces.

Well, the beauty of any road in the One-Lane-Shelf-Road-with-Switchback category is that once you're on it, there's no turning back. You just watch for opposing automobiles—and places where you, or he, can turn out. As luck would have it, we had the road all to ourselves that particular afternoon. Helen drove, silently. I watched, silently. By the time we reached the crest, we felt we had "passed" from amateur collector to something at least approaching semipro status. We admit, however, to have been just a bit shaken by the sign at the top reading "McClure's Sheep Trail." Incidentally, when we drove it last summer, the state was putting the finishing touches on a rerouted, redesigned pass road. It's beautiful. But we sort of missed the excitement of the sheep trail. We even talked to each other on the way down.

THE TOPS OF THOSE MOUNTAINS

But one's mountain-climbing experiences need not be limited entirely to passes. There are, for example, at least two noteworthy mountain-*top* roads you might like to investigate.

Pikes Peak, out of Colorado Springs, of course is world famous. As well it deserves to be, with its 14,110-foot crest reached both by auto road (all 125 twists and turns of it) and cog railroad.

But *Mt. Evans,* west of Denver, is equally deserving. With its crest officially pegged at 14,260 feet, Evans has always claimed to be North America's highest motor road. From the "summit house," however, even the Evans partisan—sipping his "boiling" coffee, which at this altitude is only lukewarm—admits to having to look *up* to the mountain's summit. Perhaps as much as 150 feet or so, which enables the Pikes Peak booster to claim highest honors for his own cloud-scraper. If you can't drive both, we'd recommend Evans. Modern engineering, in contrast to Pikes Peak's sharp curves and steep grades, makes it quite easy to drive. It carries about half the traffic of its Colorado Springs rival. And it's free.

There are many other mountain-climbing roads which if they do not reach the summit, "top out" on a ledge or shoulder from which one commands a view of more than enough scenery to make the getting there worthwhile. Some of these are more or less local affairs, a little scenic extra provided by a visitor-oriented city to give its guests something to enjoy, remember, and perhaps even come back to. Colorado can field an inordinate number of these.

In Trinidad, it's *Simpson's Rest* overlooking the Purgatoire River valley.

Castle Rock has built a road to the top of the flat-top bluff for which it was named.

Salida provides visitors with a *Spiral Mountain* loop above the Arkansas River valley.

In Boulder, it's *Flagstaff Mountain* that provides the thrills; in Glenwood Springs, *Lookout Mountain.*

And unique (if we may use that abused and often misused word) is Cañon City's *Skyline Drive,* a one-way strip of asphalt, three miles long, that threads the rocky crest of a "hogback" ridge 800 feet above the town, and the Arkansas River valley. You'll enjoy this one. Never mind that it's a "scenic road to nowhere." It was constructed mainly by men with plenty of time on their hands—convicts at the nearby Colorado state penitentiary.

More ambitious are our last two recommended mountain climbs: the spectacular toll road to the top of *Cheyenne Mountain* out of Colorado Springs and the twisting Lariat Trail to the top of *Lookout Mountain* above Golden. (As out-and-out byways, several others are noted later, in the last two chapters.) Features of the former are the famed Cheyenne Mountain Zoo, the Will Rogers Shrine of the Sun, and a lodge.

The Golden road is a regular highway, connecting U.S. 6 and U.S. 40, but a soaring one. It sweeps 1,695 feet up the east face of Lookout in a series of exhilarating loops tied together by fairly straight stretches of breathtaking shelf road. At the top: the concrete-protected grave of William F. ("Buffalo Bill") Cody and a spectacular, at-one's-feet panorama—especially effective at night—of all Denver and much of eastern Colorado as well.

And this, of course, is the one unifying thread that runs through all these mountain tours: the magnificent view one gets from the top. Fear, awe, exhilaration, surprise, pure delight—whatever one's subjective reaction to the scene, it more than compensates for the time and effort invested in achieving it. Biblical characters in writing of their "mountain-top experiences" knew whereof they spoke.

HERE LIES...

Don't go away. Collecting cemeteries isn't as ghoulish as you might think.

Death, after all, is a universal phenomenon. A tombstone in one Colorado ghost town cemetery puts it this way:

> My good people, as you pass by;
> As you are now, so once was I.
> As I am now, you soon must be—
> So prepare yourself to follow me.

This cautionary inscription echoes the sentiment of the Black Prince and is similar to an earlier one on the grave of one Elder Samuel Waldo in New York:

> A dying preacher I have been,
> To dying hearers such as you.
> Though dead, a preacher still I am
> To such as come my grave to view.
> Let this to you a warning be
> That quickly you must follow me.

Either or both may well have been cribbed from one in New England, from all available evidence the font of American tombstone wit and wisdom. And the original, according to our report, had had a coda laboriously chiseled under it by some graffiti-minded stonemason, who added:

> To follow you I would not consent,
> Unless I knew which way you went.

Death's rites and customs are an intimate part of a people's culture. By browsing through their cemeteries, studying the kinds of monuments they contain, and—perhaps most importantly—reading their inscriptions, one learns much about the people themselves. Consider this one:

> Reader pass on, ne'er waste your time
> On bad biography and bitter rhyme.

132

> For what I am, this cumb'rous clay ensures,
> And what I was is no affair of yours.

Need anyone be told that this slap at the curious was, like the one above, carved on the stone of a New Englander? (Topsfield, Massachusetts, 1797, according to our records.)

Stone immortality, of course, has been a concern of man throughout history. Consider Shelley's poor Ozymandias, and the creators of the pyramids. The desire to have a last, final word is a strong one. And it is found in the strong and mighty as well as in those who merely want to say their say. This is apparent from the "suggested" inscriptions some of them have jotted down for family and friends.

A few, perhaps, are intended only to provide a last wry grin, like humorist Dorothy Parker's "Excuse My Dust," or G. B. Shaw's "Who the Devil was He?"

But Frederic Remington, one of the great Western artists of all time, was probably serious when he said he could ask for no finer epitaph than "He knew the horse."

And who can doubt that the irascible H. L. Mencken sought to get in one final spear-thrust by suggesting for his memorial the admonition: "If, after I depart this vale, you ever remember me and have thought to please my ghost, forgive some sinner and wink your eye at some homely girl."

Also telling a good bit about the philosophy of the writer is this suggested epitaph by a twenty-three-year-old printer:

The body of Benjamin Franklin, Printer,
Like the cover of an Old Book
Its contents worn out,
And stripped of its lettering and gilding,
Lies here, food for worms,
But the work shall not be lost,
For it will, as he believed, appear once more
In a new and more elegant edition,
Revised and corrected
by
The Author

STRAIGHT TALK FROM THE WEST

But where except in the storied American West (in this instance, San Diego's Old Town) would you expect to run onto such exposition as:

> . . . sacred to the memory of
> John Stiles who came to his death
> from a bullet from a revolver it
> was one of the old fashioned kind
> and brass mounted and of such is
> the kingdom of heaven

As for grim political summation, why bother to roam beyond the confines of stanchly Republican Kansas?

> Through this inscription
> I wish to enter my
> dying protest against
> what is called the
> Democratic party

> I have watched it
> closely since the days
> of Jackson and know
> that all the misfortunes
> of our nation has
> come to it through
> this so called party
> therefore beware of
> this part of treason.

If you want to make sure we didn't make that one up just to needle our Democrat friends, go to Attica. The stone is there. And it's dated 1890.

Just to show that Kansas has no monopoly on strong political convictions, we should include this epitaph from our own native Oklahoma. It's found on a stone at Cherokee—albeit up near the Kansas line. The grave is that of a grain dealer who in life was vigorously opposed both to co-operatives and to federal interference with the grain business. Not wanting his views lost to posterity, he left orders for them to be detailed on his tombstone; and originally this was done. But his heirs, alas, have since replaced his lengthy statement with a stone bearing the simple statement: "There Is No Substitute for an Independent Grain Dealer."

It's still a rather nice testimony to the kind of rugged individuality that helped explore, tame, and build the West. And we're glad his "image-conscious" family didn't completely bowdlerize him. Still, we're tempted to add: "There Is Also No Substitute for the Deceased's Own Wording on His Tombstone."

BATTLES ON STONE

But reading quaint epitaphs on tombstones is only one aspect of the enjoyment and enlightenment to be gained from cemetery visiting. Not to be overlooked are the graveyards themselves. And there are many kinds of them scattered over the country, from well-manicured plots in major cities (like storied Forest Lawn in Los Angeles) to weed-grown, virtually abandoned graveyards in the hundreds of ghost towns of the Rocky Mountain West; from idyllically peaceful national cemeteries to dusty, flower-strewn burying grounds that mark humble Spanish-American settlements of the Southwest.

To one interested in history, particularly in the wars our country has engaged it, our national cemeteries are especially rewarding. At Vicksburg, the statuary is outstanding. At Shiloh, there's a quiet dignity and beauty to the cemetery, on its wooded hillside overlooking the Tennessee River, that helps in small measure to compensate for the bitterness and suffering that brought it into being.

History comes to life for you, too, with almost startling vividness, on a certain ridge above the Little Big Horn River in south-central Montana. From this vantage point, as a recorded voice drones out the cold facts, you can follow the fateful course of General Custer's last battle by tracing out the pattern of plain white stones that dot the wind-tossed grass at your feet. No history buff, whether Custer fan or detractor (and no one seems to be neutral in his judgment of the flamboyant cavalryman), can escape the poignancy of that century-old tragedy, re-enacted in stone.

OTHER WAYS OF LIFE

Then there are the cemeteries that definitely reflect our cultural diversity. We're thinking here of the old burial grounds of New Orleans with their ornate crypts above ground and their French inscriptions—inscriptions that reflect not only another language but another way of life. Here one can find notations like "Mort sur le champ d'honneur" and "Pour garder intact le nom de famille."

Violence, of course, is an aspect of every culture. But the reasons behind it can vary wildly. Consider this inscription over a concrete mold of a face in Dodge City's famed Boot Hill:

> Shoot-em-up Jake
> Run for Sheriff 1872
> Run from Sheriff 1876
> Buried 1876

Indian cemeteries are often distinctive, too. At Eklutna, between Anchorage and Palmer, the Indian burial ground contains row upon row of graves, each covered by a small wooden structure about the size of a large dollhouse. Similar cemeteries can be found among the Chippewas in northern Wisconsin. And we've discovered only recently that Oklahoma has its share of these strongly characteristic grave markers. Just recently we discovered two perfect specimens, within sight of U.S. 70, near Hugo in the southeastern corner of the state.

As for the Western mining towns, one could spend most of a lifetime visiting their cemeteries alone. (Lambert Florin is one who would seem to have done just that in his fascinating *Boot Hill* and *Tales the Tombstones Tell*.) Even at their most blunt, these mining-camp epitaphs often prompt a wry chuckle at their humanness. These are most frequently found in the so-called Boot Hills, particularly in ghost towns newly discovered by the tourists. This means places like Tombstone (how about this one: "Here lies Lester Moore, four slugs from a .44, No Les, No More") and Virginia City—either in Nevada or Montana, take your pick—or various and sundry others. Here one can sometimes find a crude board marker so freshly refurbished that the black paint is, unauthentically, still tacky. (Unfortunately such hanky-panky has become increasingly necessary. Nevada's Virginia City still has some of its old headstones. But such is the semi-depraved nature of all too many of us that over fifty of the original ones, at a recent count, have now been stolen by souvenir hunters!)

One Virginia City classic the town fathers have our permission to repaint as often as necessary:

> Here lies the body of Virginia Marlotte.
> She was born a virgin and died a harlot.
> For eighteen years she preserved her virginity—
> That's a damned good record for this vicinity.

RANDOM NOTES FOR THE COLLECTOR

Then there are the real McCoys, the unvarnished burying grounds that still guard their dead, after a fashion, with no apparently recognized need for appealing to the curious tourist. These old cemeteries are not always easy to find. (An unfortunate truth: directional signs often, though not inevitably, indicate a certain amount of commercialization.) But they can be well worth the extra effort required, despite the fact that most tend to follow certain recognizable patterns. Many states have an old-cemetery association, and all have an historical society. A query to either or both will bring advice about locations.

There's the random scattering of fenced lots, for example, mostly of weathered pickets. But now and then, in the case of the more affluent, there is the protective fence of wrought iron. Usually it will bear the name, or at least the initial, of the deceased worked into the ornamental gate. Often as not the gate, broken or rusted from its hinges, will be propped against its support post.

There are the faded wooden crosses, garlanded with sprays of brightly colored artificial flowers, the hallmark of the dusty Spanish-American cemeteries that dot the Southwest. One we remember most vividly, as we write this, is the cemetery at Terlingua, a picturesque quicksilver ghost deep in the Big Bend country of Texas. Brooded over by crumbling adobe ruins, the weathered wooden markers festooned with gaudy paper flowers are perhaps more moving as testimonials to a simple, abiding faith in immortality than the elaborate marble monuments with their more sophisticated inscriptions.

There are the touchingly universal sentiments for their times ("We Miss Him So" or "She Is Not Dead But Asleep"); the inevitable tree-trunk stone fashioned to look broken off a few feet above the ground, and so to dramatize the tragedy of a premature ending (not an uncommon phenomenon in the 19th century, especially in the West); the occasional pine growing straight and tall from a tumbled-in grave, an altogether fitting fulfillment of the "dust to dust" intonation at the time of burial.

In Cripple Creek, Colorado, there's a rough stone bearing no name, only: "He called Bill Smith a Liar." And in the old Glenwood Springs Cemetery there's a marker with the simple inscription: "Doc Holliday / 1852–1887 / He Died in Bed." This end was no inconsequential feat, considering the caliber of the enemies the dentist from Georgia had acquired through his extraprofessional activities—particularly at the side of his friend Wyatt Earp at the O.K. Corral in Tombstone in 1881.

The historic Jacksonville cemetery in southern Oregon offers a trove of pioneer history along its gentle pathways.

COLORADO

Larger and better kept than many of those old cemeteries in Colorado is Dory Hill, off Colorado 119 north of Black Hawk. In it lie many early settlers of the Black Hawk-Central City district. And west of Crested Butte is Irwin Cemetery, snatched from oblivion a few years ago and marked with a special granite monument. Abandoned in 1885, the plot is now almost the only remaining evidence of "the bright promise of ruby silver (which) drew 5,000 people to this area in . . . 1879 from as far as England and Scotland." (Near by is the ghost of Ruby, born on the strength of that same "ruby silver.")

But the state has many interesting plots like this. In the mountains west of Boulder are nearly century-old graveyards at Sunshine, Ward, Nederland, and Caribou. A neatly kept old pioneer cemetery rests quietly against the slope of Blanca Peak below the Great Sand Dunes, on the eastern edge of the San Luis valley.

And consider these two Colorado ladies:

Sophie Dupuy has already appeared, in the chapter on boomtown hotels; she was the wife of Louis Dupuy, eccentric builder of the gemlike Hotel de Paris in Georgetown. Dupuy, as we noted, was something of a misogynist, among his other attributes; in his lifetime he seems to have made few friends, male or female. Yet he married Sophie Galet, a widowed countrywoman. When he died in 1900, of pneumonia, he left her all his worldly possessions, which by then included a ranch as well as the hotel. Her affection for her benefactor was touching, and obviously genuine. She stayed on at the hotel, but lived only four months longer than her brilliant husband. They are buried together in Alvarado Cemetery. Their headstone reads: "Deux Bons Amis."

Laura Evans was something else again. One of Colorado's most famous madams, her story can be picked up in many of the boom mining camps of the late 19th century—Leadville, Alma, Cripple Creek, Central City. But she spent her last fifty-two years in Salida and was almost ninety-one when she died in 1953 (which should provide some commentary on the wages of sin!).

One explanation of this final move to Salida has a curiously modern ring. She was working in Leadville in 1896, at the time of the Maid of Erin strike. And when armed pickets prevented the payroll from getting in to the men who were defying the strike, one of the mine owners asked Laura to slip the money in. She agreed. Well known in the camp as a horsewoman, she donned a full-skirted side-saddle riding habit, fastened the canvas bag containing $27,000 under her skirt, and rode up to the mine gate. When challenged and asked where she was going—according to Colorado historian Carolyn Bancroft—she answered truthfully: "The Maid of Erin Mine. I want to see a friend that you fellows won't let come down to town." It was an appeal any man could appreciate and, with laudable chivalry, they let her go through the picket line. But her smuggling in of the payroll helped to break the strike. When word of it spread, the miners blacklisted her. She had, in effect, scabbed.

Such was her fame over the years that her funeral made the front page of the Denver newspapers and merited inside photo spreads. Mattie Silks, Jennie Rogers, Lillian Powers, Pearl de Vere . . . Laura Evans was one of many who made life just a bit more bearable for miner and mine owners alike. And looking up their final resting places can provide one with an interesting specialty. For unlike the identifying red light or the open crib-window during life, they have no telltale identification tag in death to make the seeker's quest easier. Indeed, most seem deliberately to have sought a kind of respectable anonymity through modest markers and the use of initials or correct, though seldom-used, family names. And Miss Bancroft notes that one, with conventional feminine coquetry, even "forgot" to put her birth date on the stone so the prurient would not learn she was fourteen years older than her husband. Still, such subterfuges and trail-covering merely make the searching more exciting, the finding more satisfying.

On a more sober note, it often takes but a single grave to bring history to life. Consider that aging wooden fence beside Colorado 115 south of Colorado Springs. It guards the mortal remains of one Henry Harkins. Only recently did the state historical society erect a sign to inform the curious that Harkins "was murdered in March 1863 by the notorious Espinosa gang who terrorized central Colorado for months." Thus does one get at least a hint of the "Bloody Espinosas" saga—two brothers who in the late 1860's announced that the Virgin Mary had told them in a dream to kill all gringos. The gory project did not end until thirty-two people were dead and frontiersman Tom Tobin had delivered the head of the last Espinosa

to the authorities in Fort Garland in a gunny sack. Thus, too, does the traveler get an explanation as to how Deadman's Gulch, through which the road passes, received its name.

ALONG THE GREAT TRAILS

But isolated stones and markers are strung like beads along all the West's pioneer trails. Mentioned earlier is the impressive monument beside the old California Trail (U.S. 40 today) in the High Sierras that recalls the tragedy of the Donner Party. And the massive stone near Alcove Springs, Kansas, that honors Sarah Handley Keyes, whose death delayed the party and became at least a contributing factor to that tragedy.

Because the Mormons feel so strongly about history, they've done an unusually fine job of commemorating the heroics and tragedies that mark their own Mormon Trail to Utah. One of the most impressive of the memorials is the beautiful bronze of a weeping pioneer mother which guards the old Mormon Cemetery in North Omaha (as expanded in the chapter on trailside graffiti).

WYOMING

Near Devils Gate in Wyoming, southwest of Casper some 60 miles, there's a monument that recalls the trials of Captain Howard Martin's Handcart Company. Surely the pathetically brave trek of this band of 576 newly converted English "Saints" is one of the true epics of the Western migration. Lacking almost everything but faith, they piled their meager possessions on pushcarts and set out to walk from Iowa City to their promised Zion. Here beside the Sweetwater, while awaiting the rescue party sent from Salt Lake City by Brigham Young, more than one hundred of them died in nine days. They were buried in a single trench.

A few years later an eighteen-year-old girl climbed to the ridge above Devils Gate (a remarkable, sheer-walled crack in the rock), slipped, and fell to her death in the gorge. For years a simple board marked her grave. The epitaph read:

> Here lies the body of Caroline Todd
> Whose soul has lately gone to God;
> Ere redemption was too late,
> She was redeemed at Devils Gate.

Near by is yet another simple roadside grave that manages to include all the elements that make cemetery collecting worthwhile: single grave, rough protective fence, cryptic legend, and a dash of mystery. We spotted the unpainted board fence at once, high on the shoulder beside Wyoming 220 just south of Devils Gap, and stopped to examine it. The grave itself is covered with rocks. The inscription, cut in the large stone at the head of the grave, reads: "T. P. Baker 1864." No one, so far as we know, has ever determined who Baker was. Nor, for that matter, does the Wyoming State Archives and Historical Department know who fenced the grave.

Mrs. Ellen Sun, whose famed Tom Sun Ranch now embraces much of this richly historic area, says she can't help much, and that the same inscription, name and date, is carved on a rock in the Devils Gate. Archives director Neal E. Miller says that the late Tom Sun told him years ago that Baker was simply a friend of *his* father (also Tom Sun) who had asked to be buried there. But Mrs. Sun doesn't know. "There are a number of graves across the road from the ranch-

house, but no markers," she says, "and almost all have been obliter-
ated by drifting sand. My husband's mother said she could count at
least forty mounds when she first came here in 1883."

But that's enough to establish the picture. Forty trailside graves,
forty personal tragedies, forty individual stories of stirring adventure, of hopes and dreams, of striving and, in many cases, of eventual
failure; and all this along just one short stretch of only a single pioneer trail. Multiply at will: the field is limitless. And often the story
behind the marker, unlike Baker's, is there for the asking.

NEW MEXICO

To strike a more individual note, there are also the graves of those
men and women who contributed notably in a particular way to the
winning of the West. Two come readily to mind. Of interest, at least
to the reader who has borne with us this far, are the graves of Kit
Carson in Taos, New Mexico, and of Jesse Chisholm near Geary,
Oklahoma.

Few indeed are the Southwesterners who were better known, in
the notable rather than notorious sense, than Carson. Mountain Man,
soldier, statesman, friend of the Indian, he contributed to the development of the West on all counts. And nowhere can one get a more
dramatic insight into the kind of man he was than in Taos, long the
base of operations for the early fur trappers and traders, and often
their home after they'd hung up their traps.

Under ancient cottonwoods there in the old Taos Cemetery—
within easy walking distance of the colorful plaza—is the Carson
family plot. And just outside the iron fence is the grave of a retired

army officer, its stone noting matter-of-factly that he wanted to "Rest for Eternity by My Idol Kit Carson."

From innumerable published accounts, Christopher Carson was famous for his integrity, as well as for his ability as a scout. Indians, the Spanish (his wife Josefa was a New Mexican-born heiress), his fellow fur trappers and traders—all agreed he was a fine fellow. And somehow it's comforting to know that even in this brash, all-knowing, often cynical age there are still those who can respond to a simple, honest, straightforward, natural man from the past.

OKLAHOMA

Jesse Chisholm, whose name is assured immortality because of the storied Chisholm (cattle) Trail, was no rancher, but a trader, a freighter, and a manufacturer of salt. He was also, like Kit Carson, an honest friend to the Indians. Part Indian himself, he knew and understood them, and was in turn respected by them. And so it was altogether fitting that while returning to his trading post in present-day central Oklahoma, from an inspection of his saltmaking operations to the northwest, he should stop to visit Left Hand, one of his Arapaho Indian friends. There he became suddenly ill (probably from food poisoning, though medical examiner's reports were rare in the Indian Nation at the time), and died, March 4, 1868.

The grave site, now preserved as a small natural park by the Oklahoma Historical Society near Geary, is as impressive as that of Kit Carson, though for a different reason. There is no iron fence, no heavy headstone, no nearby grave of a latter-day admirer. Instead there is only a small weathered slab on a grassy knoll overlooking what is now called Left Hand Spring, with the simple inscription: "No One Left His Home Cold or Hungry."

We'll leave our roundup of cemeteries and headstones at that. We'll end it here because in a very real sense Jesse Chisholm's creed was that of the West: a generous, unquestioned sharing of what one had. It was a philosophy born of necessity, true, and common in varying degree on the frontier. But it was a nonetheless admirable philosophy. If it lasted longer in the West, it's simply because the frontier itself lasted longer. And insofar as our complex, present-day society in the 20th century does not—indeed, cannot—live by it, society alone is the poorer.

RUNNING
THE RIVERS

One thing emerges when one collects rivers: scenery and history are nearly always combined. And the phenomenon is no coincidence; nor, with a moment's reflection, should it come as any great surprise. From the dawn of history rivers have been all-important to man, who managed to fashion a boat long before he learned to make a wheel. Water thus became his first dependable source of transportation, for himself as well as for his belongings. And thus was determined, for the most part, the direction and scope of his cultural development.

Our great early civilizations flourished along such rivers as the Nile, the Tigris and Euphrates, the Ganges. In more modern times there were the Rhine and the Danube, our own Hudson, Delaware, and Potomac. Traveling largely on water, man located his cities accordingly. It is hard to think of a major city throughout all history that was not located on navigable water, either salt or fresh. And when improved transportation facilities were finally developed—in the last century, actually, with the railroads first, and then in this century with auto roads—man built cities more often than not along the water-level course of the rivers he had traditionally used.

What we're getting at is, that some of the most interesting areas in the country, both as to the scenery they offer and the historic events they evoke, lie within arm's length of water. And today, though vista-domed railroad cars have nearly gone the unhappy way of the packet boats, much of this beauty and history can be soaked in from one's car. This is true even in the arid West, where water transportation has always been pretty much of a sometime thing under the most ideal circumstances.

Lewis and Clark did, as noted in the early chapter on the great migration trails, manage to pole and float their way across the West with only a minimum of portaging over the Continental Divide. But steamboating was never too satisfactory on the Upper Missouri. Or on other major Western rivers like the Colorado, Rio Grande, and

Columbia. And it has taken a billion latter-day federal dollars to make the Arkansas navigable as far as northeastern Oklahoma.

The Indian and the Mountain Man, even when they walked, tended to follow the waterways. Miners and settlers followed them, so the West tended to develop for the most part along its rivers.

Let's see, then, how we can best "run" some of these rivers so as to sample the pleasures and satisfactions they have to offer.

MAJOR POWELL'S RIVERS

. . . The scenery is on a grand scale. The walls of the canyon, 2,500 feet high, are of marble, of many beautiful colors . . . a beautiful view is presented. The river turns sharply to the east and seems enclosed by a wall set with a million brilliant gems. What can it mean?

We are now ready to start on our way down the Great Unknown. . . . We are three quarters of a mile in the depths of the earth, and the great river shrinks to insignificance as it dashes its angry waves against the walls and cliffs that rise to the world above; the waves are but puny ripples, and we but pigmies . . .

The writer is Major John Wesley Powell, still in constant pain from the amputation of his right arm in the Civil War, who is about to begin the first successful river passage of the awesome Grand Canyon of the Colorado. On May 24, 1869, his party embarked from Expedition Island in the Green River of southwestern Wyoming. Down the Green they floated, into Utah, through a corner of Colorado, and back into Utah again, where they picked up the Colorado River. Then they entered Cataract Canyon and an almost endless procession of similarly impressive gorges before they finally ended their nearly 900-mile journey.

Major Powell was greeted here by Mormon fishermen on August 30, 1869. When he'd started three months before, he'd had four boats and nine companions. Five were trappers and adventurers; only one was a trained boatman. Two boats were lost along the way, and four men. One quit a month out, and lived. Three others, fearing for their lives in Grand Canyon, walked out the North Rim and, ironically, into a Shivwits Indian ambush. Despite the losses, the expedition was a complete success. And an impressive feat as well. (It would be eighty years before the 100th individual had duplicated Powell's journey.)

There were no Flaming Gorge and Glen Canyon dams to smooth vast stretches of the river. The route was uncharted, truly a "Great Unknown." Even the names of the canyons through which they traveled reflected their mixed mood of excitement and anxiety, of wonderment and foreboding: names like Lodore, Whirlpool, Desolation, Marble, and Labyrinth. Even some of the rivers they picked up along the way contributed to the mood—silt-laden streams like the Paria and the Dirty Devil.

Well, we salute Major Powell for his magnificent accomplishment. And we extend our best wishes to the several thousand intrepid visitors who nowadays run the Colorado through the Grand Canyon each year. Theirs is quite an adventure. But while we envy them their water-level view of the canyon's awe-inspiring depths, we envy them precious little else.

A chapter or so back we were extolling the benefits of trading in one's rope, axe, and piton for an automobile before attacking mountain passes. Here we are equally enthusiastic about the rewards to be found in leaving rubber boats and life jackets to skilled boaters, and doing one's river-running by car. Surprisingly enough, it can be done more often and more easily than one might suppose. And quite satisfactorily, too. We've driven several stretches of the Green and Colorado along Powell's route. We've enjoyed them thoroughly—and in relative comfort.

THE GREEN

True, that narrow shelf road leading down Sheep Creek into Flaming Gorge on the Green in northeastern Utah was something else again. Coming to a gate marked "Private Property—No Trespassing Beyond This Point" and locked to emphasize the dictum, obviously necessitated a U turn. And with the road little more than a car-length wide, this was no mean accomplishment. Helen still rates it as one of her better driving feats, her own Major Powell conquest of the Green. But this spectacular stretch beside the river was well worth the extra driving effort, especially so now that it is under several hundred feet of water, piled up behind Flaming Gorge Dam. A

Spectacular overlooks—like the Green River seen from Harpers Corner
in Colorado—are prizes for "running the rivers" by car.

handful of other river-running roads along Powell's route remain, however. Here are some of the possibilities:

For two views of the Green you won't quickly forget, go to the Dinosaur National Monument area of northeast Utah and northwest Colorado. From the visitor center north of Jensen, Utah (on U.S. 40), follow the National Park Service road to Split Mountain Gorge, where the dirty river (a silt-laden gray rather than green) emerges from the Uinta Mountains. Such is the perspective from the pebble beach at the end of the road that the river does indeed seem to be flowing from an actual "split" in the granite mountain. It is not at all difficult to imagine the relief Powell and his men must have felt when they reached this idyllic spot and realized the canyon-slashed Uintas were at last behind them.

To begin to appreciate just what they'd been through, follow the Park Service's now greatly improved Harpers Corner road to a magnificent desert overlook several thousand feet above the Green. From here—if you enjoy the challenge of a rugged mountain road— you can wind precipitously down into Echo Park, coming to rest finally on the narrow spit of sand where the Yampa and Green rivers join, virtually in the shadow of towering Steamboat Rock.

> . . . Standing opposite the rock, our words are repeated with startling clearness, but in a soft, mellow tone, that transforms them into magical music. Scarcely can one believe it is the echo of his own voice. . . .
>
> We have named the long peninsular rock . . . Echo Rock. Desiring to climb it, Bradley and I take the little boat and . . .

Thus does the one-armed explorer begin the harrowing account of their climb, and his getting stranded on a narrow ledge. There, he found, "I can get up no farther and cannot step back," and Bradley's lifesaving rescue—effected by taking off his drawers and swinging them down to Powell, enabling him to scramble to safety. "Then we walk out on the peninsular rock," he continues calmly, despite the fact that his life had just hung in the balance—or in Bradley's drawers, if you like—"make the necessary observations for determining its altitude above camp [about 700 feet, he decided], and return, finding an easy way down."

The incident is as incredible as the man himself; and, for that matter, as Echo Park. The road down, to repeat, is a 13-mile-long

RUNNING
THE RIVERS

breath-quickener: first a rather exhilarating series of switchbacks, then a pleasant sheep meadow, followed by another sharp descent, this time through a narrow rocky defile called Sand Canyon. Along the way are Indian petroglyphs on a nearby cliff, a lonely ranch, and Whispering Cave. Finally you are amid the willows beside the river in a tiny park. Except for the car, the scene is almost unchanged from Powell's day. (And your own car may be the only one you see. It was the day we visited Echo Park, this but a few years ago.)

THE COLORADO

There are several other spots along Powell's route one can reach much more easily, these on the Colorado. Two of the best are up- and downriver from Moab, Utah. In each case you drive only a few feet from the river's edge while vividly red sandstone canyon walls, streaked with the black stains of so-called "desert varnish," tower a thousand feet, almost sheer, overhead. Utah 128 upriver from Moab follows the Colorado all the way to U.S. 50 near Cisco. As for Utah 279 down the Colorado to Texas Gulf Sulphur's new mine, dubbed the Potash Road, it has been hailed by some Eastern writers as one of the most beautifully engineered roads in the West. We wouldn't argue the point. We drive it every chance we get; it's particularly beautiful late in the evening.

FROM UTAH INTO ARIZONA

As for the Lee's Ferry road beside the Colorado, in extreme northern Arizona, it too provides a near-perfect blend of scenic and historic values. You leave U.S. 89–A near the west end of Navajo Bridge, one of the West's first high steel-arch structures. Spanning Marble Canyon, some 470 feet above the Colorado River, the bridge is something to see in its own right. A 30,000-acre section of the canyon here, incidentally, has only recently become a national monument. The informal road to Lee's Ferry swings north up the canyon, soon drops down to the river's bank. A curious feature here is the huge goblet-shaped stone rearing up from the flood plain just a few feet off the road. (We trust that no mindless vandal has destroyed it since we were there. Several similar erosion formations have been toppled, in Utah—the exquisite creation of centuries destroyed in a senseless moment. Those who have seen the Flower Pot formations on New Brunswick's Bay of Fundy will know what to expect.)

Still visible on the opposite side of the river is what's left of the rocky shelf-road which wagons and, later, automobiles had to climb to get out of the canyon before Navajo Bridge finally retired the ferry in 1929.

The ferry itself was a remarkable operation. For almost two thirds of a century, it provided the only, and tenuous, link between downstate Arizona and No Man's Land, its virtually uninhabited northwestern corner, cut off by the Colorado River and including the Grand Canyon's lofty, forested North Rim. The motorist need make but a simple trek across this vast, empty, incredibly colorful corner of the state—combining one of the West's most enjoyable forests (the deer-filled Kaibab) with one of its most forbidding desert ranges (the starkly beautiful Vermilion Cliffs)—to understand why it was for years the refuge of outlaws.

Which brings us to John D. Lee, who was on the rather remarkable side himself.

MR. LEE & HIS FERRY

A Mormon stalwart, John Lee was on the lam for his role in the vicious Mountain Meadows Massacre, which occurred in 1857 as the so-called "Utah War" between the U.S. government and the Mormons was about to begin. A wagon train that included some one hundred and forty California-bound emigrants, mostly from Arkansas, was moving through southwestern Utah. With help from some Piute Indians, a zealous band of misguided "Saints," led by Lee, slaughtered all but seventeen small children. Lee was implicated the following year and exiled by the church. Eventually he was sent to

operate the Colorado River ferry previously established by Jacob Hamblin, the famed Mormon missionary, explorer and colonizer.

Lee came to this isolated retreat in 1872 with a sizable family entourage that included at least five or six of his eighteen wives. Here, where the Paria flows into the Colorado, he took over the crude ferry—and an old boat left over, curiously enough, from the first Powell expedition. Soon he had brought timbers from the Kaibab and built a second ferry. Whatever his character shortcomings in other areas, Lee apparently set a good table (even granting that competition could not have been too keen in this corner of No Man's Land). Visitors, including members of Powell's second expedition, thought highly of the fresh vegetables, milk, fresh butter, and other comestibles his wives managed somehow to come up with. And overnight guests invariably commented on the evening ritual of prayers and protestations of innocence.

But it ended for Lee in 1874, and all because of conjugal loyalty. In his two years at the ferry, no U.S. marshal had tried to arrest him, perhaps because one of his wives maintained lookout from a small rock fort on the canyon wall. A marshal, however, did capture him in Utah while he was visiting one of the wives he'd had to leave behind. His 1875 trial ended in a hung jury, but a second trial, in 1876, convicted him and he was executed by firing squad the following year —quite fittingly, at Mountain Meadows.

Emma, wife No. 18, operated the ferry for a time, after which it was leased by polygamous brothers, Price and Elmer Johnson. From a population consisting mainly of Lees, Lee's Ferry became a settlement of Johnsons. Public opinion, though officially scandalized by polygamy, was often a bit more tolerant in practice. The story is told that an Arizona governor in the 1920's, finally pressured into riding up from Phoenix for an inspection, took one look at the awesomely isolated setting and blurted, "Hell, if I had to live here I'd want more than one wife myself!"

Be that as it may, it's an altogether pleasant place to visit today. And will be even more interesting when, as a national historic site, John Lee's old stone fort is restored and other Park Service developments are completed.

TWO CROSSINGS

Much less convenient to reach by car but still accessible are two other historic Colorado River crossing sites. Best known perhaps is that at Hite, on Utah 95 between Hanksville and Blanding. Had not Glen Canyon Dam and the backed-up waters of Lake Powell necessitated the building of several bridges, the picturesque Hite Ferry would probably still be in business.

The second crossing, used but briefly (and with good reason, as the motorist who reaches it will quickly agree), is famed Hole-in-the-Rock. The west-bank access to the river—via some 60 miles of dirt and gravel out of Escalante, where initial inquiry should always be made—is actually a dugway (i.e., a wagon trail chiseled out of solid rock, usually with a single sunken track to serve as guide and/or anchor for the wheels). The route was pioneered in 1879–1880 by dedicated Mormons ordered by Brigham Young to establish a mission in the San Juan River valley of southeastern Utah.

The two-hundred-mile "short cut" across an unsurveyed and virtually unexplored desert took the eighty-wagon caravan of two hundred and fifty men, women and children from mid-October to early

April. Surprisingly, no pioneer was lost—nor wagon nor horse, for that matter—and three babies were born en route. Stand at the top of the cliff looking down into Hole-in-the-Rock—actually a "cleft in the solid rock wall," according to the expedition's chief chronicler, Platte D. Lyman—and you marvel that the so-called "road" was used even a year. You'll begin to appreciate why historian David E. Miller calls the San Juan mission expedition "an excellent case-study of the highest type of pioneer endeavor that broke the wilderness and brought civilization to the West." The excitement and drama are still there, virtually undiluted by the passage of nearly a century.

IN COLORADO

We shouldn't leave the Colorado without a few comments on the joys of exploring it in the state where it is born. If you've crossed Colorado by car, train, or bus, you have perhaps already seen several of its more scenic stretches. U.S. 40 picks up the infant, though already lusty, river at Granby, follows it through black-tinted, at times almost forbidding, Byers Canyon to Kremmling. Here the river plunges southwest through rugged, virtually uninhabited canyon country to Dotsero on U.S. 6–24. (In a later chapter we'll take a byway short cut, called State Bridge Road, through this rugged stretch. Meanwhile, though, we'll resume our river-running at Dotsero.)

And now begins a 90-mile stretch of winding canyon-bottom highway—smooth, gently curved, a pleasure to drive all the way—that's as beautiful as anything to be found in the West. Almost sheer walls of rock line the route much of the way to Grand Junction, first vividly red, then red and cream, then cream, and black. Through this colorful conduit are strung road, river, and railway, intertwined here and there as each struggles for a foothold on the narrowly confined floor of the canyon. One recommended stop is at Grizzly, a railroad siding just east of Glenwood Springs. Here beside the road, in the heart of Glenwood Canyon, the silver replica of a glass-roofed railroad car atop a stone monument memorializes the birth of the vista-dome idea. For many years, when they were running on schedule, the pioneering *California Zephyrs,* eastbound and westbound, met dramatically at Grizzly.

At Grand Junction we can continue on U.S. 6–50 west to Cisco,

Utah, and pick up the river route through Moab, described a short while ago.

THE MISSOURI

Books could be (indeed, have been) written on all the important rivers of the West. And a separate chapter on each could be written on the various ways one can discover that particular river by car. We have only one chapter for all of them, and the Green and the Colorado have already claimed over half of it. What follow, then, are some random suggestions, a few personal favorites. And as we have already touched on a couple of these elsewhere, perhaps we should consider them first.

The Missouri, as we noted early, was the main avenue of Western conquest. Starting with Lewis and Clark and the fur traders, and continuing right up to the coming of the railroads, it helped mightily to shape the course of empire. But how does one run it by car? Well, you can start by driving north of St. Louis to the point near the old Chain of Rocks bridge where the Missouri joins the Mississippi. Here at its mouth you can best appreciate, from the massive gray arc of silt-laden water it pushes into the blue Mississippi, why it is called the Big Muddy. From Nebraska to Montana, however, extensive dam building has now converted many vast stretches of the river into one long lake.

STARTING IN MONTANA

To get an interesting look at its far humbler origins, you need to go to Three Forks, just off U.S. 10 in southwestern Montana. A modest state park preserves the spot. Walk to the water's edge, then put yourself in Meriwether Lewis's shoes that midmorning of July 27, 1805. Here, some 2,475 miles from the Mississippi, he suddenly saw the country open up "to extensive and beautiful plains and meadows which appear to be surrounded in every direction with distant and lofty mountains." Here at his feet three streams—now called the Gallatin, the Jefferson, and the Madison—joined to form the stream he and his party had followed for just over a year. He correctly assumed it to be "the three forks of the Missouri." The first leg of his journey to the Pacific had been successfully completed. Today the scene appears to be little changed from Lewis's view. It's a pretty spot and, if we may use the term once more, it's also an exciting one.

GATES OF THE MOUNTAINS

Three other Missouri River spots offer the same exciting blend of scenic beauty and historic significance. Inaccessible by car (though well worth driving as far as you can) is Gates of the Mountains, just off Interstate 15 north of Helena. Even from a distance, the striking cleft in the rocks into which the river disappears seems bleakly forbidding, especially so as you recall Captain Lewis's description:

> . . . this even we entered much the most remarkable clifts that we have yet seen. these clifts rise from the waters edge on either side perpendicularly to the hight of 1200 feet. every object here wears a dark and gloomy aspect. the tow[er]ing and projecting rocks in many places seem ready to tumble on us. the [Missouri] river appears to have forced it's way through this immence body of solid rock for the distance of 5¾ Miles and where it makes it's exit below has th[r]own on either side vast collumns of rocks mountains high.

Excursions into Gates of the Mountains, now preserved as a wilderness area, can be arranged. Deep inside the gorge, sitting around a smoky campfire late at night, one would feel the Lewis and Clark mood even more completely, we suspect.

Less forbidding—more on the idyllic side, actually—is the view of the placid Missouri from the flat, grassy riverbank at Fort Benton, Montana, on downriver from Helena and Great Falls. Here the crumbling remains of a single bastion of the old trading-then-military post help one shuck off more than a century of civilization and absorb something of the fur-trade feel.

Nostalgically satisfying, but historically important only in the sense that it's the last of its breed on the Big Muddy, is the Running Water Ferry. It still carries mostly local traffic and junketing sentimentalists across the upper limits of Lewis and Clark Lake between Niobrara, Nebraska, and Running Water, South Dakota.

THE RIO GRANDE

The Rio Grande is another storied river of the West, though many may more readily associate it with Texas and Mexico, whose border it forms from El Paso/Juarez to the Gulf of Mexico below Browns-ville. But the river heads above Creede, cuts through a large chunk of southern Colorado, and divides New Mexico north to south before reaching El Paso. And from at least three roadside vantage points along the way one gets dramatic, yet totally different, views.

Above Creede, the Rio Grande is an inviting trout stream, mean-dering through a broad mountain valley that shelters some of Colo-rado's finest cattle ranches.

INTO NEW MEXICO

Not until the river reaches northern New Mexico does it begin to take on its strongly characteristic Spanish-American complexion. One's access road here is New Mexico 111, his vantage point the new steel-arch Rio Grande Gorge bridge. Here, some 600 feet be-neath where one stands, the river, by now gray with silt, scours its way southward through a rough, near-desert wilderness. The sight is more than a bit fearsome, especially in late evening as shadows be-gin to fill the yawning crevice. The canyon's deepest, most inaccessible section is now protected as Rio Grande Gorge State Park (which might well set some kind of configuration record with a total length of 70 miles and a width of two!).

Only a few highway miles farther south, however, through Taos and then, on U.S. 64, down into a less precipitous section of the can-yon, the leisurely motorist begins to savor the Spanish-American West at its pepper-string-on-adobe-wall best. Here one is delighted by the steady procession of towns and villages with melodious names like Pilar, La Cienega, Rinconada, Embudo, Velarde, Alcalde, San Juan, and Española. And gradually, provided one refuses to be hurried or harried by the ever increasing traffic, one comes to appreciate the soothing recurrence of peaceful settlements, neatly spaced orchards, and postage-stamp fields of irrigated corn, beans, and peppers. Tamed now, yet exotic too, the Rio Grande presents the warmth and agelessness of both the adobes that line its banks and the soft-spoken, friendly people who live in them.

INTO TEXAS

It's well below El Paso, below Presidio actually, from that tiny sun-baked border town to wildly beautiful Big Bend National Park, that one begins to feel the power and majesty of the river and the dreadfully desolate country through which it has carved such impressive canyons. El Camino del Rio is a relatively new road, superbly engineered, and as yet only beginning to attract the traffic that will inevitably diminish its basic charm. But that's still in the future, happily. The river road simply isn't on a route *to* any place—at least *from* any place one is likely to be, unless of course he goes there on purpose. That is to say, this "short cut" between Presidio and the Big Bend promises to remain a lightly traveled byway for some years to come. And it alternates smooth riverside stretches with occasional climbs to vantage points that give one a soaring canyon panorama of quiet beauty amid almost frightening emptiness— a vividly exciting byway indeed.

THE SNAKE

No collection of Western rivers would be complete without at least two or three samplings of the Snake. Next to the Colorado, it boasts the most awe-inspiring canyons, if not in number, then at least in magnitude.

With a depth below Sheep Mountain on the Oregon/Idaho border of some 7,000 feet, Hell's Canyon is easily the continent's mightiest. And from the top of the notorious Kleinschmidt Grade, below Cuprum on the Idaho side, it must certainly be one of the most impressive. We finally cleared the straggle of trees that covers the crest and swung to the left to begin the descent.

Suddenly the world beyond the right car window simply dissolved into a vast, shimmering, lavender nothingness. The dark-tone Oregon side of Hell's Canyon and the river itself more than a mile below us finally penetrated the velvety haze to register on our somewhat numbed consciousness. But that first breathtaking view of the gorge remains one of our most vivid travel memories.

However, the Snake, like the Rio Grande, has many faces. And many different view points from which to enjoy them—some quite accessible.

Where it heads, for example, in relatively flat ranching country near the south entrance to Yellowstone Park, the river is on the idyllic side. Even below Idaho Falls, as it grows both in size and economic importance, it remains an interesting stream. Neither idyllic nor awesome, it's a workaday provider of sugar beets, potatoes, and electricity. And if the production of these useful commodities, made possible only by dams, has diminished appreciably the onetime magnificence of Shoshone and Twin Falls, it has also made this arid southern half of the state not only habitable but prosperous as well. U.S. 30 parallels the Snake from Pocatello to the Oregon line beyond Boise, offering an occasional splash of beauty, like Thousand Springs (a cliffside cascade of white water stemming presumably from various of the state's "lost" rivers) and a continuous panorama of Western irrigation economy at its best.

HUNTING HEADS & TRANSFORMATIONS

Hinted at, but not recommended explicitly up to now, is an interesting subcategory in our rivers collection. Rivers, like everything else, have to start *some* place. And running down some of the geographical heads of famous rivers can be thoroughly interesting, too. Already mentioned is the excitement one feels standing at Three Forks in southwestern Montana and seeing the Jefferson, Madison, and Gallatin merge to form, officially, the mighty Missouri.

IS THIS THE MISSISSIPPI?

Less impressive by far, though fully as pretty, is the birthplace of the even mightier Mississippi. The State of Minnesota, not unmindful of the dramatic incongruity, has provided an appropriate designation. Where Lake Itasca spills across a few flat rocks (scattered just haphazardly enough to provide stepping-stones for the reasonably agile) and becomes thereby a trickling stream, the 0-milepost (zero miles) marker solemnly notes the start, 1,475 feet above sea level, of the Mississippi's 2,552-mile course to the Gulf of Mexico. After you've savored the thrill of "walking on the Father of Rivers," and wish to appreciate just what you've done, journey 75 miles below New Orleans, southeasterly into the delta, and take the Pointe à la Hache ferry. Without resort to a boat, you will have thus bracketed the continent's mightiest river, crossing its sparkling headwaters and, some 2,500 river miles to the south, its broad, dirty-gray mouth. In between crossings it has drained half the country and changed from a playful thing of beauty to an unknowably powerful, almost frightening, economic workhorse.

BY OTHER NAMES

Every collection has its oddball items—the ash tray made of Confederate currency and the cuckoo clock that pops out to say "Drop dead" in German. A river collection should be no different. So what about a couple of cases of, say, philological metamorphosis?

Drive U.S. 20 north out of Shoshoni (in northwestern Wyoming on one of the principal roads to Yellowstone Park) and you are following *Wind River* in the pleasantly scenic canyon of the same name, a rugged water-worn notch in the Owl Creek Mountains. Suddenly you're at the "Wedding of the Waters." Beyond, though still rolling along beside the same coursing stream, you are following the *Big Horn River*. It's not something dreamed up for the tourist, so far as we can tell. Rather, it's a simple reminder of the day not too far back when people, unable to travel far or often, unwittingly gave different names to the same river because they didn't know what other folks called it.

A similarly curious transformation takes place underneath the

U.S. 10 bridge between Moorhead, Minnesota, and Fargo, North Dakota. Here the *Bois de Sioux,* coming up from the south, magically metamorphoses itself into the *Red River of the North* for the remainder of its journey to Canada and, eventually, Hudson Bay. Or so says the sign. And who are we to knock a good story?

THE GREAT RIVER ROAD

A word or two on the Great River Road and we'll abandon you to your own river collecting. That the G.R.R. exists—and is receiving increasing recognition as one of the country's most rewarding motoring experiences—is proof enough that we're on the safest possible ground in recommending it for both scenic and historic values. Started a decade or so ago with relative modesty, the G.R.R. idea envisioned the use of existing roads—federal, state, and county— along both sides of the Mississippi from its source in Lake Itasca to its mouth in the Gulf below New Orleans. Just a roll call of the cities and towns along the way is enough to stir the blood of most Americans. Besides the major cities of Minneapolis and St. Paul, St. Louis, Memphis, Baton Rouge, and New Orleans, there are the in-between cities with historic, economic, or cultural characteristics all their own. Places like Vicksburg with its Civil War significance, Natchez with antebellum charm as thick as the river mud at its doorstep, Cairo at the mouth of the Ohio, Prairie du Chien and Ste. Genevieve with their heavy French backgrounds, Hannibal with Mark Twain and Huckleberry Finn, Nauvoo with its rich Mormon history, the museum town of Galena.

But it really makes little difference where you strike the Mississippi, whether you head upstream or down, on the east bank or the west. The states have all got interested now. Roads have been improved, smoothed, and in many cases hard-surfaced. Great River Road signs have been put up, maps distributed. And, inevitably, there's now talk of a magnificent parkway along both banks, which naturally would tend to negate the whole project.

For as it stands now, or so it seems to us, the Great River Road is a Concept, not a Thing. It's this broad land of ours as it was, as it has been, as it is today—the bad with the good, the ugly with the beautiful. To "pretty it up," to remove the Copenhagen Snuff sign, to straighten the road where it had to jog around the abandoned ice plant, to set out shrubs to hide the railroad yards: these things could help to create a "parkway," but they could also help to destroy the Great River Road as a mirror of the nation's heartland.

Anyway, touring rivers can be both enjoyable and instructive, both entertaining and educational. The jet plane largely shapes our civilization today. But yesterday it was the riverboat and the iron horse. You're reminded of these historic values time and again as you explore the Mississippi and the lower Missouri. On beyond, as you penetrate the Rocky Mountains, the scenic values are more likely to command your attention. Either way, you're ahead. For rivers reflect more than sky and overhanging rock—they also reflect the country itself. And in the American West, when you combine scenery with history, you have a rare bargain indeed.

THE SOUTHWEST INDIAN: YESTERDAY & TODAY

If you would test the effectiveness of "atmosphere" as a sauce for food, Western style, pack a simple lunch in to Arizona's Canyon de Chelly (regional pronunciation: duh-*shay*). Stop at the White House ruins, on the opposite side of the narrow, steep canyon to get a little perspective. If the sun is right when you start eating, if your inner spirit is congenial—and you aren't interrupted by a flatbed-truck load of sightseers on their way up the canyon—it could well be the most satisfying meal you've ever eaten.

Never mind what you take. We had, as I remember, Vienna sausages and Longhorn cheese, soda crackers, dill pickles, and a bottle of milk. Perhaps an apple. But it didn't really matter. For with it we had a magnificent setting, and almost ageless peace and serenity in which to enjoy it. The long-abandoned cliff house itself was set like a fine jewel—small, but flawlessly cut—in a crevice of the red-and-yellow-streaked canyon wall. We soaked in its beauty, almost wordlessly, as we munched our food, wondering if the harsh austerity of their existence kept its builders from seeing, as we did, the incredibly perfect blend of form and color that went into the creation of their compact little world.

Prosaic? Foolish? Perhaps prosaic. It's simply not in us to dash off a deathless ode in such circumstances. But we're not quite ready to concede foolishness. For looking up Indians in the American Southwest—whether yesterday's, as here in Canyon de Chelly, at nearby Mesa Verde, and Chaco Canyon, or today's, as on the sprawling Navajo Reservation, in the Hopi villages, and amid the pueblos of New Mexico—offers at least one unique reward only the most insen-

164

The Antelope House in Arizona's Canyon de Chelly ruins has not been inhabited since A.D. 800.

sitive visitor can fail to claim. Along with striking, often overwhelming beauty, this business of getting acquainted with the American Indian provides the non-Indian traveler with an insight into his own background. And the experience may well be humbling.

Not only was the American Indian here, as he rather enjoys reminding chauvinistic visitors, to greet the *Mayflower*. He had already created for himself a culture and civilization that, while lacking certain creature comforts we have now grown accustomed to, was peculiarly well suited to his needs. A hundred or so miles southwest of the Canyon de Chelly, at Casa Grande, one can still trace out the remains of a simple but quite efficient irrigation system that was old when our *Mayflower's* forebears were still enduring the darkest part of the so-called Dark Ages.

The Indian, then, is the native American. And nowhere can one learn to know more about him—his past achievements as well as his present-day accomplishments; his amazing multistoried apartment houses that date back to the 12th century, as well as his intricately designed and handcrafted jewelry of the 20th—than in the Southwest, from Oklahoma west through New Mexico and Colorado to Arizona and Utah.

YESTERDAY: RUINS IN "FOUR CORNERS"

Where and how does one begin? By rifling the time vault of the National Park Service, just as if one were collecting mountains, canyons, waterfalls, glaciers, forests, geysers and other Western specialties. More than a score of significant archeological sites are now preserved by the N.P.S. For the most part they are clustered conveniently around the Four Corners area—where Colorado, Utah, Arizona, and New Mexico join.

But starting one's discovery tour of the American Indian here has more than geography going for it. It is historically logical to do so as well. For in this congenial region the Indian, after millennia of wandering about North America, settled down to develop his highest culture. And the physical reminders of that culture—some still impressively preserved after many centuries, thanks to the dry atmosphere in the Southwest—have been carefully studied and analyzed by Park Service experts, then skillfully interpreted and displayed so that one can more easily understand what he is seeing. Visiting

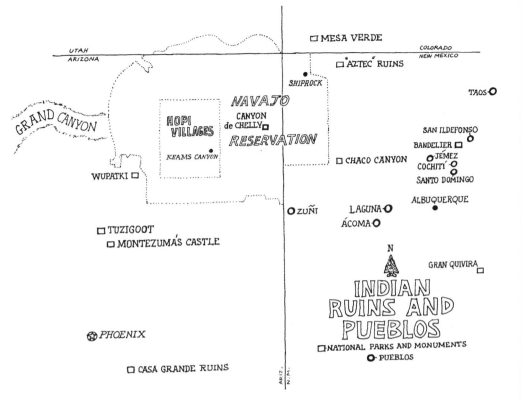

one or more of these archeological preserves, then, and learning more about the American-Indian-That-Was, will better prepare you for moving on to the pueblos and reservations inhabited by the American-Indian-That-Still-Is.

MESA VERDE
(COLORADO)

Mesa Verde National Park is the most famous (and most visited) archeological site in the United States. It is also perhaps the most important, if considered by weight of numbers alone. The 80-square-mile park in southwestern Colorado is essentially a giant mesa ("green table," in Spanish), gashed by twenty or so deep side canyons and towering 2,000 feet above the surrounding arid plain. It was occupied by succeeding Pueblo Indian civilizations from the time of Christ until about A.D. 1300, when an unprecedented twenty-four-year drought

drove the last inhabitants (once believed to number as many as 70,-000) to new locations to the south. Hundreds of pit houses (their earliest homes) and surface pueblos (built before A.D. 1000) dot the top of the mesa. And in giant caves or niches along the sheer canyon walls are as many as four hundred known major cliff dwellings. These were built from A.D. 1000 to 1300 during the so-called Classic period.

Everyone who has ever thumbed through a picture-book on travel is familiar with some of these amazing ruins. Cliff Palace is the largest and best known. It contains over 200 living rooms, 23 *kivas* (ceremonial chambers), and many storage rooms, all on eight floor levels and all within a single cave. But you can visit this one and many other ruins at Mesa Verde. It's one of the most fascinating properties N.P.S. owns. And a leisurely Mesa Verde visit, plus some homework time spent in the excellent museum, will give you a fine short-course indoctrination for further visits and explorations.

Increased visitation over the years has brought inevitable changes, of course—some for the better, some otherwise. If your last visit was ten or more years ago, you may well rejoice that the Knife's Edge is no longer your spine-tingling introduction to the mesa top. Though it was consideration for the Park Service budget as much as for your nerves, we suspect, that prompted the present ascent, marked by a gentler grade, wider roadway, and a long upsweeping tunnel. (Unquestionably more scenic, the old road against the sheer northern face of the mesa was simply too costly to maintain, while posing an ever present threat to the unwary motorist.) But another change, also the inevitable by-product of increased traffic, is far less felicitous.

The old Spruce Tree Lodge complex for visitors—including intimate dining room, cluttered gift shop, and rustic cabins scattered among the piñon and juniper at the very southern tip of the mesa— is no more. Visitor accommodations and services have been pulled back mid-way on the mesa top. They're new, attractive, and comfortable. But they lack the exciting intimacy of the old cabins where you slept, if not in as great comfort, at least in the rather awed awareness that you were within easy walking distance of a giant apartment complex (the *original* Spruce Tree House) which accommodated as many as two hundred people eight centuries ago, when most of our ancestors still believed the world to be a flat pancake centered on the Mediterranean, and were capable of doing away with those who thought otherwise.

So great has the Mesa Verde visitor-count grown that N.P.S. is preparing to open additional archeological ruins on nearby Wetherill Mesa, a western neighbor to Chapin Mesa that contains the cliff houses now open to visitors. It is not yet ready for use.

AZTEC RUINS
(NEW MEXICO)

Let it be said at the outset that Aztec National Monument has much the same relationship to the Aztecs as the hot dog does to a pack of poodles. "Aztec" was bestowed on these impressive ruins— just southeast of Mesa Verde and over the line into New Mexico— by the Mexico-based Spaniards who discovered them. It is a complete misnomer. (But the Spanish can perhaps be forgiven. They knew nothing about the Indians whose civilization they were destroying. And, if possible, cared even less. What's the Spanish equivalent of General Philip Sheridan's "The only good Indians I ever saw were dead"?)

The Indians who built this giant three-story, 500-room pueblo in the early 1100's were not even related to the Aztecs, at least as relatives are figured these days. They were hard-working contemporaries of the Mesa Verde builders. The most interesting feature of the monument, aside from the museum, is the restored Great Kiva. It represents the peak of construction of religious edifices among the Pueblo Indians, past and present.

CHACO CANYON
(NEW MEXICO)

Chaco Canyon National Monument lies still farther south. And if access roads are on the primitive side, not so the ruins themselves. Here against the steep walls of a narrow, river-cut canyon, prehistoric Indian architecture and culture reached their peak. Most remarkable of the monument's ruins is Pueblo Bonito, a semicircular structure, originally five stories high, 667 feet in length, and covering more than three acres. Sometimes called the largest apartment house built anywhere until the late 1880's, it contained 800 rooms and 32 kivas, and may have housed as many as 1,500 people in the 12th century.

Then came drought, heavy erosion, and the inevitable flash floods. By A.D. 1200 the valley, once green and prosperous, was barren and deserted. The amateur archeologist will be intrigued by the many ruins, spanning at least six centuries, and find himself fascinated by the evolutionary development they show. But even if your interest doesn't go quite that deep, reflect for a moment on the miles of inhospitable semidesert you crossed to reach the site, and on the stark harshness of Chaco Canyon itself. Browsing through the visitor center will further help you realize the magnitude of what was accomplished here.

CASA GRANDE
(ARIZONA)

These memorials to yesterday's Indians dot western New Mexico and much of Arizona. You'll need to pick and choose carefully if you're to have any time for today's Indians. One more N.P.S. property you should visit, in any event, is Casa Grande National Monument. Lying between Phoenix and Tucson, and the farthest south of the important ruins, it is noteworthy for its four-story watchtower-apartment house sheltered today from the elements by an umbrella-like covering of steel poles and sheet iron.

The watchtower is unique among Indian structures, protecting as it did the nearby walled villages (now in ruins) and the extensive irrigated fields that surrounded them. Interestingly enough, irrigation here in the arid Gila valley (as noted above) is believed to have started about the time of Christ. Traces of the canals—some of them 25 feet deep, 15 feet wide, and up to 25 miles in length—can still be seen.

RANDOM, IN THE AREA

If you choose to ride this particular "collection" with any abandon at all, you'll want to visit other N.P.S. holdings in New Mexico and Arizona. Offhand we recommend these:

Bandelier, north of Santa Fe. It boomed in the 14th century, when the 1270–1299 drought emptied the more elaborate Cliff Palaces and Pueblo Bonitos to the north. It wasn't abandoned until the late 16th century.

Gran Quivira, southeast of Albuquerque and representing a more recent phase of Pueblo Indian life. Its ruins also include an impressive old Spanish mission, for the Indians didn't leave this area for good until the 1670's.

Montezuma Castle, south of Sedona, Arizona. Another misnomer, like "Aztec," but a perfect 12th-century jewel nonetheless. Well preserved, its ruins sit like a cameo in a 445-foot-high concave limestone wall.

Tuzigoot, west of Sedona. This is a personal favorite of ours, not only for its spectacular hilltop setting and magnificent museum, but—perverse creatures that we are—for its name as well. With a name like Tuzigoot, it's bound to please.

Wupatki, north of Flagstaff. As Oklahomans, we're intrigued by this one for the evidence it shows of having been settled by a curious Oklahoma-style "land rush." The time was the 11th century; the cause, an abundance of fertile land created by an eruption of nearby *Sunset* volcano (itself an interesting national monument). Some eight hundred homesites in all are known to have been developed in this area as a result, largest of which was the three-story, 100-

room Wupatki. In the 1200's, however, all were abandoned, perhaps in favor of the pueblos now inhabited by the modern Hopis (who are believed to be their descendants, at least in part).

This is perhaps as easy a way as any to leave the Indians-That-Were and consider the Indians-That-Are.

TODAY: THE RESERVATIONS

But first, a bit of "Amy Vanderbilting."

Alas, thousands of people each year invade Indian reservations in much the same way they would visit the zoo. They stare, giggle, point, make comments, snap pictures, and otherwise act as if they were around some interesting new species of animal. True, they don't always mean to be rude. They simply fail to recognize (1) that Indians are human, (2) that when they open their reservation to a visitor, it is as host to guest, and (3) that as a guest the visitor is obliged to display at least a modicum of ordinary good manners.

Trips into Canyon de Chelly can now be made only with an authorized guide. Why? Because present-day Navajos, who graze sheep and tend a few tiny fields and orchards in protected corners of the canyon, eventually tired of visitors who poked around in empty hogans, ate all-too-scarce fruit, and plucked ears of corn to take home as souvenirs. That they also took pictures without asking permission, goes without saying. They're "just Indians," aren't they? Don't they encourage folks to come and buy their blankets and turquoise jewelry, their gas, film and soda pop?

Well, yes and no. The Navajos have admittedly changed with the times. They've traded in most of their wagons for pick-ups. They've built some modern roads; and they've dotted those roads not only with motels and restaurants but with even such things (here and there) as soft ice-cream emporiums and drive-in banks. The land, however, is still theirs. And they are still the hosts. No matter how much or how little money we may care to spend with them, we are still obliged, as guests, to mind our manners.

Despite the ubiquitous pick-up, one still sees plenty of them walking. Most have too much pride to thumb a ride. Most, though, will gladly accept one if it's offered. And the experience can be both interesting and rewarding.

THE HOPIS

(ARIZONA)

Our own policy against hitchhikers permits almost no exceptions today. However, we were more tolerant when we ran onto Cordelia. And we've always been glad of it.

We picked her up with her sick baby in front of the Polacca (Arizona) trading post and took her to the hospital in Keams Canyon. We've kept up with her, albeit haphazardly, ever since. Curiously enough, we saw her that first time after we'd come down off First Mesa with our initial, semi-awed look at *Walpi,* the starkly beautiful Hopi pueblo that so completely dramatizes the Indian's successful adaptation to a harsh and hostile environment. Our impressions of both Walpi and Cordelia remain strong to this day.

It is relatively easy these days to visit the Hopis. Approximately 4,000 of them live in eleven mesa-top villages entirely surrounded by the reservation of the Navajos, their traditional enemies. (The almost inaccessible location of these villages until modern times is a picturesque indication of their centuries-long enmity.) A 60-mile stretch of Arizona 264 roughly bisects Hopi-land and, even allowing for its roller-coaster nature, you could drive it in little more than an hour. But a full day is not too much time to give it. There's a café in a corner of the Keams Canyon trading post; we suggest you plan a lunchtime stop, not so much for the food as for the color. A summer ago we even rated a personal welcome from Second Mesa's Chief Joe, who was conducting tribal business at a nearby table. "Where are you from?" he asked. And when we said Oklahoma— "Oh, yes; that's where the wild Indians come from."

No, we protested, the *rich* Indians.

And he nodded with mock gravity: "That's what makes them wild." Lo, the taciturn, humorless Red Man!

The Hopis are an agricultural people and they live in autonomous villages something like the old Greek city-states. They are Arizona's only pueblo dwellers and Walpi, built out on the very tip of sheer First Mesa, is a breathtaking testimonial to their architectural perseverance. Living on top, many of them cat-crawl down perilous rocky paths to tiny terraced plots of corn, beans, and squash that even a Japanese gardener would admire. Among the many arts of the Hopis are pottery (to our thinking as fine as any to be found), basketry,

Monument Valley (Arizona) in the heart of Navajo-land.

and blankets (woven by men, incidentally—the only North American Indian males to indulge in such housewifely pursuit).

The Hopis differ from the sheep- and cattle-raising Navajos in other ways too. In appearance, they're likely to be shorter and heavier, with rounder faces. In demeanor, they tend to be friendlier and more talkative. And of course they have their distinctive customs and ceremonies, best known of which is the spectacular Snake Dance. Each village has its own, an eight-day affair to which visitors are permitted only the last two days. And then only on condition that they leave cameras behind—and bring along their manners.

THE NAVAJOS
(ARIZONA-NEW MEXICO-UTAH)

If geographic compression into a handful of conveniently clustered villages makes the Hopis easy to visit, not so the Navajos. The fastest-growing tribe of Indians today (population 120,000)—and perhaps the richest as well—they are pretty well scattered over a vast 16½-million-acre desert domain the size of West Virginia. True, a massive road-building program in recent years, as oil-gas-coal-and-uranium wealth has begun to flow in, has made most tribal areas relatively easy to reach in an ordinary automobile. But their reservation spreads north into Utah and east into New Mexico, so a good bit of driving is involved even if one wants only a once-over-lightly look. And in 1953, when we made our first serious attempt to learn about Navajo-land, there simply was no such thing as a once-over-lightly. Instead, that empty northeastern corner of the Arizona map was a web of dash lines with the challenging notation "Primitive Road— Inquire Locally." We saw what was involved almost the moment we left U.S. 666 on the outskirts of Shiprock, New Mexico:

WARNING TO PUBLIC

Travel Beyond This Point
Uncertain Due To Bad Road
Conditions

TRAVEL AT YOUR OWN RISK

In the finest "damn the torpedoes" tradition we plowed right on, though we had, admittedly, made local inquiry beforehand, secured the best maps available, checked the car, filled the gas tank, and got an early-morning start.

Rainfall is woefully inadequate in the desert country. But when it comes, it tends to come all at once. It is not too unusual for an area to get as much as half its average *annual* rainfall in a single shower. And splashing down viciously on land with precious little ground cover to trap and store the water, these "gully washers" are often just that—scouring, silt-laden torrents that sweep everything before them, including cars and people. August is a likely season for these locally destructive cloudbursts; afternoon is the most likely time for one to let loose. Hence morning driving—when it's cooler, too—is usually the best for off-pavement exploring. But any time you are driving in this area keep an eye on the weather, watch for sudden storms, and respect all dry, seemingly innocent draws and arroyos.

Late that afternoon, when we had finally reached Kayenta (in Arizona), we were reminded of an uncle who'd driven to California from Oklahoma in a Model T in the early 1920's. A wonderful experience, he always said: he wouldn't take a million dollars for it; nor would he take that to do it again. Well, the going wasn't quite that bad for Helen and me. At least it didn't last as long!

For a few miles beyond the pavement the graded road was even deceptively smooth. Behind us was the agency town of Shiprock.

Ahead of us beckoned the 1,400-foot, shiplike peak that soars up dramatically from the desert floor to tower over the Four Corners country, give the village its name, and provide the whole reservation with a kind of mystic, half-forbidding symbol. Then we topped a gentle rise, dropped down on the other side, out of sight of "civilization" as we figured it. Promptly our road, no longer pretending to be something it wasn't, became more of a trail—a trail that clambered down into and then out of countless dry washes across a land as colorful and spectacular as it is vast and lonely.

Here and there we saw a solitary octagonal hogan, and near it perhaps a few sheep, watched over by a Navajo woman in brightly colored velvet skirt and jacket, or by a couple of children. (Depending largely upon sheep even today, Navajos rarely live together, preferring to scatter out, family by family, in search of hard-to-come-by grass and water.) Occasionally we saw small bands of horses. Occasionally, too, we saw an Indian walking. Several we picked up, and carried along—for the most part silently—until they indicated they wanted out. And as far as the trading post of Mexican Water in Arizona, about halfway to Kayenta, there were no difficulties. But beyond we crossed one of the reservation's then rare steel bridges (over Walker Wash), forded a hard-bottomed tributary, and we were on our own. Another mile or two and we had our first official introduction to "slickrock," the smooth red shale from which rain and wind over the years have eroded virtually all of the thin gray soil.

The 15 miles from Mexican Water to Dinnehotso were marked *unimproved* on even the Tribal Council's official map. However, since a flash flood a week or so before had in some places erased even the car tracks, the road was somewhat more "unimproved" than usual. We felt a bit like Daniel Boone as Helen inched the car along in low over the worst spots. And we covered the strip safely in a little over two hours, counting the discretionary fifteen minutes we spent beside a Laguna Creek ford, waiting for a pick-up load of Navajos to splash across to prove its passability. (This, incidentally, is a precautionary—"chicken," if you like—technique we have used elsewhere from time to time, and recommend highly.)

Beyond Dinnehotso the road was a road again, and graded. And the last 24 miles on in to Kayenta were as relatively uneventful as any section of road can be through such spectacularly beautiful country.

Stark Agathla Peak, looming up over the serrated rim of Comb Ridge, led the way. Another hour and we were in Kayenta, 175 miles from the nearest railroad and in front of the most isolated post office in the forty-eight contiguous states. Perhaps because it was so isolated, it was also one of the friendliest. In 1953 it boasted only a few guest rooms in a modest tourist court; a trading post and small café rounded out the "business district." After a leisurely dinner we drove out on the desert and, under a full moon, soaked up our first impressions of *Monument Valley.*

Books have been written trying to describe its breathtaking beauty, but none is too successful. The fantastic shapes of the monuments— shadowy and ghostlike in the moonlight, but multicolored and ever changing by day—means something different to everyone who sees them. Much of their beauty and their significance lie in the eye and heart of the beholder. Soak its beauty into your system for a while, and, at least until the spell begins to wear off, everything else you see is anticlimax.

To begin to appreciate just how much Navajo-land has changed, keep the above in mind while driving this route on what is now called "The Navajo Trail," officially U.S. 164. Relocated here and there and completely re-engineered, it is a legitimate "short cut" now, a high-speed road actually preferred by Colorado truckers bound for California. But while it symbolizes the change that has swept both the Navajos and their reservation, it does not signal an end to the excitement and satisfaction to be found in visiting Navajo-land. The same incredible beauty is still there. The network of paved roads, the scattering of modern motels and restaurants merely make the visiting easier and, to most people, more enjoyable. Now all one needs is an interest, a concern, an honest desire to learn, and a willingness to slow down, look carefully, and listen. That lacking, one might better spend his time on the Interstate.

THE PUEBLOS
(NEW MEXICO)

Visiting New Mexico's eighteen Indian pueblos ("villages," in Spanish) is similarly easy to do or to avoid. Nowhere is this better dramatized than with *Laguna* pueblo, lying west of Albuquerque *between* old U.S. 66 and Interstate 40. The leisurely, curious motorist can spend a delightful half-day between interchanges by visiting the trim little pueblo itself, and the various churches, schools, missions, trading posts, and other points of interest beside the now semiretired highway. Meanwhile, the Disneyland-bound motorist can zip by at 70+ mph and, if he watches closely from his slightly elevated grade, can get a fleeting glimpse of the beautiful Laguna church and its surrounding cluster of neat adobes. Most of the other pueblos offer much the same major highway convenience, either of access or by-pass.

It really doesn't matter where we start. So far as we're concerned, all the pueblos are interesting, if for different reasons. Though all have certain characteristics in common, they differ sufficiently to make it rewarding to hunt up as many of them as possible. And, too, though all but one lie in a rough oval along the Rio Grande that is scarcely 150 miles from top to tip, they offer an interesting variety of settings—from the water's-edge of San Juan to the arid mesa-top of Ácoma—styles of architecture, traditional ceremonials, and handicrafts.

It was four centuries ago that the Spanish nominally conquered the Pueblo Indians and introduced them to the Catholic religion. Except for the Zuñis, most of the tribes accepted the new faith without too much protest. Characteristically, however, they added it to, rather than exchanged it for, their old faith. And the happy result is a year-long calendar of colorful masses, processions, and feast days, combined with a just as long, just as colorful schedule of traditional dances and ceremonials.

The Pueblos have always been agriculturists, and this is an area where drought and heat make farming difficult, not to say downright problematical. So it is not surprising that their religion (and their art, for that matter) has centered on producing more and better crops. There are ceremonies commemorating the opening of the *acequías* (the irrigation ditches), the planting of the corn, beans, squash, and other crops. And there are rain dances and harvest festivals.

Because the health of these crops is all important, Pueblo art and religion is filled with what anthropologists call "life forms"—representations of living things, from ears of corn to butterflies, from owls and eagles to deer and bear. These show up colorfully as decorations on pottery, as designs in silverwork, and as elaborately masqueraded figures in the various dances.

Most of these dances and ceremonies, whether religious or purely secular (they like to get together just for fun, too), are open to the respectful visitor. However, because dates vary from year to year—as do regulations concerning fees and picture-taking—we suggest that you write the State Tourist Bureau (State Capitol, Santa Fe, New Mexico) before leaving home.

One final suggestion: if you plan to attend an Indian ceremonial, try to do so without prejudice or preconception. Erna Fergusson, one of New Mexico's most perceptive writers, has put it this way: "No act in daily life is too ordinary to be dignified by ritual; no magnificence of God or nature too awe-inspiring to be explained by myth or influenced by prayer." And to the Indian his ceremonial is just that—a symbolic representation of his relationship to God . . . in short, a prayer.

No two Pueblophiles would offer you the same preferred list; or perhaps even the same reasons where their personal preferences overlapped. But for what they're worth, here are our suggestions.

Taos you must see if for no other reason than that it is the best known and most photographed! But this is for good reason, of course. Just three miles north of the town of Taos (which we visited for the old fur trade), it consists of two large communal houses, four and five stories in height and so handsomely picturesque as to resemble a Hollywood movie set. If you're sensitive to commercialization (it's inevitable to a certain extent; we're blaming no one), don't get too close; wander away from the access road and let the impressions soak into you slowly.

Taos is the farthest north. Collecting picks up around Española, some 50 miles to the southwest. Here near the Rio Grande is *San Juan,* a typical farming community where the Spanish established their first capital of New Mexico, in 1598. Currently, archeological work is under way at nearby San Juan de los Caballeros, to add interest to a pueblo that is neat, friendly, and prosperous-looking.

Also well worth a visit while in this area are *Santa Clara* (a sprawling community that produces some good pottery) and *San Ildefonso* (best known perhaps for Maria, the potter whose artistically decorated black pieces are now found in leading museums everywhere).

Southwest of Santa Fe are a half-dozen more pueblos, most of them on or near the Rio Grande and requiring a bit more of a detour from U.S. 85. Two of the most rewarding, we feel, are *Cochití* (with its excellent pottery and silver jewelry) and *Santo Domingo*. The latter also features turquoise jewelry, excellent pottery, and some weaving. Santo Domingo is famed, too, for its elaborate Corn Dance (August 4); the pueblo is one of the most conservative of all the villages and has held on more closely than most to the ancient customs and traditions. Also noteworthy is the frescoed church.

Of the pueblos north of Albuquerque, we like *Jémez,* for the fascinating back country it opens up (along recently rebuilt New Mexico 4).

Of the pueblos west of Albuquerque, both Ácoma and Zuñi stand out. *Ácoma,* the "Sky City," is in some respects the most unusual of them all, a breathtakingly picturesque community of rock and adobe perched atop a sheer-sided, 357-foot mesa. Ancient when the Spanish arrived (some of its excellent masonry is known to be 700 years old), it is one of the oldest continuously inhabited communities in the United States, saved from almost total desertion a few years back by construction of an auto road! The handsome Ácoma church, built sometime before 1644, is one of the state's most remarkable mission structures and would, almost alone, make a visit to the mesa top worthwhile.

Zuñi lies south of Gallup against the Arizona line. Aside from an unusually pretty setting, amid mountains and forests, it has several additional distinctions. Zuñi turquoise-inlay silver has long been the pace-setter in the Indian jewelry field. The Zuñi Shalako dances, in late November or early December, are among the most elaborate, and the most admired by aficionados. And it was a Zuñi pueblo, now abandoned—Hawikúh—that Coronado's advance men saw in 1539 and thought to be, such apparently was the effect of the sun on its adobe walls, the long-sought-for Cíbola.

A SCATTERING OF TRIBES

One can visit many other Indian tribes in the West, of course. We've already mentioned the Sioux, in connection with the Battle of the Little Big Horn, where General Custer died with his men in 1876. We'll poke through at least a corner of the sprawling Apache reservation in Arizona when we consider the Coronado Trail in the next chapter. In addition, every state's historical society and tourist bureau will send material for the asking about the accessibility of Indian communities on one's route. Regional and local museums are troves of information and of ancient and modern artifacts (one of the most interesting new ones being the Museum of the Five Civilized Tribes—Cherokee, Chickasaw, Creek, Choctaw, and Seminole—in Muskogee, Oklahoma). A look around such centers is an ideal introduction to the nearby Indians one hopes to visit.

Most Indian tribes these days are becoming increasingly aware of the benefits to be gained from travel. And regardless of the way they feel about it inside (unfortunately their attitude toward non-Indians has in recent years often hardened perceptibly), they are making an increased effort to entertain and—perhaps in the process—enlighten the visitor. The Cherokees around Tahlequah, in Oklahoma, are doing an excellent job of this, both with a Cherokee village, vintage 1700, and with a colorful historical drama which premiered in 1969 in a striking outdoor amphitheater.

So wherever you go, if you're interested in Indians, just inquire locally. Whether the Indians are particularly enchanted about it or not, they'll be expecting you!

FOR THE
BYWAY LOVER

A flat tire had slowed our day's exploring. It was nearly dark when we stopped in front of the two-story stone Folsom Hotel, built in 1900 when Folsom was still threatening to become the commercial center of northeastern New Mexico. But depleted mines, a disastrous flood, and other adversities had long since wilted the town's pretensions. As we'd noted somewhat apprehensively driving in, about the only thing it was currently threatening to do was give up the ghost. Hoping for the best, we went in and asked if we could still get dinner.

Mrs. Crabtree, the old-time Folsomite who owned the hotel, broke it to us apologetically. It was Labor Day weekend; most of her regular guests had gone elsewhere for the holiday; she'd given her help the day off. We thanked her and said we'd go somewhere else.

And that, presumably, did it. Her still very much alive sense of Western hospitality was apparently pricked. "But, my dears, where would you go?"

With that she dragged us (figuratively—it really wasn't all that difficult) into the empty dining room and proceeded on into the kitchen to fix us a dinner for two. When it was ready, she brought it in herself, served us, then sat down to answer our questions about life in Folsom "in the good old days."

As we've said before, it's only on the back roads you're likely to encounter such spontaneous manifestations of simple, honest, person-to-person friendliness, and even then, of course, but rarely. Still, the fact that one *can* stumble upon such heartwarming travel discoveries (more about them in the last chapter) by leaving turnpikes and superhighways helps explain the increasing popularity of byways today. Here, away from the numbing impersonality of numbers, people can still treat one another as fellow human beings, as individuals.

It's this, we feel, as much as—if not more than—the back-country scenery it reveals, that constitutes shunpiking's real charm. True, the improved road—broader, smoother, perhaps on a higher grade—

182

many times offers the motorist a better, more expansive view of the countryside (and one the driver, especially, is better able to enjoy); yet this *plus* is often more than canceled out by the sheer weight of numbers.

A case in point is that "Travel at Your Own Risk" sign greeting us as we left the pavement at Shiprock, New Mexico (in the preceding chapter). Even today we feel our excitement at reading those words, and can recall the slow, soundless savoring on our lips of the "towns" we would soon be encountering (provided of course we didn't get lost, or stuck, or both)—exciting names like Teec Nos Pos, Mexican Water, Dinnehotso, and Kayenta. It was enough to set one's heart pumping in anticipation. Now, however, a modern highway slashes across this corner of the Navajo Reservation. And while it admittedly shows off the spectacular countryside to much better advantage, having to wait for a couple of tractor-trailer rigs to roar by before one can even pull onto the roadway tends to weaken the "byway" illusion more than a little bit.

Which brings us to this reluctant disclaimer: Today's byway, alas, may well be tomorrow's thruway. It's that simple. Some of our most memorable byways have been turned into high-speed raceways, at least for those inclined to make them such. As we write this, one of the nation's biggest corporations talks of building a city of 250,000 people at Four Corners, the spot where New Mexico, Colorado, Arizona, and Utah join, and which you almost needed a guide to find until the so-called Navajo Trail was built. And that high-speed "trail" is far from unique. Superhighways are to be found now throughout the West, on and off the Interstate system. And often the contrast between their broad, divided-lane hurly-burly and the narrow, bumpy intimacy of the road they replaced is fully as dramatic.

TEN FAVORITE SHUNPIKES

Still, all is not lost. The gradual upgrading of most Western roads isn't really that all-encompassing, and a rather surprising number of them are—wonder of wonders—essentially unchanged. Consider for a moment, if you will, the following excerpt from a shunpiking article we wrote for our travel series in *The Sunday Oklahoman.*

Off-the-Road Explorations

We made our bed; now we'll lie in it. Here are ten shunpikes that we have, at one time or another, enjoyed very much. Most of them are gravel; a few are dirt. All of them, we believe, are well worth your exploring one of these days, if you haven't already done so.

◀ The famous State Bridge road—Kremmling to Dotsero along beside the young Colorado River and the old Denver & Rio Grande Western main-line tracks.
◀ Boise City to Raton—via U.S. 64 and New Mexico 72.
◀ The Nambe Pueblo road (above Santa Fe) north through Cundiyo, Chimayo, and Santa Clara.
◀ The Tioga Pass road—Yosemite's "back door" to the east.
◀ The Shirley Basin road from Medicine Bow to Casper—unmarked Wyoming road.
◀ Utah 44 across the Uintas.
◀ The Douglas Pass road (Colorado 139) between Rangely and Loma.
◀ The Little Laramie River drive from Chambers Lake, Colorado, north on unmarked Forest Service roads to Woods Landing, Wyoming.
◀ Golden Gate Canyon out of Denver—Colorado 58.
◀ Slumgullion Pass from Lake City to Creede—Colorado 149.

Now perhaps the most curious thing about that list is that it is, to our way of looking at it, still a pretty exciting bunch of byways— and it was drawn up almost twenty years ago! Several of the roads, according to my latest maps, are still not completely paved. Several of those that are hard-surfaced, nominally, are just that—paved, but not redesigned or re-engineered. And right now, although some attract sufficient traffic so that calling them unqualified "byways" would require a bit of semantic license, none is a thruway or even a major highway.

Before we go any farther, then, let's look at each of these, note why we prized it so highly then, and see how it can still delight and satisfy the byway lover today.

STATE BRIDGE ROAD

(COLORADO)

State Bridge traditionally is the Colorado byway that separates the men from the boys. Handy as a rule of thumb for driving proficiency, it has often been used over the years by Old Colorado Hands to determine whether or not to recommend a particularly rugged road to a friend whose tastes and abilities in mountain driving were still in question. "Ever drive State Bridge?" you ask casually. If the answer is No, accompanied by a blank stare, the issue remains in doubt. But if there's an affirmative answer—and a noticeable paling of the cheeks or a slight nervous twitch of the lips—then the questionable routing is discouraged. Only if the friend answers Yes, with obvious and unmistakable enthusiasm, is the inquired-about road recommended without reservation. In short, State Bridge was—and to a certain extent remains—the epitome of the ruggedly exciting mountain-and-canyon-country byway.

Another criterion might well apply to several of the byways covered in this chapter. When some years ago we submitted a tentative schedule for some travel articles we were preparing for *The Sunday Oklahoman,* the State Bridge piece elicited this succinct reaction from Leland S. Vance, then business manager of the Oklahoma Publishing Co.: "State Bridge Road . . . is a fine place for goats. I took a 12-cylinder Lincoln half a block long on this particular goat trail about 12 years ago and would recommend that no civilized person attempt this drive."

But that was some years ago. And he was, after all, driving "half a block" of automobile. Perhaps Dr. M. L. Wardell, our history professor at the University of Oklahoma, put it best, though in a slightly different context. Cleopatra, he always liked to say, was "a mighty nice sort of girl, if you happen to like that sort of girl."

And that's pretty much the way we feel about it. If you happen to like that sort of road, you just can't beat State Bridge.

Some grading and a few miles of paving in the immediate area of State Bridge itself have tamed the route somewhat in recent years. But they haven't completely eliminated the breath-quickening stretches that make the Dotsero Cutoff (to borrow the railroad name for it) between U.S. 40 and U.S. 6–24 so exciting. (And you'll still want to inquire locally if it's been raining.) Leaving U.S. 40 at Kremmling, the route follows generally the course of the Colorado River, already showing promise of becoming a major stream, and the main-line tracks of the Denver & Rio Grande Western Railroad.

State Bridge itself is, simply, the tiny settlement that sprang up at the bottom of the canyon some 30 miles southwest of Kremmling. Here a picturesquely modest state-owned bridge crosses the river, and if you've had enough nonpaved roads by this time, you can escape via Colorado 131 to the south, coming out on U.S. 6–24 at Wolcott.

But the entire byway, continuing on along the river to Dotsero, on U.S. 6–24, is an exciting adventure. Alternating are bits of dizzying shelf road with canyon-bottom stretches where you have the river and the railroad tracks all to yourself for miles at a time.

BOISE CITY TO RATON

(OKLAHOMA–NEW MEXICO)

This is the Folsom road. It offers not spectacle, so much as color; not excitement, so much as human interest. Wandering north and west from Boise City, Oklahoma, the route crosses the Cimarron (or Dry) Cutoff of the old Santa Fe Trail, ruts of which are still clearly visible a century and more later (see "A Clutch of Western Trails"). Beyond, it crosses rough, rolling ranch country to tiny Kenton and Black Mesa, Oklahoma's highest point.

Easy to visit is Black Mesa State Park. Requiring more effort, and local co-operation, are isolated caves containing prehistoric Indian petroglyphs, dinosaur quarries from which important museum specimens have been taken over the years, remarkable erosion formations, and the flat top of 4,978-foot Black Mesa itself, its stone marker noting the three-state junction of Oklahoma, Colorado, and New Mexico.

On westward, in New Mexico, the byway pushes up the broad, virtually uninhabited valley of the Cimarron River to Folsom. Be-

yond lies the *Folsom Man site,* one of several important archeological "digs" that, over the years, have probed and defined the cultures of our continent's first settlers.

The last leg of the route runs across the flat green top of Johnson Mesa, as pretty a ranch country as you'll find anywhere, and affording magnificent top-down views into both Colorado and New Mexico. Then the road passes a few once important coal mining towns, drops down off the mesa finally into the bustling town of Raton, with its popular horse track and abundant visitor facilities. And all this after a 125-mile junket that could well have taken you most of a day and, if luck was with you, let you encounter well under that number of automobiles, most of them driven by natives who will almost surely have waved as you passed.

NAMBE PUEBLO ROAD

(NEW MEXICO)

Only within the past few years has the Indian/Spanish area north
of Santa Fe and east of U.S. 64 been made readily accessible by
paved roads. But the essential charm of these centuries-old settlements remains unchanged. Just get a good map and strike out almost
at random. In a few instances the village itself has now been by-
passed, thus speeding the passage of those on business and tending
to preserve the picturesque peace and serenity of the old adobe villages themselves. *Chimayo* is far-famed for its weavers, an ancient
sanctuario from which many miraculous cures have emanated, and,
our favorite, an old adobe ranchhouse that serves magnificent Spanish
food. As for *Cordova,* it has so successfully resisted the onslaught of
machine-age modernization that only two summers ago we got "lost"
in the village, ended up on a dead-end shelf road over the creek, and
were compelled to back a hundred yards or so to get out of the way
of a grinning, pick-up-mounted native who knew where he was going.

Jewels of the route, perhaps, if you choose to push up New Mexico
76–3 all the way to Taos, are *Truchas* and *Las Trampas.* The latter
is a three-century-old museum piece, an almost perfect example of
Spanish Colonialism carried intact into the middle of 20th-century
America.

We get excited even today just recalling our personal discovery of
this virtually untouched corner of Spanish New Mexico. The single
dusty access road, eroded red earth, tiny fields, scrubby forests, and
ever watching mountains; the hollowed-out log still carrying precious
irrigation water across a deep arroyo; proud geraniums in the narrow
windows of weathered adobes; the quietly beautiful San José de
García Church in Las Trampas.

Even then, however, the paved road was approaching and people
were beginning to worry. Admittedly, the village's economy was no
longer viable. But what was to be done about it? Find an "angel"
who could buy up the area like a small Colonial Williamsburg, preserve it as a living museum, whether residents wanted it so or not?
Or, abandon it to the asphalted, neon-lighted commercialism to which
some felt it was already doomed? Well, the details of the problem
and assorted solutions are not germane here. Let's just say that a

delicate compromise has been effected, as of now—and this byway is still tremendously rewarding.

TIOGA PASS

(CALIFORNIA)

Tioga Pass is the "back door" to Yosemite and provides what is undoubtedly one of the West's most exciting motoring experiences. True, it was even more exciting before they "improved" it. And more fun, too, especially the *Tuolumne Meadows* section, on top, in Yosemite National Park and west of the pass itself.

Frankly, we have never been able to understand why engineers can see the virtue in separating the lanes of a busy multilane highway, yet fail—as they frequently do—to see equal virtue, not to say charm and economy, in allowing individual lanes of a lightly traveled road to wander apart at will, the better to avoid chopping down a century-old tree or bulldozing into existence an earth-scarring cut. Which is to say that the Tuolumne Meadows part of the Tioga Pass road has been straightened a bit, widened more than a little bit, and hard-surfaced. Gone, in the process, are the delightful one-way stretches that never failed to delight the leisurely-minded motorist. But despite this completely unjustified sacrifice on the altar of drawing-board correctness, the striking scenery—flower-carpeted alpine meadows, ice-rimmed lakes, and awesome sweeps of the naked Sierra Nevadas, California's backbone—makes the drive a memorable one.

Then, if you're headed east out of Yosemite, you come to the pass and that abdomen-tightening series of loops in the shelf road that drops you almost 3,000 feet down an incredibly bare mountainside to Mono Lake, on the floor of the desert, and the town of Lee Vining. The road has been improved in recent years—though many a bemused flatlander, we suspect, having negotiated it as his "introductory offer" to the pleasures of mountain driving, might well demand to know *how*. Certainly from the top the series of looping descents resembles nothing so much as the graceful tracings of an artist's brush on the black mountainside itself. It is obvious, such are the distances involved and the tricks the desert plays on one's eyes, that the alleged road is wide enough only for a small motorbike, if that. Here and there, where perspective allows, the squeamish motorist will not fail to note that the whole thing has been projected out from the wall by ingenious rock undershoring, thereby adding yet another touch of picturesque, if not too reassuring, artistry.

Still, other foolhardy motorists are obviously attempting it and soon, fascinated—though perhaps hypnotically so, like the moth circling the flame—you are on your way down. A few hundred yards, perhaps a quarter of a mile, and a kind of narcotic fatalism begins to take over. You've come this far, your car is still on the road: perhaps, with luck . . . and gradually then the truly stupendous nature of the descent begins to soak into you. You forget the road and begin to see the curious white-rimmed lake (white from salt spray whipped up out of the briny water by the strong desert winds) and the Lilliputian town at your feet. Improved it has been, but the Tioga Pass Road is still a byway *par excellence.*

SHIRLEY BASIN
(WYOMING)

For those of us who were raised on Owen Wister, this is *The Virginian* in living color—the fabled West of one's boyhood dreams brought to life just beyond the car's fender. It starts at the U.S. 30 town of Medicine Bow, Wyoming, home of the Virginian Hotel, where Wister frequently stayed and where he undoubtedly wrote at least part of his most famous novel. It ends at Casper, near which was located the celebrated Goose Egg Ranch, setting for his hilarious baby-swapping chapter.

For about 100 miles the unnumbered road cuts through a vast mountain-rimmed basin that, until oil was discovered some years back, was given over almost exclusively to ranching. When we crossed the Shirley Basin almost twenty years ago it was gravel and dirt all the way and as isolated as the most confirmed shunpiker could desire. We saw far more sheep than we saw people in the three or four hours the trip took us to complete. And far more curious antelope than sheep and people combined. There are many fine byways in Wyoming—vast and sparsely populated—but the Shirley Basin is still one of the best.

The only sad note, actually, is that the Goose Egg ranchhouse itself is no more. When we first saw it, the two-story, square-to-the-world stone house was abandoned. Though going down (one corner had crumbled and the roof was sagging badly), it was still proudly impressive. To its credit, it did not give up of its own free will. The owner of the ranch, fearful of suits that might result if visitors were hurt while roaming through it, dismantled the structure, storied stone by storied stone. Allegedly he even numbered them so that they could some day be reassembled, were a wealthy history buff to appear. And the last we heard they were stored some place, against that day.

But whatever develops—and we doubt anything will—we have our memories of the Goose Egg. You'll simply have to reread *The Virginian* and when you get to the site, suitably marked, supply your own mental re-creation of that scene when the party broke up and the various scrambled babies began their journey to the wrong homes. Let this much be said: though the house is gone, Wister would have no trouble finding his way around the Shirley Basin. It really hasn't changed appreciably.

ACROSS THE UINTAS
(UTAH)

Utah 44, across the Uinta Mountains in the extreme northeastern corner of the state, is one of our ten byways which has, at least in part, actually disappeared. The most spectacular section of it, the magnificent canyon bottom where idyllic Sheep Creek flows (or flowed) into the Green River, is now under water backed up from the dam that takes its name from the colorful rock crevice it flooded: Flaming Gorge. Uinta byways still exist, however: specifically we'd recommend *Utah 150,* only a few miles to the west. As for Utah 44, it is still interesting and highly scenic, even if the *Flaming Gorge National Recreation Area* traffic is a bit heavy to qualify the road as a true byway.

DOUGLAS PASS ROAD
(COLORADO)

The Douglas Pass road is now a half-and-half affair. A connecting road between U.S. 40 and U.S. 50 in northwestern Colorado, it has been considerably improved, particularly the northern section out of Rangely. But the southern part, from the pass itself in the pines at the crest of the *Book Cliffs Plateau,* down on to the arid flats again near Grand Junction, is a legitimate shunpiking favorite. The shelves aren't too bad, what with generally light traffic. And the constantly changing panoramas of colorful bluffs, mesas, escarpments, and assorted desert country scenery along the Colorado/Utah line more than compensate for the extra driving effort required.

ALONG THE LITTLE LARAMIE RIVER
(COLORADO–WYOMING)

The Little Laramie byway is so much still what it has always been that you'll need a good map even to find it! Two summers ago, Colorado highway department crews had finally pushed up the Cache La Poudre almost as far as Chambers Lake. So prospects that the Cameron Pass road, Colorado 14, will now be improved all the way, in our lifetime, have brightened appreciably.

But the Little Laramie detour only begins in this area. Striking off from Colorado 14 near the lake, it picks up and then follows that pleasant mountain stream, first along the east slope of the Medicine Bows and then, as it emerges from the forest and swings northeast into Wyoming, out on to the flats where it finally joins the Laramie itself. The road serves a few isolated resorts and, with turnoff trails, offers access to several small summer-home areas, back-country fishing streams and lakes, and a lot of just plain, off-the-beaten-path Colorado mountain real estate.

GOLDEN GATE CANYON
(COLORADO)

The Golden Gate Canyon byway west of Denver—Colorado 58 when we first saw it in 1940 and still so numbered—is yet another Colorado rarity: the relatively undiscovered road (though, virtually in Golden's back yard, it has always been something of a local favorite). We've liked it for the glimpse it offered of rural living in the mountains—as opposed to urban living with a cabin in the hills for weekending. Golden Gate has always had a few small farmers and ranchers. Driving up the canyon—to return via the modern Clear Creek road to the south (U.S. 6), or via much improved Coal Creek on the north (Colorado 72)—gives one a pleasant, even relaxing, loop. This is the kind of loop, incidentally, that shows off the back-country quietness and beauty that convinces the natives that they live in the finest of all possible states.

SLUMGULLION PASS
(COLORADO)

What's in a name? Plenty, if it's Slumgullion Pass. Colorado 149 between Creede and Lake City is just that—a slumgullion—a collection of a half-dozen or more assorted ingredients that add up to a delightful ragout of savory vacation travel lore. There's the mountain stream, of course, the headwaters of the Rio Grande, a sparkling trout stream here that gives no hint of the gray, silt-laden river it is soon to become. And there's the lush high-valley ranch country that flanks it, as well as the snowy mountains that beckon in all directions just beyond the road; a waterfall or two; two distinct mountain passes (Spring Creek is almost as high as Slumgullion and fully as beautiful, but lacking the "name appeal" to make it as well known); and the interesting old mining towns that guard each approach.

Like most Colorado roads, this one attracts far more traffic today than it did even a few years ago when it was gravel-surfaced from end to end and Slumgullion itself was still a wandering path cut through the forest. But it remains a byway nonetheless. Not on the direct route from anywhere to anywhere, it's spared the idle traffic of those who really don't want to be on the Slumgullion Pass road. And that's all to the good. The driver who inadvertently stumbles onto the Pasadena Freeway, say, at five in the afternoon, isn't likely to be too happy about it; and as a result he's very likely to become a traffic hazard, so everyone around him is soon unhappy too. We've seen this happen on mountain roads any number of times: the motorist stumbling onto a road he is psychologically unable to enjoy, thereby ruining it for others.

As an example:

Amusing now, but not then, was the contretemps in Yosemite—on the stiff climb up to Glacier Point—that brought us into direct bumper-to-bumper confrontation with a woman from the East. She was driving a long, wide, low-slung car that must have ridden beautifully on the Merritt Parkway, but was hardly the ideal personnel carrier for this particular road—even had the driver been enjoying herself, which she obviously wasn't. Her grip of the steering wheel appeared vicelike; her jaw was set, her eyes fixed straight ahead. Fortunately she was little more than crawling as she came up the mountainside. So when we met her on the curve—on our side of the road—we were both able to stop. But then began the frantic, hugging and pulling as she worried her big car to the outer, drop-off side of the road to let us edge past her on the cliffside.

We scanned the papers next day and found nothing. So we presume she got to Glacier Point (obviously there was no turning around!) and made it back down into the valley without killing herself or anyone else. But that look of sheer terror in her eyes is still with us, and leads us to repeat what we've said before: When driving in the mountains, know what kind of road you like and what kind you do not like, then try to find out beforehand what you are letting yourself in for.

REMOTE & REWARDING

Well, those were a few of our shunpiking favorites of nearly twenty years ago. As you can see, most of them, while no longer strictly undiscovered byways, are still worthy of attention. If and when you've run through them, and want more, here are some other favorites.

BLUE RIVER LOOP & CORONADO TRAIL
(ARIZONA)

The Blue River Loop (our own name for it) is what most would call a byway-within-a-byway. It's a half-day circle trip off the Coronado Trail out of Alpine, in east-central Arizona.

The *Coronado Trail* itself, of course, is a beauty all the way. If you've never driven it (U.S. 666), do so the first chance you get. It climbs up from idyllic high-mountain valleys, like *Hannagan Meadows,* to Arizona's unique Mogollon Rim, then drops down precipitously to the flat desert country that is most of southern Arizona. But it has now been modernized, making it much too easy to drive much too fast—and thus to miss the deer, elk, wild turkey, and other highlights of the route when it was a narrow gravel trail.

But our Blue River Loop is still that—a narrow gravel trail—and great fun. You leave U.S. 260 some 3 miles east of Alpine, drop south on a Forest Service road to Blue (just a post office). Here you ford the Blue River (a U.S.F.S. marker says "Coronado Trail, 12 miles") and come out on U.S. 666 just below Hannagan Meadows, 33 miles in all. But the bare statistics give no idea of the amazing variety of scenery you encounter along the way.

Within a few miles you drive from lush pine forests to desertlike mesa tops covered with piñon, juniper, sage, prickly pear and yucca. At Red Bluffs you find yourself amid vividly colored headlands reminiscent of famed Oak Creek Canyon and the Sedona area to the west near Flagstaff. Beyond the ford you climb onto a high desert ridge with a 50-mile view to both the north and the south.

And then of course there's the wildlife. Last time we flushed four deer before we'd gone a half-dozen miles. Elk and wild turkey are common sights throughout this area. But variety is still the one word for this Blue River byway. Rarely in so few miles is it possible to drive into and out of so many different life zones—with the flora and fauna, geological and climatological features, and other distinctive characteristics of each—all in such a satisfyingly beautiful setting. An ecological museum could not have been conceived or developed more masterfully.

UNAWEEP CANYON
(COLORADO)

Unaweep Canyon, in far west-central Colorado, is in the Slumgullion Pass category. No short cut *to* some place else, it attracts, for the most part, only those motorists who are there by choice. That can mean uranium or vanadium miners, for the far side of this circle route serves a mining area that has enjoyed something of a boom in this atomic age. It can also mean countless fishermen and hunters, for this *Uncompaghre Plateau* country is one of the last big wildernesses in Colorado. But the entire byway—Colorado 141 and 145 through Gateway, Uravan (for *Ura*nium and *Van*adium) and Norwood to Placerville, then Colorado 62 to Ridgway and U.S. 550 again, eventually, near Ouray—is still free and uncluttered. And magnificently colorful, particularly the full length of Unaweep Canyon itself, remarkable geographically by virtue of being one of the very few canyons in the world with two mouths and a stream flowing from each.

You drive up East Creek, cross a divide so shallow you have to watch for it, then follow West Creek (if not imaginative, the creek names are at least forthright) downstream to where it flows into the Dolores River at Gateway. Yet all the way you are driving between high rocky walls that tower from a few hundred to a thousand feet overhead.

The rest of the loop is fully as interesting, though entirely different. To watch for particularly: the rotted remains of a mountainside flume that pays silent tribute to the vision and raw courage of those who wrestled the mountains for their wealth in an era that had not yet dreamed of bulldozers and helicopters.

RUBY MOUNTAINS
(NEVADA)

The Ruby Mountains we recommend to all who are inclined to think of Nevada as one long, unbroken desert, dotted here and there with neon-fronted casinos. This delightful half-day detour from U.S. 40 south of Elko reveals to the unhurried motorist a side of the state that all too few ever discover in their mad dash from one bank of slot machines to another. For here, even in the middle of the summer when shimmering heat waves distort the pavement ahead of you and leave distant mountain ranges hanging from the sky over a vast nonexistent lake, you can enjoy forested canyons, meadows bright with wildflowers, sparkling rocky streams, modest waterfalls, and an occasional patch of snow. As an unbelievable sight to the first-time visitor to Nevada, it ranks right up there with the Las Vegas "strip."

Just drop south and east from Elko, inquiring at Lamoille, if necessary, for the *Thomas Canyon* road, a dead-end detour that serves a newly developed recreation area. Back at Lamoille you loop north to pick up Nevada 11, which carries you over the Ruby Mountains (via *Secret Pass* which, secret or not, is now paved) and through some lush green ranch country to U.S. 93. A few more miles and you rejoin U.S. 40 at Wells.

You'll never again have the same feeling about Nevada. For an extra, strictly gustatory fillip, try a hearty family-style Basque dinner at the ramshackle Star Hotel in Elko.

EVEN MORE BY-THE-WAY

There are many, many more roads we'd like to recommend, for a variety of reasons, some of them purely personal. They include:

For an exciting look at back-country Utah, drive *Utah 54* from Escalante north and east to Fruita and *Capitol Reef National Monument.* The crossing of the yellow, deeply eroded Escalante River, the sharp shelf-road climb up Calf Creek to Boulder, and the up-and-down vaulting of Boulder Mountain—these are just three reasons why this, in our opinion, is one of the Beehive State's finest byways. And if you should happen to run into Mrs. Ormund at Boulder (see the next chapter) your byway cup would indeed overflow.

For a bit of old-fashioned, twisting, mountain shelf road, slow but absolutely safe, try Colorado's *Russell Gulch* road. (This is now the back-door approach to Central City; once it was the only door. We prefer to visit Central first, then take Russell Gulch going down.) Not the least unusual feature of this picturesque reminder of road building a century ago is that it now leads almost directly onto the Idaho Springs ramp of Interstate 70.

For another exciting corkscrew shelf road, try the *Fish Creek* section of the *Apache Trail* that skirts Arizona's Superstition Mountains.

For a glimpse of pleasant Montana back country that serves a modest resort playground seemingly known only to the natives, drive the *Swan Valley* road, Montana 93, primarily south of Flathead Lake and Glacier National Park.

For a close look at the *Wallowas,* which many think are among the most beautiful mountains in the West (certainly they are among the least publicized), take the day-long drive from La Grande, Oregon, to Lewiston, Idaho.

For an example of one of the nicer contributions a volcano can make to life on this often troubled planet, visit *Valle Grande,* New Mexico. Long believed to be just that, a Great Valley, it has now been identified as what it really is—the extinct crater of a volcano. And with an area of 176 square miles, it is one of the world's largest. New Mexico 4 west from Nambe skirts the lower rim of the bowl and shows it off to best advantage: the incredibly flat, incredibly lush green range dotted with cattle and sheep, the fringe of darker green forests on the mountains rimming the bowl, and the intense blue of the sky overhead.

The full loop west and south to New Mexico 44 north of Albuquerque, including the shiny new atomic city of Los Alamos and the ancient *Jémez* Indian pueblo, provides a fascinating study in geographic and cultural contrasts. New Mexico 4 has been rebuilt in recent years, which takes away some of the isolation and remoteness one felt on the original dirt-and-gravel trail. Pavement, however, has not yet increased traffic sufficiently to take away its status as a preferred byway.

BACK DOORS & DEAD ENDS

But all good things must come to an end. Let's just summarize it this way:

Where there's a will to get away from the seemingly inevitable press of commercialism and fellow travelers, there's a way. A "back way" into even such crowded favorites as Yellowstone (the *Beartooth Plateau* route via Cooke City); the Grand Tetons (via *Teton Pass* on the west); Grand Canyon (via *Pipe Springs* on the northwest); Yosemite (via Tioga Pass); Rocky Mountain National Park (via Colorado 7, the so-called *Peak-to-Peak Highway* from the southeast) . . . and so on.

And we haven't even begun to mention favorite "dead-end" byways:

The fantastic, 5-mile shelf road that runs mostly west—and up—from Ouray to the *Camp Bird Mine,* monetary godfather to Evelyn Walsh McLean's Hope diamond. (This one, we admit, comes perilously close at times to that imaginary line between the road that is passable and the one that is only jackassable. But you can always inquire in Ouray. The trip up and back is eminently worthwhile.)

The *Eureka* road north and east of Silverton, in far southwestern Colorado.

The *North Creede*-and-points-north road that probes gingerly into that famous old Colorado mining district.

The new *Kings Canyon* road in the California Sierras. And many others.

But you get the idea. If you really like byways, and enjoy exploring them, you'll find them. Plus many we probably haven't discovered yet ourselves.

"AS THE
SPIRIT LISTETH"

There would seem to be a certain mystical element in successful vacationing, just as there is in successful living. The unforeseeable chance event . . . the unexpected fortuity . . . the undreamed-of serendipity . . . these are the things that seem often just to happen, for no apparent reason at all, to lift an ordinary travel experience into being a memorable adventure. We say "seem" just to happen because we can't be sure. We're not going so far as to say one can actually plan on the unplannable. (Or, as the old-timer preacher used to promise, "to unscrew the unscrutable.") But we do believe, honestly and at the same time humbly, that one can put himself in a position where the unforeseeable and the unexpected *can* happen. A minister would probably call it being responsive to the working of the spirit within one. We'll call it simply wooing the serendipitous.

This is not to suggest a vacation trip should be undertaken without a plan. We do suggest, however, that plans and itineraries be considered as something less than Holy Writ, handed down on tablets of stone at the beginning of each day. Obviously we do not counsel foolhardiness in the matter of reservations. One who enjoys the security they offer will want to continue getting them. And even those who, like us, do not like being restricted, will be wise to break over occasionally in certain popular vacation areas or under special circumstances. But we shun reservations for the most part, preferring to start out early in the morning when the roads are relatively uncluttered and stopping early in the afternoon before accommodations are picked over. In all the years we have sought a place to sleep at night, without a reservation (and we say this not to boast, but to reassure you), only once have we been obliged to sleep in the car.

Therefore if you plan on enjoying each vacation without concentrating too strongly on just when and how you'll go about it, we suggest that you can be virtually assured of some pleasant surprises.

Consider our introduction to the Schroeders.

199

All day we'd simply poked along, idly following our impulses. By midafternoon we decided to go into Colorado's North Park, entering by way of Muddy Pass. (This was a number of years ago when that particular U.S. 40 crossing of the Continental Divide west of Denver was, at least when it rained, muddy.) We had no clear idea of where we wanted to go, how we proposed getting there, or what we wanted to see en route. At least four times we stopped at crossroads, debated the possibilities briefly, then impulsively chose one of the two or more roads that were offered, and drove on.

We ended up late on a Saturday night—when by all the laws of common sense we should have been reduced to sleeping in the car— in the only remaining cabin of the only for-rent accommodations within some mountainous twenty miles in any direction. Not only did we have a bed for the night, we had a free trout dinner that night, a delightful evening with congenial companions in front of a roaring fireplace (on the eve of a day it registered an official 114° F. at our hometown in Oklahoma), and, next morning, a six o'clock breakfast, also free, to send us on our way. We've kept up with the Schroeders ever since, needless to say. They're dear friends. Was it chance? Who can say . . . for sure?

Of course friendships don't have to be so lasting as this in order to make the serendipity pleasant or worthwhile. (Nor, we might add, do they necessarily involve freeloading!)

PUNKIN CENTER FLAVOR

Take our visit to Punkin Center. You probably won't find Punkin Center on your Arizona map. You'll have to look for Tonto Basin— and even then you'll need a pretty good map. But Punkin Center or Tonto Basin, it's there, in the center of a vast ranching area northeast of Phoenix: post office, general store, community hall, all wrapped into a single nondescript building. Outside and in, though, it radiated Western hospitality and frontier friendliness. We turned in—on a hunch—almost automatically.

Now at first blush our reception was not auspicious. "Who sent you up here?" a grizzled native demanded from the porch. But it was all right. He simply had us confused with two other people, which wasn't too surprising, when you consider the way he had apparently spent the morning. He was a fine old gentleman for all that. And once past the initial misunderstanding we got along famously.

He'd been in this country since 1892 or thereabouts. "I was thirty-five years old," he confided, "before I knew there was anything on the other side of these hills. And then I went to New York." To which his partner—a quiet Gary Cooper-type straight man—grinned and said, "I'll bet he got lost." They had been ready to leave, of course. But we were old friends by this time: when we went in, they came along.

The woman behind the bar was just as friendly. As was the sun-bronzed man standing beside a table loaded with rock specimens.

"How's uranium hunting around here?" we asked, and he was soon explaining to us the relative merits of carnotite and yellow-streaked torbonite.

He'd been a rancher all his life, he admitted. But he was sure as hell a miner now. That's where the money was. He grinned, gave us a choice chunk of torbonite (he assured us it was choice) and his name and address. "When you get home, show this to any rich friend you might have. Tell him I've got tons of the stuff."

We were all part of the family by now. And when we mentioned lunch, the woman readily agreed to fix sandwiches for us. But she confided that there was a nice new place just twenty miles or so up the road. She thought we'd like it better.

We thanked her, saying we were headed that way, toward Verde Hot Springs. And that got our tippling friend to reminiscing about the eight-mule freight wagons he'd driven into that isolated canyon bottom when the dam and power plant were being built. After still more talk, he and Gary Cooper finally said goodbye and roared off in their jeep. When they disappeared to the north they were still waving to us out of a cloud of dust. We told the folks in the store how much we had enjoyed the visit and then we left, too.

But that wasn't the end of the meeting. At the point where a trail took off for the towering Mazatzal Mountains to the west, the jeep was parked beside the road and our friend was waving us down. Perhaps he wanted to warn us of the dangers of the Fossil Creek Gorge road ahead. Perhaps it was only that he wanted to talk some more. Anyway, he'd just remembered the car in the bottom of the canyon on our way up to Punkin Center. Had we seen it? He had.

Well, he wanted to tell us about it. He'd gone down to Tortilla Flat—"for a cup of coffee," he explained, with a broad wink—and it happened just ahead of him on his way back. Everybody killed. He gave us all the details. Then more goodbyes, a last word of caution about the road ahead, and finally we were on our way again.

Yes, the lunch at Rye was quite satisfactory. And *Fossil Creek Gorge*—just as the old man had promised—was almost as beautiful as Grand Canyon (and a byway we really should have recommended in the last chapter). But that was merely icing on the cake. We had explored a delightfully isolated ranch country, made a number of new acquaintances, and discovered the genuine frontier friendliness that still exists in the West, like gold, where you find it.

Adding a shivery tang to the entire experience, of course, was consciousness of the fact that this friendly latter-day reception was in rather sharp contrast to what a couple of strangers might have expected back in the late 1880's when the Graham-Tewksbury feud, the so-called Pleasant Valley War, was unfolding here in a seemingly endless procession of duels and ambushes. The details of the war are controversial to this day, but by the time Tom, the last of the Grahams, was killed in Tempe in 1892, the five-year bushwhacking feud had claimed at least nineteen lives for sure, and was blamed for a number of others. Pleasant indeed today, the valley was considerably less so when, according to one account, "an enemy was hunted like a wild animal and death was the penalty for an unguarded moment."

MRS. ORMUND & FRIENDS, OF UTAH

More meaningful perhaps than our Punkin Center encounter are several fragmentary insights we've gained into Mormon life and the fierce devotion Utahns—Mormon or otherwise—often have for their harshly beautiful state. It was Brigham Young who said, in 1847 when he first saw the desert floor where Salt Lake City now stands, "This is the Place!" And Utahns have been echoing his judgment ever since, some in words, others simply by their actions. We encountered both these responses in a single memorable junket a few years back into the spectacular Escalante River/Boulder Mountain country.

As a byway, this day-long swing from *Bryce Canyon National Park* to *Capitol Reef National Monument,* via the towns of Escalante and Boulder, is a memorable one (as indicated earlier). But even more vividly than the striking Red Desert scenery it unfolds along the way, we recall the people we met. It started with the friendly, efficient woman who serviced our car from a lone curbside pump in Boulder. Together we had agreed it was a shame that "progress" had closed Capitol Gorge to automobiles. And not too surprisingly, when you stop to consider the matter.

Long the only way to get through the monument, the gorge itself wasn't really a road, but a route. You drove it simply because it was there and you wanted to get to Hanksville; the only other way to do so was a 100-mile loop to the north. As for the "road," it was a creekbed—usually dry, fortunately—that ran for a 15-mile-long course between multicolored cliffs towering 500 to 1,000 feet above one's head. At times the defile was little more than car-wide. At times, too, following a hard rain, it could run car-deep. After that, for a time, its "floor" would be dotted with manifold-cracking rocks that had to be rolled out of the way before one continued.

But you could make it to Hanksville—usually—after fording the Dirty Devil River that awaited you at the east end of the gorge. And the adventure was one you didn't quickly forget. Happily, you can still drive into Capitol Gorge several miles, from the west end, where the National Park Service headquarters is located, then follow a trail the rest of the way into its most breathtaking section.

The closure, of course, was done for safety's sake, and we must approve of it; but we're still thankful we had the chance to drive it when it was just a creekbed.

So far as we were concerned, our bond about closing the old Gorge road made us fast friends with the gas station attendant immediately. Then, too, it was she who suggested we go to Mrs. Ormund's for something to eat. She serves meals—good ones, she assured us; just go on in. And we did, although it looked like a private home—probably because that's what it was, with a few tables and a plain counter added at the end of the living room nearest the kitchen.

Mrs. Ormund greeted us by peeking around from behind the stove.

"I've been cutting willows all morning, but I'll fix you something if you'll let me clean up." Fifteen minutes later she reappeared, potatoes in hand. Soon we were eating corned beef sandwiches on thick homemade rolls and warming not only to the food, but to reminiscences of a pioneer who still appreciated the "good old days when daddy footed the bills and there weren't many bills to foot."

Her father bought a ranch in this area in 1902. He taught her at home her first year, because she was too young for the five-mile horseback ride to the nearest school. She remembered being put on a sure-footed horse with her sister and going to Escalante with her father—thirty miles the way we'd come; but only fifteen via Hell's Backbone and "the world's highest wooden bridge over the world's deepest dry holler," she told us proudly.

Then the Robinsons came in for coffee and talk. He was a native returning from California to introduce his wife to the beauties of the desert country. He told of running Angora goats with his father and uncle in the rugged Henry Mountains to the east. "Some eight thousand of them. And the only ones in Utah." He struck the same note of quiet, matter-of-fact pride. He loved this area, and it was obvious he wanted his wife to love it, too.

Oh, yes. In the course of our visiting with Mrs. Ormund we told her of our conversation with the woman at the gas pump down the street, and how we'd agreed it was a shame Capitol Gorge had been closed to auto traffic.

"Uh-huh," she nodded. "She's a Wayne County girl." As if to say, "Of course she would agree; she's one of us and has a feel for this Red Desert country." It gave us a sudden insight into the make-up of Utahns who are born and reared in this bleak, colorful, spectacularly beautiful basin of the Colorado River.

Still later, after we'd left Mrs. Ormund and climbed to a crude, turnoff observation point high on the east flank of Boulder Mountain, we met yet another group of native Utahns—two couples, middle-aged, apparently hard-working farmer/ranchers enjoying a day of sightseeing. Their car was one of a handful we encountered that whole afternoon.

From a grassy ledge there on the side of the mountain you look out over what appears to be all of southeast Utah, a shimmering, colorful wasteland of shadowy escarpments, knife-edge ridges, and twisting canyons. It's a vast empty wilderness stretching east and south to the horizon, and we were both fascinated and awed. We soaked it in as best we could, from our limited firsthand experience with the area. Then, just as we were about to leave, the natives came —overalled and gingham-clad—to share the scene with us.

And "share" it they did. The two men had been over much of the areas, on horseback in the early days, later in a jeep. Soon they were describing trails that cut through the shadowy notch off there to our left, dropped down behind that low purplish ridge there to the right. They swapped tales of adventures, and misadventures, in the Waterpocket Fold area; passed on to us, casually, unconsciously, their love for this land and its rugged beauty, their pride—unspoken, but nonetheless real—in its vast emptiness and the harsh challenge of its terrain and climate. We learned much about the region and its history as we listened.

But we learned even more about the people who had accepted its challenge, wrested a living from its hostile soil, and loved it enough to drive a hundred miles of poor road to be able to see it spread out at their feet. That evening we realized fully just what we had done: We had traveled an entire day through an awesomely beautiful region and had managed, fortuitously, to see it four different times through the eyes of native Utahns who loved the land and wanted others to love it too.

ARTISTS IN SHARING

So far as we've been able to tell over the years, that's the "why" of travel serendipities. The one unifying thread drawn through all these experiences seems to have been woven of love, pride, and loyalty, in about equal proportions. These people we've encountered along the way have known and loved their particular area, region, or state. That's why they've been willing, even eager, to share with us their insights and their enthusiasms, and their prejudices as well.

"Is everyone treating you all right?" a perfect stranger asked us on

the street in downtown Winnipeg. He'd seen our Oklahoma car tag
and just wanted to make sure we were enjoying ourselves. His love
for Manitoba and his desire to have us get a good impression of
his province and the Dominion was echoed by the proverbial "sweet
little old lady" in a nearby town, in the days when the excellent
Trans-Canada highway was still pretty much of a dream. She interrupted her enthusiastic recital of the attractions of her particular
corner of Manitoba to offer an apology. "You know, we're proud
of just about everything we have here in Canada—but our roads."

What happens in these cases is that—to borrow some of today's
jargon—we are given a kind of "instant understanding" of a particular area by being allowed to "relate" to a native who already understands, and loves what he understands. All we've been required to
give in return was a willingness to listen, to try to understand, to be
seduced, if you will.

We can still recall listening to old-time prospectors reminisce
about the glory days of their particular mining area. At Mogollon, a
remarkable ghost in extreme west-central New Mexico, we were so
entranced by the re-creation of the scene—in the eyes, words, and ges-
tures of an oldster who seemed to be the town's last surviving resident—we could almost hear the roar of the stamp mills as they ran
round the clock, trying to keep up with the rich ores being gouged
from the surrounding hills by thousands of feverish miners. We had
an almost identical experience in North Creede years before that.
And our present mind's-eye picture of both these camps is still a
curious blend of the scene we actually saw and that re-created for us
by an old-timer who remembered it "back when."

THE "MOVING OF THE SPIRIT"

Let's leave it at that, then. When you set out to collect the American West, take along all the beforehand knowledge you can acquire
—especially as it pertains to your particular fields of interest. But
then, after you've laid out a general plan, keep yourself free and
open to the "moving of the spirit." Don't be upset by developments
that seem to interfere with your master plan. Be a fatalist. Try to
convince yourself—as, say, a Fundamentalist preacher might—that
whatever happens is for the best. Or can be, if you're determined to
make it so.

Had it not been for a flat tire that Sunday morning in Forks, Washington, for a last example, we might never have had such a revealing insight into lumber-camp social amenities as they have survived into what some have concluded to be a somewhat effete 20th century. Delayed by the service call (probable cause of the delay was not learned until later), we adjourned to what appeared to be the town's most popular café. And there, from an unobtrusive booth, we watched the leisurely flow of holiday morning coffee-drinkers and listened to the easy, gossipy banter of old friends so characteristic of small-town life. Quickly it became apparent, even to strangers, that the previous night's soirée had been no ordinary Saturday-night affair. Not only were eyes bleary; one was definitely black. Another coffee-seeker, also greeted with good-natured needling, sported a neck patch that covered one ear. Then came the third veteran of the party, a husky still in his twenties, his right arm in a sling. Just what happened? We heard them discuss it briefly, and then the sling-wearer summed it up with both admirable conciseness and complete logic. "I really don't know," he said. "After a couple of double shots around things got a little confused."

Looking back over the years' accumulation of travel memories and experiences, we know the feeling. We're a little confused by some of them, too, without benefit of double shots around. But we have yet to recall a really unpleasant experience, at least when considered in perspective. We have yet to recall a development that actually ruined a trip for us, or even a significant part of it.

Perhaps we've been lucky. But we're inclined to believe that, within certain bounds, one is pretty likely to get what one expects. Certainly the person who goes through life confident everyone else is out to cheat him seems to run into more than his share of bunco men. And the one who starts out on a trip convinced he's going to be miserable (probably because the whole thing was his wife's idea) is not likely to be disappointed.

But the law of "self-fulfilling expectations" works both ways. Plan to have a good trip when you start out—not *how* you're going to have that good trip, specifically, just that you *are*—and we believe, firmly and unalterably, that you will.

Try it and see for yourself, next time you set out to tour the Old West.

BIBLIOGRAPHY

"Bibliography" is rather a fancy word for what follows (requested by the publisher, an Easterner who loves the West), but it does try to answer two questions: 1) Where can I get more information on some of these places you talk about?—and 2) How can I find them without getting lost?

It is sketchy, informal, and admittedly opinionated: but it tries to give straightforward answers—and to this extent it is a Bibliography.

MAPS

Here we admit to an overriding prejudice. Unless in your travels you have no intention of getting off the Interstate System, or the major *major* highways, insist on maps prepared by the H. M. Gousha Company.

A number of the leading oil companies patronize this established California mapmaker; you can check for the name on the "legend" section. If at first you don't succeed, try again. And again. It's worth the effort. Carefully read, they help you know exactly where you are, what you're seeing, and what to expect down the road. They're the best general maps we know.

If you plan extensive excursions off federal and state routes, you'll want maps even more detailed. A good possibility here, for the Western states, is the United States Forest Service. Each national preserve has its own map, showing not only the roads but also giving much other useful information. They are usually available at U.S.F.S. offices throughout the area, and often from local Chambers of Commerce.

If you are in California—and are an AAA member—you'll find the California Auto Club maps, specially made and prepared on extra-large scale, a real delight—greatly detailed and highly informative.

TOURING INFORMATION

As for tour information, the answer is not quite so simple. Perhaps the most used sources (free, too) are the various state tourist promotion offices. All are helpful, some more so than others of course. Write to the tourist bureau/development department at the capital of the state involved.

Another source of information we invariably depend on is the travel club guide. Perhaps the two most widely distributed are the *AAA Tour Books* and the *Mobil Guides*. (The former are not sold, of course, but given free to AAA's over 10 million members.)

209

BOOKS

This brings us to regular trade books, such as this one.

First on the list, as far as we're concerned, are the various state volumes in the American Guide Series. Some are out of print by now and available only in libraries or through O.P. book dealers. In any case, they are excellent, particularly for the detailed background material they contain. Our personal library contains the volumes for all the Western states (and most of the others). We take a box of them along with us on every trip.

What next? Each field of interest boasts its own library of helpful books, reading of which—before you go, as you drive, or after you return home—is almost sure to double your travel fun.

In Chapter 2 we followed old Western trails. Here Bernard DeVoto's one-volume look at the expedition, *The Journals of Lewis and Clark* (Houghton Mifflin, 1953), is always exciting, and first-rate reading. For the Oregon Trail there is a special American Guide Series volume (Hastings House, 1939), not easy to find but containing a wealth of mile-by-mile information. To get the flavor of the old Sante Fe Trail there's nothing like Josiah Gregg's *Commerce of the Prairies* (University of Oklahoma Press, 1954).

The booklist on the fur trade for Chapter 4 is a sizable one. Jim Colter, Kit Carson, Jedediah Smith, the Bent brothers, John Jacob Astor, Jim Bridger, John McLoughlin—all the well-known figures, whether trapper or trader, have their own volume or volumes. If you would read a single book simply to savor the color and excitement of the trade, try DeVoto's *Across the Wide Missouri* (Houghton Mifflin, 1947). For distaff color there's *Daughters of the Country* by Walter O'Meara (Harcourt, Brace & World, 1968).

In Chapter 5 we explored military posts around the West. Robert W. Fraser provides a rather prosaic listing of pertinent details on these installations in *Forts of the West* (Oklahoma, 1965). For more of a backdoor view there's *Army Life on the Western Frontier* (Oklahoma, 1958). In it Francis Paul Prucha edits some of the official reports turned in 1826–1845 by Colonel George Croghan, the army's Inspector General. His field notes, they get down to such basics as bedbugs and such. In the picture-and-text field there is also an excellent new series on Western forts by Herbert M. Hart (Superior Press). Inherent modesty does not quite prevent a recommendation for *Great Day in the West* by K. Ruth (Oklahoma, 1963), a close look at nearly 150 trading posts, forts, *and* mining towns, all at the time they were enjoying their "great day." It too is helpful, if we say so ourselves.

Ghost towns (Chapters 6 and 7) boast a shelf that stretches from here to there and halfway back. Almost everyone with a pen, camera, or sketching pencil seems sooner or later to fall under their spell. One of the first to recognize their charm—and still one of their finest chroniclers —is Muriel Sibell Wolle. With her sketches, as well as in words, she has captured literally hundreds of these Rocky Mountain ghosts and near-ghosts. You can't help but be fascinated, not to say informed, by *Stampede to Timberline* (privately published, 1949), *The Bonanza Trail* (Indiana University Press, 1949), and *Montana Pay Dirt* (Sage Press, Denver, 1963). Perry Eberhart's *Guide to the Colorado Ghost Towns and Mining Camps* (Sage, 1959) is art-less, but none the less interesting. James E. and Barbara Sherman have entered the field recently with *Ghost Towns of Arizona* (Oklahoma, 1968), and Lambert Florin has produced photographic studies of Western ghost towns (Superior).

In Chapter 8 we turned from ghost towns to some of the more interesting institutions they spawned and left for the latter-day visitor to enjoy —mainly hotels and opera houses. One book stands out in this field, for our money: Sandra Dallas's *No More Than Five in a Bed* (Oklahoma, 1967). She limits herself to fine old Colorado hostelries.

When it comes to Chapter 9, we could smother you with reading lists, since we chronic rail buffs are avid nostalgiacs with a penchant for collecting all sorts and sizes of books on all aspects of railroadiana. What follows is a selective list containing at least one book that concerns itself primarily with each of the roads we've mentioned in the chapter.

Rio Grande: Mainline of the Rockies by Lucius Beebe and Charles Clegg (Howell-North, 1962) takes care of the Denver & Rio Grande Western nicely. *Narrow Gauge in the Rockies,* also by Beebe and Clegg (Howell-North, 1958), considers the D&RGW's ancestor, the D&RG, along with its competitors among the three-foot-gauge roads in Colorado.

The Giant's Ladder by Harold A. Boner (Kalmbach, 1962) covers the most spectacular stretch of yet another D&RGW antecedent, General Palmer's Denver & Salt Lake. Just to the north of the D&SL there was the old narrow-gauge Denver, Boulder & Western, beautifully written up in *The Switzerland Trail of America* by Forest Crossen (Pruett Press, 1962).

Other interesting one-volume histories of famous Colorado railroads include: *The Uintah Railway* by Henry E. Bender, Jr. (Howell-North, 1970); *The Rio Grande Southern Railroad* by Josie Moore Crum (San Juan History, Inc., 1961); *Colorado Midland* by Morris Cafky (Rocky Mountain Railroad Club, 1965); *Denver, South Park & Pacific* by R. H. Kindig, E. J. Haley, and M. C. Poor (Rocky Mountain Railroad Club, 1959); and *The Argentine Central* by Frank R. Hollenback (Sage, 1959).

In Chapter 11 we dip into one of the faster growing hobbies among travelers—exploring old cemeteries for the interesting insights they give on the life of the community that "supported" them. The publisher of this book has done as much as any to popularize tombstone-hunting— with *Over Their Dead Bodies* (1962), about New England, and *Sudden & Awful* (1968), across the country; both by Thomas C. Mann and Janet Greene. Superior has picture-and-text volumes by Lambert Florin, *Boot Hill* (1966) and *Tales the Western Tombstones Tell* (1967).

INDEX BY STATES

WYOMING

Devils Gap (grave
inscription) 143
Devils Gate 10, 143
Forts (*map 45*):
Bridger 53
Laramie 51
Fur trade posts 34-5:
Museum 35
"Rendezvous" 35
map 39
Inscriptions (pioneer):
Independence Rock 15,

17, 25, 27, 31
Names Hill 30
Register Cliff 30
map on endpapers
Medicine Bow 190
Mining camps/towns:
Atlantic 61
South Pass City 61-2
map 59
"Mountain Men" 34-5
Mountain passes:
South 11, 17-8, 28,
61, 118
Teton 198

Togwotee 34, 118-9
map 187 & endpapers
Parks, Nat'l:
Grand Teton 34
Yellowstone 4, 115, 119,
160-1, 198
Rivers (running):
Big Horn 161
Green 34-5, 147, 191
Snake 34, 159-60
"Wedding of the Waters"
161
Wind 35, 161
map 157

GENERAL INDEX

Ācoma (N. Mex.) pueblo
178, 180
Ajax mine (Colo.) 81
Alcove Springs (Kan.)
30-1, 142
Alder Gulch (Mont.) 73-5
Alma (Colo.) 60, 180
American Fur Co. 33, 35,
38, 51, 53
Angels Camp (Cal.) 64;
map 59
Antelope House (Indian
ruin, Ariz.) *ill. 165*
Apache(s) 47, 50, 76, 171
Apache Trail (Ariz.) 197
Applegate, Jesse 14-5
Arapaho(s) 48, 145
Archeology (ruins/relics)
23-4, 166-72 *passim,*
187, *see also* Index
by States
Arkansas River 7, 21, 38,
52, 110, 125, 147
Aspen (Colo.) 57-9, 68-9,
81, 93, 123; *map 73*
Astoria (Ore.) 13, 35, 36
Aztec Ruins (N. Mex.)
169-70; *map 167*

Ballad of Baby Doe, The 82
Bandelier (Indian ruins,
N. Mex.) 171; *map 167*
Beaumont Hotel (Colo.)
88, 95-6
Bent's Fort (Colo.) 38
Big Bend country (Tex.)
159
Bird Cage Theatre (Tomb-
stone, Ariz.) 75-6

Black Hawk (Colo.) 59, 77,
106, 140
Blesser, Nick 43-4
Blue River (Ariz.) 194-5
Bois de Sioux River 162
Boothills 58, 74, 76, 134,
136-7; *see also* Grave
markers
Bridger, Jim 30, 118; *see
also* Mountain Men
Brown, Molly (unsinkable)
82
Bryce Canyon (Utah) 34,
203
Bucket of Blood saloon 72

Calico (Cal.) 72
California ("Overland")
Trail 18-9, 27, 30, 51-2,
61, 142; *map on
endpapers*
Canyon de Chelly (Indian
ruins, Ariz.) 164, 166,
172; *ill. 165, map 167*
Capitol Reef (early Indian
art, Utah) 24, 197, 203
Carson, Kit 18, 30, 40, 144,
145; *see also* Jaramillo,
Josefa
Casa Grande (Indian ruins,
Ariz.) 166, 170-1;
map 167
Casper (Wyo.) 25, 27, 184,
190
Central City (Colo.) 59,
77-82 *passim,* 85, 86,
87-9, 92-3, 96, 106,
140; *ill. 79, map 73*
Chaco Canyon (Indian ruins,

N. Mex.) 164, 170;
map 167
Chapin Mesa (Indian ruins,
N. Mex.) 169
"Chateau de Mores" 71
Cherokee(s) 46, 135, 181
Cheyenne Indians 48
Chickasaw(s) 46, 181
Chimayo (N. Mex.) 184,
188
Chimney Rock (frontier
inscriptions, Neb.) 10,
15-6; *map on endpapers*
Chippewa grave markers 137
Chisholm, Jesse 21-2, 144,
145
Chisholm Trail 9, 12, 21-2,
72; *map on endpapers*
Choctaw(s) 46, 181
Cimarron Cutoff (Santa Fe
Trail) 10, 20-1, 128
186; *map on endpapers*
Clark, Capt. William 3, 12-
4, 29, 146; *see also*
Lewis & Clark Trail
Cliff Palace (Indian ruins,
Mesa Verde, N. Mex.)
168
Climax mine (Colo.) 82
Cochiti (N. Mex.) pueblo
180
Cody, William F. ("Buffalo
Bill") 30, 131
Coloma (Cal.) 63; *map 59*
Colorado Central RR 104,
106; *map 107*
Colorado Midland RR 104,
109; *map 107*
Colorado Railroad
Museum 113